Achieving QTS

Teaching Foundation Stage

edited by
Iris Keating

Learning Matters

First published in 2002 by Learning Matters Ltd
Reprinted in 2003

British Library Cataloguing in Publication Data
A CIP record for this book is available from the British Library.

ISBN 1 903300 33 9

Cover design by Topics – The Creative Partnership
Cover photo reproduced by permission of Educational Solutions (sales@edsol.co.uk)
Text design by Code 5 Design Associates Ltd
Project management by Deer Park Productions
Typeset by PDQ Typesetting
Printed and bound in Great Britain

Learning Matters Ltd
33 Southernhay East
Exeter EXI INX
Tel: 01392 215560
Email: info@learningmatters.co.uk
www.learningmatters.co.uk

CONTENTS

Wendy Baker is currently a Senior Lecturer in Mathematics Education at Manchester Metropolitan University. She was formerly Advisory Teacher for Mathematics in Lancashire. She is enthusiastic about teaching in the Early Years.

Jo Basford is Senior Lecturer in Childhood Studies and Early Years at Manchester Metropolitan University. She has extensive experience working within Early Years, and has a particular commitment to the High/Scope curriculum approach.

Rosemary Boys is a Senior Lecturer at the Institute of Education at Manchester Metropolitan University. She currently teaches English and Teaching Studies.

Joy Coulbeck is Senior Lecturer in Education Leadership and Management at Manchester Metropolitan University. Initially trained at Bretton Hall and Leeds University, she has spent 25 years in primary education and was a primary headteacher in Cheshire for six years before moving into higher education.

Sue Egersdorff is a Senior Primary Adviser for Cheshire Education Authority. Previously she was headteacher of a large infant and nursery school in the Cheshire town of Winsford.

Angela Harnett is a Senior Lecturer in Education Leadership and Management at Manchester Metropolitan University.

Elaine Hodson is a Senior Lecturer at Manchester Metropolitan University where she teaches Child Development and Literacy. She was formerly a headteacher, first of a nursery school and then of a primary school.

Iris Keating is a member of the Early Years team at Manchester Metropolitan University, working in CPD and on the Best Practice Research Scholarship scheme for the DfES. She was a nursery teacher for 12 years.

Brenda Keogh has worked as a primary teacher, lab technician, resources officer, advisory teacher and National Curriculum co-ordinator. She currently lectures in science education at Manchester Metropolitan University where she is Leader of Flexible Programmes. She is the joint creator of the innovative concept cartoon strategy.

Norma Marsh is currently a senior lecturer in Mathematics Education at Manchester Metropolitan University. Formerly, she was deputy head teacher of a large infant school where she learnt most of the important things she knows from playing alongside four year old people.

Nell Napier is a Senior Lecturer at the Institute of Education at Manchester Metropolitan University. She teaches on a variety of courses including BA (Hons) Primary with QTS, BA (Hons) Childhood Studies and CPD.

Stuart Naylor has worked as a secondary teacher, lab technician and advisory teacher as well as teaching in the USA. He currently lectures in Science Education at Manchester Metropolitan University where he is Head of the Sciences Education Centre. He is the joint creator of the innovative concept cartoon strategy.

Tony Poulter is Senior Lecturer in Primary ICT at the Institute of Education at the Manchester Metropolitan University.

Elaine Spink is a Senior Lecturer in Primary Science Education at Manchester Metropolitan University, teaching on undergraduate and postgraduate courses.

This book has been written to meet the needs of those of you who are planning to work with young children and by this we mean children aged from three to five years. The Early Years are an area of great interest and concern. The foundations that are laid at the beginning of children's early education stay with them for the rest of their lives. One of the major characteristics of the Early Years is the variety of locations where children can be engaged in learning. There are the informal situations, with parents, carers and childminders, and there are the more formal venues: playgroups, day nurseries, nursery schools and units and Reception classes. The focus for this book is on the formal locations.

The Foundation Stage was introduced to meet the needs of three to five year old children in a range of settings. It is discussed in detail in Chapter I and should not be confused with Foundation subjects, which are the National Curriculum subjects, geography, history, art, PE and RE. Its introduction was very significant in the education of young children since for the first time a distinct stage was identified with a specific philosophy, expectations and underlying principles. These principles are at the heart of this book and in the chapters that follow you will see them developed in a range of areas. One of the central principles, and one which this book is built around and upon, is that the Foundation Stage is concerned with more than the just the *content* of what children learn, but also includes the *process* of learning and with this the four key elements of learning:

- **concepts;**
- **knowledge and understanding;**
- **skills;**
- **attitudes.**

The Foundation Curriculum is organised into six distinct areas of learning.

- **Personal, social and emotional development.**
- **Communication, language and literacy.**
- **Mathematical development.**
- **Knowledge and understanding of the world.**
- **Physical development.**
- **Creative development.**

By the end of the Foundation Stage, most children will be expected to have reached a number of goals in each of these areas of learning. Some will have exceeded these goals, others will be working towards them. These are the Early Learning Goals. Because children develop at different rates and in different ways, a number of developmental Stepping Stones have been identified which relate to the relevant knowledge, understanding, skills and attitudes needed to achieve each Early Learning Goal. This information is all contained in the *Curriculum Guidance for the Foundation Stage* (DfEE/QCA, 2000) and described and explained in detail in Chapter I.

In Chapters 2 and 3 we recognise that children live in a complex world, surrounded by a variety of influences and players. The contribution of parents and carers in the education of their children is considered as well as the importance of establishing sound partnerships between settings and parents/carers. We also explain the variety in the roles and responsibilities that other professionals have in the lives of young children.

Chapters 4 and 5 are concerned with the development of young children and here we consider not only their physical and creative development but also their personal, social and emotional development. We also address how best to plan to meet the needs of young children in order to help them develop as independent and confident learners.

There is more of a focus on the Early Years curriculum in the next four chapters, when we address in turn: communication, language and literacy; developing mathematical understanding and the foundations of numeracy; knowledge and understanding of the world; and information and communication technology. These four overlapping areas do not represent the whole Early Years curriculum but we believe that they will allow you to experience many of its central features.

In Chapters 10 and 11 we lead you into a consideration of some of the challenges that exist for Early Years teachers, first concerning monitoring, assessment, recording, reporting and accountability and then asking what makes for an effective teacher of young children. We hope that this will encourage you to think about and reflect upon the principles that underlie your own personal philosophy of teaching.

Each of the eleven chapters makes explicit reference to the Professional Standard/s addressed in that chapter and these are, of course, a requirement prior to achieving Qualified Teacher Status.

As you can now see, this book is structured to take you through the central features of the Foundation Stage. In order to do this there are a number of tasks in each chapter that we hope will allow you to think carefully about placing some of the theory that you have read into your experience of practice. This is further aided by the inclusion of classroom stories and case studies. We have also provided you with details of further reading, which will help you to learn more about this important and fascinating stage of children's learning.

In writing this book we have been aware of the very special challenge for those working with children in Reception classes. Here is the interface between the Foundation Stage and Key Stage 1 and in some ways this can result in competing demands on staff time and children's experiences. A particular example of this is the importance of play in the different settings. As you will see from your reading of this book, play is central to the Foundation Stage, underpinning the activities and experiences contained within it. We would argue that play should continue to have a part in the lives of older children too, but as children get older there are further pressures placed on then and in order to meet these demands, play can sometimes be squeezed out of the children's school experiences. However, in the Reception class we maintain that play continues to have a vitally important role.

1 THE FOUNDATION STAGE AND MEETING THE EARLY LEARNING GOALS

Jo Basford

Professional Standards for QTS

(→) 2.1a

This Standard states that in order to gain QTS, teachers must know and understand the aims, principles, six areas of learning and the early learning goals described in the DfEE/QCA Curriculum Guidance for the Foundation Stage and, for Reception children, the frameworks, methods and expectations set out in the National Numeracy and Literacy Strategies. These are considered in detail in Chapters 6 and 7.

You may find it helpful to refer to the appropriate section of the Handbook that accompanies the Standards for the award of QTS, for further clarification and support.

What is the Foundation Stage?

The establishment of the Foundation Stage by the DfEE (DfES) in 1999 was a major landmark in the education of young children. For the first time, the education of children between the ages of three and five was recognised as a distinct and very important stage of education. The general aim of the Foundation Stage is to prepare children for learning in Key Stage 1, by providing them with activities and experiences that will help them make progress and develop in all areas of learning. Your role as a teacher in the Foundation Stage is crucial in helping every child to develop skills, knowledge and understanding, attitudes and concepts which will prepare them not only for entry into full-time school but for the rest of their lives.

The Foundation Stage begins when children reach the age of three, and continues until the end of the Reception year in school. When a child enters a Year 1 class the following academic year, he or she becomes part of Key Stage 1, and begins to study the National Curriculum.

The range of Foundation Stage settings

Many children will have attended some form of pre-school setting before they enter the Foundation Stage. In order to ensure that all children have equal access to high-quality provision, once they reach the Foundation Stage, the government provides nursery education grant funding. This means that all children are entitled to a free part-time nursery place until they begin school. Parents are entitled to choose which setting they would like their child to attend. There are a wide variety of settings, each catering for the diverse needs of children and their parents. The range of settings that children may attend includes:

- playgroup;
- childminder;
- day nursery;

- private nursery;
- local authority maintained nursery;
- combined nursery centres.

In addition to a Reception class, you may be employed as a specialist Early Years teacher in any of the last four settings. Whichever setting you work in, it is important to remember that the children in your care will probably attend two or more separate settings within the Foundation Stage. In addition to this, the expectations we have of children as they grow older increase. For example, children are expected to leave their parents for longer periods of time and greater learning demands are made. It is therefore vital that all settings work in partnership with one another, so that children's previous learning and experiences can be built upon (see Chapter 10).

An Early Years teacher must be very sensitive to the differences a child may experience in each setting, which may consequently affect the way in which they settle into a new setting. Factors such as adult:child ratios, the organisation of the learning environment and the daily routine can all have a huge impact on a child's personal, social and emotional well-being (see Chapter 4).

The following classroom story illustrates the range of settings one child encountered in the Foundation Stage. Try to identify the factors that may have contributed to the way in which he settled in each new provision.

Classroom story

Tom had attended playgroup for two morning sessions per week, from the age of two and a half. The playgroup was situated in the local village hall. There was usually a ratio of at least five children to one adult. These consisted of the employed playgroup staff, and parents who helped out on a rota basis. During the session, the children were free to play with any of the toys that the adults had selected. The adults planned a specific practical activity each day. Groups of four children at a time were invited to join in with the activity, under the careful direction of the supervising adult.

At the age of three years and eight months, Tom was eligible for a place at the local education authority nursery, which was attached to the school he would later be attending. Tom was allocated five afternoon sessions. The nursery was a purpose built building, and had its own outside play area, which was shared with the Reception class. The staff consisted of a teacher in charge, and two fully qualified nursery practitioners, equating to a ratio of one adult to 12 children. The nursery was organised using a specific daily routine. Time was allocated for separate adult-directed and child-initiated activities, where the children were engaged in a plan–do–review process in which they made decisions about what they wished to play with.

When Tom first joined the nursery, staff were concerned that he seemed tired and somewhat tearful – especially near the end of the week. During the child-initiated activities, Tom also needed a lot of encouragement to select his own toys. Through sensitive intervention with his key worker, and regular opportunities to share information with his parents, Tom soon became an active member of the nursery class.

Tom joined the Reception class the following year. He remained happy and settled, and particularly enjoyed helping the new nursery children to find a bicycle to play on, during the outside play sessions. Tom's parents were delighted with the apparent ease of his transition from the nursery to the Reception class.

The Foundation Stage curriculum

Unlike the National Curriculum, the Foundation Stage does not consist of a set of programmes of study of curriculum subjects that have to be covered. The curriculum for the Foundation Stage is more concerned with the four key elements of learning:

- **concepts;**
- **knowledge and understanding;**
- **skills;**
- **attitudes.**

Although there are areas of learning which children are required to experience (see the Early Learning Goals), there are a number of principles which form part of good Early Years' practice. To be an effective Early Years teacher, these principles should be reflected in your practice. This will then enable all children eventually to achieve the Early Learning Goals. The DfEE and QCA have produced a document called *Curriculum Guidance for the Foundation Stage* (DfEE/QCA, 2000). It includes useful information which will help you to deliver the Foundation Stage curriculum. You may find it helpful at this point to briefly familiarise yourself with this document. It will be referred to throughout this book.

The principles for the Foundation Stage

The principles for the Foundation Stage have been amended and supplemented over the past ten years by a number of authoritative people in the Early Years field (see DES (the Rumbold Report) (1990) and Bruce (1997) for example). They form part of the curriculum that you provide for young children. These principles look beyond the content of what children learn, concentrating more specifically on the process of learning. They are concerned with our beliefs and values regarding how young children learn and the skills we need to be effective teachers.

Thinking about these principles in relation to your own beliefs and practice will help you develop your own philosophy of learning and teaching in the Early Years. It is important that you begin to develop your own philosophy. This may change either subtly or dramatically as you gain more experience and develop your own understanding of teaching in the Foundation Stage. By the time you become a fully qualified teacher, your philosophy should be evident in everything you do.

Practical task

Look at the 'Principles for Early Years education' below. What examples of Early Years practice have you seen that illustrate any of these principles?

Principles for Early Years education

- *Effective education requires both a relevant curriculum and practitioners who understand and are able to implement the curriculum requirements.*
- *Effective education requires practitioners who understand that children develop rapidly during the Early Years – physically, intellectually, emotionally and socially. Children are entitled to provision that supports and extends knowledge, skills, understanding and confidence, and helps them to overcome any disadvantage.*
- *Practitioners should ensure that all children feel included, secure and valued. They must build positive relationships with parents in order to work effectively and with them and their children.*
- *Early Years experience should build on what children already know and can do. It should also encourage a positive attitude and disposition to learn and aim to prevent failure.*
- *No child should be excluded or disadvantaged because of ethnicity, culture or religion, home language, family background, special educational needs, disability, gender or ability.*
- *Parents and practitioners should work together in an atmosphere of mutual respect within which children can have security and confidence.*
- *To be effective, an Early Years curriculum should be carefully structured. In that structure, there should be three strands:*

  - *provision for the different starting points from which children develop their learning, building on what they can already do;*

  - *relevant and appropriate content that matches the different levels of young children's needs;*

  - *planned and purposeful activity that provides opportunities for teaching and learning, both indoors and outdoors.*

- *There should be opportunities for children to engage in activities planned by adults and also those that they plan or initiate by themselves. Children do not make a distinction between 'play' and 'work' and neither should practitioners. Children need time to become engrossed, work in depth and complete activities.*
- *Practitioners must be able to observe and respond appropriately to children, informed by a knowledge of how children develop and learn and a clear understanding of possible next steps in their development and learning.*
- *Well planned, purposeful activity and appropriate intervention by practitioners will engage children in the learning process and help them make progress in their learning.*

- *For children to have rich and stimulating experiences, the learning environment should be well planned and well organised. It provides the structure for teaching within which children explore, experiment, plan and make decisions for themselves, thus enabling them to learn, develop and make good progress.*
- *Above all, effective learning and development for young children requires high-quality care and education by practitioners.*

(Curriculum Guidance for the Foundation Stage, DfEE/QCA, 2000)

The Early Learning Goals

The Foundation Curriculum is organised into six areas of learning. They provide a basis for you to plan appropriate learning experiences throughout the Foundation Stage.

THE SIX AREAS OF LEARNING

- **Personal, social and emotional development.**
- **Communication, language and literacy.**
- **Mathematical development.**
- **Knowledge and understanding of the world.**
- **Physical development.**
- **Creative development.**

When engaged in a planned learning experience, children will undoubtedly gain skills and experiences in other areas of learning – quite often the learning is unintended by the practitioner – but equally important to a child!

By the end of the Foundation Stage, most children are expected to have reached a number of goals in each area of learning. These are known as the Early Learning Goals. Some children will exceed the goals; others will be working towards them. Much will depend on a child's age and previous experience. Some children will have special educational needs or use English as an additional language, and therefore may not be able to achieve all the goals by the time they reach the end of the Foundation Stage.

As we have already discussed, all children develop at a different rate, and in different ways. The *Curriculum Guidance for the Foundation Stage* (DfEE/QCA, 2000) recognises this, and therefore identifies a number of developmental stepping stones which identify the relevant knowledge, understanding, skills and attitudes needed to achieve each goal. Turn to page 32 of the document for an illustration. The progression is shown through a series of sequential colour-coded bands. You would expect most three year old children to be described by an earlier stepping stone (the yellow band), and the later stepping stone (green band) would describe an older four or five year old child. The grey band at the bottom of the page represents the Early Learning Goal for that particular area of learning.

It is important to remember that:

> The stepping stones are not age-related goals and the number varies between and within areas of learning. In some cases stepping stones relate to an individual aspect of an early learning goal, in others a group of closely linked aspects have been brought together with one set of stepping stones (DfEE/QCA, 2000:26)

Practical task

Turn to page 54 of the Curriculum Guidance document. First look closely at the Stepping Stones column. Think of a child who has only just turned four years old. Can you identify which stepping stone best describes him or her? If you are not sure, look at the next column 'Examples of what children do'. You should now be able to find an example that best describes the child you are thinking about. If you were teaching this child in your setting, you would need to plan appropriate activities which would help him or her progress to the next stage. The final column, 'What does the practitioner need to do?' gives you very clear guidance, and would serve as an excellent starting point for your future planning.

Planning for the Foundation Stage

The knowledge and skills required to plan an appropriate curriculum are generic to whichever age range you are teaching. You may find it useful to refer to the book *Achieving QTS Professional Studies: Primary Phase* for more explicit and detailed guidance. Nevertheless, some guidance pertinent to planning for the Foundation Stage can be found in the next section of this chapter.

Long-term planning

Julie Fisher (in Siraj-Blatchford, 1998) discusses the importance of establishing what a child already knows and can do, before fine-tuning planning to meet the individual needs and interests of individual learners. There will be certain aspects of the learning environment and the curriculum that are generally appropriate for all children of the same age. This is your starting point for your long-term planning. It provides what Fisher describes as a 'menu' of skills, under-standing, knowledge and attitudes that will be appropriate for most of the children at that particular time.

Your long-term plan will most probably cover the learning experiences that children will encounter over a year. It is important that, over that period of time, all children will have had the opportunity to experience a broad and balanced range of experiences.

WHAT SHOULD BE INCLUDED IN A LONG-TERM PLAN?

- **The overall aims for children's development in each area of learning.**
- **Themes and topics that will form the focus of a unit of learning experiences.**
- **Information related to specific dates, events, visits and visitors intended to extend children's experiences.**

- **Overall organisational factors including: the characteristics of the class, staffing and resourcing requirements.**

Most schools have a specific format for planning. You will probably find that long-term planning documentation is already in place. You may find it useful to collect a range of long-term planning examples from during your school experience. Look for common patterns – seasonal learning experiences will almost certainly be similar in most settings.

Medium-term planning

Your medium-term planning should address continuity and progression from one stage in each area of learning to the next. Using the Curriculum Guidance document will help you do this. You will have decided on a topic or theme by this stage. This will usually last for up to half a term. You may have a series of mini-themes within your overall topic – for example, using a different nursery rhyme as a starting point every two weeks. At this stage of planning, it is important that you begin to think how each area of learning links together, so that children are able to make the most of their learning experiences. (See Figure 1.1)

WHAT SHOULD BE INCLUDED IN A MEDIUM-TERM PLAN?

- **The topic or theme.**
- **Specific learning objectives for each area of learning.**
- **Children's special needs and suggested groupings.**
- **Resources, for example storybooks, artefacts and role-play equipment.**
- **An evaluation of children's progress in relation to each area of learning, at the end of the topic/theme.**

It is important that you reflect on the progress children have made in your planned topic. You will then have relevant information that will inform you of the experiences children need next for each area of learning, to take them forward. (See Chapter 10.)

Short-term planning

Your long- and medium-term planning is concerned with the organisation of the curriculum and what is going to be taught. Short-term planning considers the specific needs of individual groups of children and how key concepts, skills, knowledge, understanding and attitudes are to be introduced to children in a relevant, meaningful and purposeful way. Julie Fisher refers to this as the 'diet', taken from the menu, which is selected, modified and customised to meet the particular characteristics of individual children.

One of the principles for Early Years education states that 'There should be opportunities for children to engage in activities planned by adults and also those that they plan and initiate themselves'. Your short-term planning can only account for the learning experiences that you have planned. The children in your class will also be engaged in their own chosen learning experiences. These will usually be in the form of 'play' activities. This is addressed in a later section of this chapter (also Chapter 8). For the moment, let us return to your own short-term planning.

TOPIC/THEME: Once Upon A Time   **Focus**: Goldilocks & the Three Bears   **TIME**: 3 weeks

	Learning objectives	Possible experiences	Resources	Evaluation
Personal, social and emotional development	• Be confident to try new experiences; initiate ideas & speak in a familiar group. • Understand what is right, what is wrong & why.	• Encourage children to share thoughts & responses to the story. • Share ideas for Baby Bear's birthday card. • Talk about Goldilocks entering the Three Bears' cottage on her own.		
Communication, language and literacy	• Listen attentively & respond to the story of the Three Bears. • Use language to imagine and recreate roles and experiences. • Show an understanding of the main events and characters of the story. • Use non-fiction books to answer questions. • Attempt writing for different purposes.	• Set up the role play corner as the Three Bears Cottage. • Use puppets to act out the story.[lg] • Write a shopping list for the Three Bears. • Make a Birthday Card for Baby Bear. • Use a selection of non-fiction books to find out about bears.[sg] • Draw pictures and make labels for a class book about bears.[sg] • Use the Internet to find pictures of bears. [p with adults' support]	• Small, medium and large sized furniture, bowls, spoons etc. • A range of 'breakfast' food packaging. • Paper, card, pencils, crayon etc. • 'Real' Birthday cards. • Find a relevant web site.	
Mathematical development	• Count reliably up to 10 everyday objects. • Use mathematical ideas and methods to solve problems. • Use language to compare quantities.	• Play counting games. [lg] • Shopping game [p] • Make a bed long enough for Daddy Bear to keep his toes warm! [sg] • Weighing Compare Bears – 'Whose bears are the heaviest?' [sg]	• Counting equipment. • Shopping game. • Construction equipment. • Compare Bears. • Balancing scales.	
Knowledge and understanding of the world	• Investigate objects and materials by using all senses. • Look at similarities, differences, patterns and change • Build and construct with a wide range of objects, selecting appropriate tools. • Observe, find out about and identify features in local environment.	• Make and taste porridge, using a variety of sweeteners. • Make toast, selecting from a range of toppings [sg] talk about and describe range of tastes and textures. • Build a dark cave where a bear can hibernate.[sg] • Walk to the local shop. Make a 3-D map to help the Three Bears find their way.[lg]	• Porridge oats, bread, jam, honey, marmite, butter etc. • Cooking utensils. • Large blocks, sheets and blankets, boxes etc. • Camera • Large paper, small world equipment	
Physical development	• Move with confidence and imagination. • Travel around, under, over and through balancing and climbing equipment. • Handle tools, objects and construction materials safely.	• Respond to the story 'We're going on a Bear Hunt.' [lg] • Set up a range of equipment for outside play. • Encourage and support children to use a range of equipment and tools when working independently.	• Story – 'We're Going on a Bear Hunt'. • Wheeled toys. • Cones, hoops, benches. • Scissors, playdoh, sellotape, stapler.	
Creative development	• Explore colour, texture, shape, form and space. • Sing simple songs from memory. • Use imagination in art and design and imaginative role play.	• Explore the effects of porridge oats added to paint and glue. • Use chalks, crayons and inks to make own bear representations – using non-fiction books as a stimulus. • Learn the song 'When Goldilocks went to the house of the Bears' – use instruments to accompany.	• Paint, porridge oats, glue. • Chalks, crayons, inks. • Choice of sized paper. • Non fiction books and pictures. • Musical instruments.	

Figure 1.1 An example of medium-term planning

Key: [p] – pairs   [sg] – small group   [lg] – large group

Context: Goldilocks & the Three Bears	
Area of learning	
Learning objectives Knowledge & Understanding	• To explore & describe similarities & differences using senses when making toast. • To be confident to try new experiences. • Use language & imagination to recreate the story of the Three Bears.

Introduction [lg]
Show the children a shopping bag containing bread, butter & a range of toppings which could be spread on toast. Discuss when these ingredients may be used & encourage children to share their knowledge of the process for making toast. Ask the children to share their own experiences & state preferences.

Adult focused activity	Supplementary activities	Resources/organisation
Making toast: Involve the group of children in the process of making toast. Encourage children to sample a range of toppings, including those which are unfamiliar. State preferences & encourage children to describe taste, consistency, texture etc. Focus language: *soft – hard – light – dark – dry – sticky – sweet – hot – cold – melt.*	(1) Three Bears Cottage: Introduce a range of breakfast cereals. (2) Writing Area: Children to choose & plan own ideas. (card, letter, story …) (3) Sand: Children may choose to recreate their own Three bears world. (4) Construction Area: Children to plan & choose.	Range of cereal boxes, empty milk carton. [T.A to support initially] Card, paper, envelopes, glue, scissors & pens. [T.A to join group later – share children's ideas & copy their ideas to make own] Compare Bears, small world house, twigs, stones etc. Encourage children to add own objects if needed. [T.A to encourage children to talk about their plans]

Assessment focus
How confident were the children to try unfamiliar toppings?
Were the children able to talk about & describe similarities, differences and the process of change?

Evaluation
Toast – children were all actively engaged (see assessments) two toasters needed to avoid children having to wait.
Role Play – many children were keen to use the role play corner need to plan more opportunities.
Writing area – children requested sellotape, many made cards and activity developed into wrapping up parcels to send for Baby Bear's birthday.
Sand – Children added foil cake cases and filled with water to make a pond.
Construction – many children were building 'tall' houses.

Figure 1.2 Short-term lesson plan

In your short-term planning, you will be planning specific activities that are intended to result in some intended learning. There are three main types of activities that will occur in an Early Years environment:

1. **Adult-focused activities** usually involve the adult working with a child or group of children, for the duration of the activity. There will be a clear learning objective, where the outcome is pre-determined.

2. **Adult-initiated activities** are usually a subsidiary activity that an adult may initiate and then leave children to complete independently. You may have a specific learning objective in mind, but when left to their own devices children's own interests may lead to a different learning outcome. In order for these activities to provide valuable learning experiences, it is important that the activity is relatively open ended, and provides opportunities for exploration and dialogue. You must ensure that you make time available at the end of the activity to return to the activity, in order for you to make judgements about what the children have gained from it, by talking, asking questions and making suggestions.

3. **Child-initiated activities** are activities where it is not possible to define a learning objective, or outcome. Children are able to take responsibility for their own learning and follow their own interests by selecting the resources and activities independently (see Chapter 8).

Your short-term planning usually only takes into consideration adult focused and initiated activities. Some settings may use some form of documentation that highlights specific resources which children may choose from in their independent activities. Attempts may also be made to highlight the potential learning outcomes which may occur in child initiated activities. This is very difficult – children are unique individuals. Their own imagination, interests and experiences can take play to a dimension that most adults would never be able to predict! (See Figure 1.2 for an example of a short-term plan.)

WHAT SHOULD BE INCLUDED IN A SHORT-TERM PLAN?

- **A clear learning objective for each area of learning.**
- **An outline of the intended activity.**
- **Organisation, such as groupings and where the activity will take place.**
- **Resources to be used, including the name of the adult.**
- **Identification of assessment opportunities, which are clearly linked to the learning objective.**
- **An evaluation of the activity, and the next steps that identify future learning needs.**

Practical task

Figure 1.2 shows an example of a short-term plan for a Reception class. You should be able to identify three different types of activities on the plan. Refer to the medium-term plan (Figure 1.1) and think about what learning experiences the children would benefit from next, in order to build upon their existing knowledge, skills and understanding. You may wish to focus on a different area of learning, or consider how the same area of learning can be extended. Try to ensure that there are opportunities for all three types of activities. Remember, it is only possible for you to focus on one group at a time.

Meeting the diverse needs of young children

The Children Act (1989) states that 'Children have a right to an environment which facilitates their development' (6.28). It goes on to determine rights in the terms of a child's sense of identity, including the right to individuality, respect, dignity and freedom from discrimination such as racism and sexism (DoH, 1991).

When we consider how we advocate children's rights in the Foundation Stage, your role is imperative in meeting children's diverse needs, and helping all children make the best possible progress.

> Practitioners should plan to meet the needs of boys and girls, children with special educational needs, children who are more able, children with disabilities, children from all social, cultural and religious backgrounds, children of different ethnic groups including travellers, refugees and asylum seekers, and children from diverse linguistic backgrounds. (DfEE/QCA, 2000:17)

Meeting the diverse needs of all children can sometimes be very challenging, for a variety of reasons. For example, you may feel you have very limited knowledge and understanding about Islam and do not know how to communicate with a child's mother who does not speak English. You may not know what strategies to employ, in order to ensure a hearing impaired child is able to engage in role play, or you may be aware that there is a very able child in your setting who has exceeded the Early Learning Goals, and you are not sure how to differentiate the activities you plan to meet his needs. These are just a few of the varied and sometimes complex situations you may encounter during your career. There will always be a number of outside agencies and specialist professionals who you will be able to contact to support you, the child and his or her family (see Chapter 3). Your role is to think about the needs of all young children in your class, and how you can attempt to meet them.

The first step is to think about what actually happens in your classroom on a daily basis. Ask yourself the following questions:

- **Do I have enough information about each child's background? Think about the family structure; the socio-cultural features; previous experiences and his or her particular interests.**
- **When planning my topic, have I taken account of each child's rich and varied background? Think about the learning experiences you are going to provide, and consider how they will extend each child's knowledge, experiences, interests and skills, as well as develop their self-esteem and confidence. This will have an overall impact on their ability to learn.**
- **What range of teaching strategies can I use that are most suitable for children's learning needs? Some children will need additional support, for example through the use of specialised resources, a differentiated task or modelled language. Children learn in different ways, and so you must use a range of teaching strategies that will address this.**
- **How can I ensure that all children will be motivated and involved in their learning, so that they can concentrate and learn effectively? You will need to consider how you structure your day; how you group children; how you organise your classroom and the role of the adults who work with your children.**
- **How can I ensure that I am providing a safe and supportive learning environment, which is free from harassment, where all children are valued, and where all racial, religious, disability and gender stereotypes are challenged? Look carefully at the resources that you use and the themes you plan. Ensure that they positively reflect diversity and are free from both discrimination and stereotyping.**
- **How will I monitor each child's progress, identify any areas of concern and decide what action to take? You may find, for example, that a child's understanding and ability seem far more advanced than her language and communication skills. It will be important for you to share your information with her parents and other members of staff, in order to devise a plan of action that would meet that child's individual needs.**

The following classroom story illustrates some of the areas of practice one particular teacher addressed, in order to meet the individual needs of all the children in her class.

Classroom story

Miss Cook was responsible for a class of 27 Reception aged children. The children had previously attended a variety of pre-school settings. In order to help the children settle into the new class, a series of induction sessions had been arranged. These occurred each week, over the final half of the term before the children started full-time school. The first session was a story time, which the children attended with their parents. Over the next six weeks, the sessions were gradually extended, culminating in the children staying in their new class all morning, and then going to the dining room for lunch. In addition to this, Miss Cook also invited parents to an informal meeting to discuss their child's first year in school. In addition to this, Miss Cook had visited the children in their own homes.

By the time the new term began, Miss Cook felt that she had already developed very positive relationships with both parents and her pupils. She felt that the information she had gathered during the home visits had provided her with valuable information regarding each child's individual experiences, interests and needs.

There were 15 boys and 12 girls in the class. One child was hearing impaired, and was supported by a teacher of the deaf for ten hours per week. Miss Cook had contacted the Hearing Impaired Services to seek advice about the support she would need to give to the child. As a result of her discussion, and a visit to the nursery she was previously attending, an individual education plan was devised. Miss Cook ensured the classroom was made acoustically sound by adding more soft furnishings to the classroom. She discussed the structure of the day with the Teacher of the Deaf, to ensure that he visited her at the times in which she would benefit from his additional support.

There were also twin boys in the class, whose home language was Punjabi. Their parents spoke English as an additional language. Miss Cook contacted the Bilingual Support Team. They helped her devise an individual education plan for the boys, which was primarily concerned with providing them with opportunities to build on their experiences of home. A member of the team was also invited to join Miss Cook in all parent meetings to ensure the parents were fully informed of their children's progress. In addition to this, Miss Cook looked at the resources in her classroom to ensure they positively reflected the diversity of languages and cultures in her classroom. This included purchasing a number of dual language books.

Baseline assessment revealed that a large number of the children in the class had very poor speaking and listening skills. Miss Cook decided that her medium-term planning needed to be amended, so that there was a greater emphasis on developing these skills. More practical games and role-play activities were included into the structure of the day.

Children with Special Educational Needs

There will be some children you teach who have very specific individual learning requirements. Some children will have already been identified as having specific special needs. They will already have an Individual Education Plan in place. In other situations, the Foundation Stage can be the first time a child's particular needs or disabilities are identified. You have a key role to play in working with parents (see Chapter 2) to identify a child's particular needs, and attempt to develop an effective strategy to address his or her needs. This will usually involve working with other agencies in devising an individual education plan (see Chapter 3). This will include specific targets for a child to meet, and an action plan which specifies the nature of support needed in order to help the child meet his or her target.

The revised SEN Code of Practice specifies the particular requirements for intervention in Early Years settings. This is discussed in greater detail in Chapter 3.

Children with English as an additional language

Many children in an Early Years setting will have a home language other than English. Some children will be multilingual from birth, as their families have communicated in more than one language. Some children will need to acquire English as an additional language. In order for this to be a relevant learning experience, a number of factors need to be taken into consideration. As with any learning experience, it must take place in a context that is both relevant and meaningful. Children need opportunities to engage and interact with others. They also need time to merely listen and experience the new language before they attempt to speak it. Other forms of communication are equally important, and contribute to the child's understanding. For example, gesture, sign, facial expression and visual support such as pictures and objects should all form part of the learning process.

The Curriculum Guidance document states clearly that you should plan opportunities that will help children develop their English, and provide support which will enable them to take part in other activities. Examples given include:

- **building on children's experiences of language at home and in the wider community by providing a range of opportunities to use their home language(s), so that their developing use of English and other languages support one another;**
- **providing a range of opportunities for children to engage in speaking and listening activities in English with peers and adults;**
- **ensuring all children have opportunities to recognise and show respect for each child's home language;**
- **providing bilingual support, in particular to extend vocabulary and support children's developing understanding;**
- **providing a variety of writing in the children's home languages as well as in English, including books, notices and labels;**
- **providing opportunities for children to hear home languages as well as English, for example, through the use of audio and video materials.**

It is always a good idea to contact the Bilingual Services Team for guidance. In addition to providing you with support in relation to teaching strategies, they can also provide you with information and contacts to purchase relevant resources.

Play in the Foundation Stage

Anyone who has observed play for any length of time will recognise that, for young children, play is a tool for learning and practitioners who acknowledge and appreciate this can, through provision, interaction and intervention in children's play ensure progression, differentiation and relevance in the curriculum. (Moyles, 1994:6)

The place of play in the Early Years curriculum is clearly defined, in the Foundation Curriculum.

Well-planned play, both indoors and outdoors, is a key way in which young children learn with enjoyment and challenge. (DfEE/QCA, 2000:25)

How does play contribute to a child's learning?

Play encourages children to:

- **co-operate, and learn from each other;**
- **explore and develop new ideas and concepts;**
- **practise, revisit and master new skills;**
- **make sense of the world through their own representations;**
- **take risks and make mistakes;**
- **explore their own emotions and relive anxious experiences in a safe and secure environment;**
- **communicate effectively;**
- **develop confidence and independence;**
- **use imagination and develop creativity.**

There are probably many more of your own thoughts that you can add to this list.

There is no question regarding the value of play, in relation to children's learning and development. Yet many teachers are presented with the problem of how to ensure that children are engaged in meaningful and valued play experiences – when the teacher is frequently engaged in other adult directed activities. Research by Bennett et al (1997) suggests that many teachers believe children are learning a great deal during play activities, but in reality, without support and intervention from an adult, the benefits of the play activity are only of a very low level. This suggests that your role in the classroom is fundamental to the benefits children gain in play activities.

How can I ensure that play experiences are meaningful and valuable?

The Curriculum Guidance document states that the practitioner plays an essential role in ensuring that children are learning when they play. Your role is crucial in:

- **planning and resourcing a challenging environment;**
- **supporting children's learning through planned play activity;**
- **extending and supporting children's spontaneous play;**
- **extending and developing children's language and communication in their play.**

(DfEE/QCA, 2000:25)

Let's take each point in turn, and consider the implications for your practice.

PLANNING AND RESOURCING A CHALLENGING ENVIRONMENT

When you plan your theme or topic, you will need to consider what play activities children may engage in that are connected to your theme, and will help develop their knowledge, under-standing and skills. Role-play, for instance, will help children understand about features of everyday life which are beyond their own experiences. This means that you will need to ensure that the resources you provide for the children are relevant and are of a good quality.

For example, you may wish to set up a health clinic in your classroom. An initial visit to a health clinic would give the children first hand experience and provide a meaningful context. The knowledge they have gained can then be transferred and built upon, through their own role-play.

It is also important that all the resources in your classroom are attractively displayed, and organised in such a way that children can access them independently. When children have ownership of their play, it will be much more purposeful (see Chapter 8 for more).

Remember, children need to experience the curriculum both indoors and outdoors. As far as possible, you need to be thinking about how play experiences can be taken outside the class-room. For further information about outside play, refer to Bilton (1998).

SUPPORTING CHILDREN'S LEARNING THROUGH PLANNED PLAY ACTIVITY

We have mentioned earlier in this chapter the three different types of activity that should occur in your classroom. On many occasions, these activities will be happening simultaneously. You need to think carefully about the structure of your day, in order to ensure that all children experience a range of activities throughout the day. In that way each child should have had an opportunity for both child- and adult-initiated learning.

When you plan an activity, think carefully about your role. There are a number of different roles you may adopt in any play situation. You may act as a guide – where you are perhaps modelling how to use a new piece of equipment, so that a child is able to use it independently the next time. On the other hand you may wish to use the opportunity to find out what a child already knows, and then help him or her build on that knowledge through further dialogue. (See Chapter 5 for more on adult/children relationships.)

EXTENDING AND SUPPORTING CHILDREN'S SPONTANEOUS PLAY

When children are playing spontaneously, it is very tempting to join in, presuming that you know what the children are thinking about. Have you ever joined a play situation with a sweeping statement or question, to find that the children greet you with a look of exasperation at the irrelevance of your statement? You then quickly find yourself alone, as the children have gone to play with something else!

The most important thing to do before joining in any play activity, is to observe silently what is happening. You need to give yourself time to understand the nature and focus of the play. Once you have established this, you can then enter the game at the children's level. It is important that you try to use the same language as them, at least in the beginning − until the children are comfortable with your presence. When the children are engaged in their own play, do not be tempted to steer them towards your own agenda. Children gain a great deal from spontaneous play.

EXTENDING AND DEVELOPING CHILDREN'S LANGUAGE AND COMMUNICATION IN THEIR PLAY

All of the issues that have been discussed in this section are pertinent to this final point. Chapter 5 explores language development in much greater depth. Play situations are an ideal opportunity to introduce children to new vocabulary, and extend and develop their communication skills. There will be times when children prefer to play on their own. Some children need these opportunities to gain confidence, before joining others. It is important that you monitor solitary play. If a child continues to play on his or her own, there may be a specific reason for this. It is important that you try to find out what the reason is, then you should be able to sensitively help the child and support him or her.

One final thought about play. Children need to know that you value their play. When planning for play opportunities, think about organising it so that you are not always engaged in an adult-planned activity. In order to really know and understand what interests a child, and how they think and learn, you need to spend some time just watching and learning about them as individuals. This will also provide you with vital information that will help you plan their future learning experiences.

The Foundation Stage and meeting the Early Learning Goals:
a summary of key points

The aim of this chapter has been to provide you with relevant knowledge and understanding about the Foundation Stage and the Early Learning Goals. We can summarise the key points in the following way:

- *The Foundation Stage is an important stage of learning, which provides the basis for all children's future learning.*
- *The aims of the Foundation Stage are to support, foster, promote and develop children's personal, social and emotional well-being; positive attitudes and skills towards learning; language, literacy and communication; mathematical, physical, creative development and their knowledge and understanding of the world in which they live.*
- *There are a number of principles related to teaching and learning in the Early Years. When put into practice, they should provide the opportunity for children to develop to their fullest potential.*

All children have a diverse range of needs, which teachers must make every attempt to identify in order for every child to achieve the Early Learning Goals as far as possible.

Play provides an exciting and challenging way for children to learn. In order for children to benefit from play experiences, the teacher has a vital role to play.

2 WORKING WITH PARENTS AND OTHER CARERS: ENHANCING LEARNING OPPORTUNITIES

Iris Keating

Professional Standards for QTS

→ 1.4

This Standard states that in order to gain QTS teachers must be able to communicate sensitively and effectively with parents and carers, recognising their roles in pupils' learning, and their rights, responsibilities and interests in this.

You may find it helpful to refer to the appropriate section of the Handbook that accompanies the Standards for the award of QTS, for further clarification and support.

The Curriculum Guidance for the Foundation Stage also makes reference to this area of interest where a whole section is entitled 'Parents as partners'. Here the focus is on the development of an effective partnership with parents with a 'two-way flow of information, knowledge and expertise' (p.9).

By the end of this chapter you should:

- *appreciate the importance of parents/carers in the educational experiences of their children;*
- *understand and acknowledge the range of roles that parents/carers can play in partnership with their children's education;*
- *realise the need for effective communication and liaison with parents/carers;*
- *understand how to manage the work of parents/carers in the setting in order to enhance the learning opportunities of the children;*
- *be aware of the importance of a two way flow of information, knowledge and expertise with parents/carers.*

Introduction

The potential of the role that parents can play in the Early Years setting has been understood since the publication of the Plowden Report (Central Advisory Council for Education, 1967) and since then there has been significant research into the benefits of involving parents/carers in the education of their children. The Plowden Report highlighted how parental attitudes towards their child's education vitally influenced the child's school performance. During the 1980s a number of research studies showed the effectiveness of directly involving parents in their children's learning, such as the Haringey Reading Project (Tizard et al 1982) and the PACT project (Griffiths and Hamilton 1984) which focused upon parents assisting in the development of children's reading skills. The 1986 Education Act, followed by the 1988 Education Reform Act, extended parents' involvement with their child's education by providing them with opportunities to become members of the school governing body. The Children Act (1989) focuses more on the responsibilities of the parent, clearly stating that all parents have responsibilities for the care and education of their children. The Act also makes it clear that parents have the right to be consulted and informed about the progress of their children and thus institutions involved in the care and education of their children are responsible to the parents. The focus today continues on the partnership between parent/carer and educational setting, and is one that is not confined to the Early Years. In the later years the focus tends to be on shared responsibility and joint action such as with homework and the development of home-school agreements and contracts.

For many Early Years settings and primary schools what is termed 'parental involvement' is seen on the surface to be unproblematic and is viewed unquestioningly. But the reality of parental involvement is highly complex and not least since the skills and abilities needed by Early Years staff to work successfully with parents/carers do not necessarily come naturally or by accident. This is the focus of this chapter.

Who do we mean by parents/carers?

On the surface this seems to be a simple question, but when we look further this is a much more complex issue. Parents under the Parent's Charter of 1991 have rights and responsibilities for their children's education. However, the status of parent extends, according to Houghton and McColgan (1995: 95), to others involved in the care and upbringing of children: 'Thus extended family members, grandparents, step-parents, child-minders or foster parents may be considered as sharing parental responsibility.'

Consequently, when we talk of parent/carer we need to be aware that it could refer to a number of people associated with the child. Also when we consider the reality of what most settings refer to as parental involvement we can see that for most of the time what we really mean by the term 'parents' is in fact 'mothers'. There has been a lot of discussion about why this is the case, not only why it is that mothers are the ones to come into school but also why it is that we tend not to reflect this in our choice of words. Why do we use the term parental involvement instead of mothers' involvement? If you would like to read more about this see the work of Reay (1998).

Why might mothers be the main carers to become involved in their children's schooling? You may think that mothers are the ones with most available free time, but in these days of a changing economic base with higher female employment and indeed lower male employment it could be argued that there are more fathers who are available to come into school. If we add that mothers tend to have the major responsibility for care of younger pre-school children, then it might be more manageable for the family as a whole for the father to go into the school. But why does this tend not to be the case? And where fathers do go into school it appears that they tend to have a specific role, such as to help with computers or to do some woodwork. This may serve to reinforce sex stereotyped notions of men's work and women's work.

We also need to be aware, as Houghton and McColgan (1995) indicated above, that there is a huge diversity of family life with children living in families with step-parents, step-siblings and a range of extended family settings. We need to ensure that not only do we address those who bring and collect children from the Early Years setting in a respectful and accurate way but that any invitations to become involved in the setting should be open to all, and not to a select few. This will be returned to later.

The following classroom story illustrates how important it is to ensure that parents/carers are addressed appropriately.

Classroom story

When Jane started to attend nursery, the class teacher and nursery nurse both made the assumption that the woman who brought her to school each day and collected her was her mother. They therefore referred to her as 'Jane's mummy' or as Mrs Brown, which was Jane's surname. This was never corrected by the woman and not commented upon by any of the other parents/carers. However, the staff were aware that 'Jane's mummy' was reluctant to communicate with staff, was always eager to leave the nursery as quickly as possible and indeed almost hurried Jane off the premises.

The staff were eager to encourage parents/carers to play a full part in the life of the nursery and believed that they made all parents/carers welcome. But 'Jane's mummy' never took up any of these invitations and appeared almost to shun them. She did not attend the nursery nativity play and despite several invitations did not come on the end of year trip to the seaside. The staff were tempted to believe that she was simply not interested in becoming involved in Jane's schooling. It was only some years later (when Jane was in Key Stage 1) that at an evening parents/carers meeting it became evident that Jane's mummy was dead and the person referred to for so long by the staff as 'Jane's mummy' was actually Jane's father's girlfriend. She was too embarrassed to correct the staff and rather than address the misunderstanding did all that she could to avoid it, feeling increasingly unhappy about not playing the part in Jane's life that she very much wanted to.

Why involve parents/carers?

Working with parents/carers clearly has many significant benefits, some of which have been indicated in the introduction to this chapter. Others include:

- aiding the accountability to parents/carers, as enshrined in the Children Act (1989);
- helping children's learning. Parents/carers are their children's first educators. They are experts on the children in their care. Staff in Early Years settings can learn a lot from them. Similarly parents/carers can also learn from Early Years staff how best to support their children's learning, without placing the children under too much pressure to achieve;
- minimising the potential for conflict between the Early Years setting and home by ensuring not only that parents/carers understand the aims of the establishment and how it sets out to achieve these aims, but also that good two-way channels of communication are opened up between the Early Years setting and home. For some parents there is distrust or even fear of school, resulting from their own experiences of school. An important function of the Early Years setting could be to overcome those fears and develop a relationship built on trust and a commitment to the growth and development of their children;

- providing support for staff by parents/carers supplying an extra pair of hands – particularly useful in adult-intensive activities. Some would go even further than this and argue that parents/carers can add to the efficacy of the educational establishment. Wolfendale and Bastiani (2000) recognise the need for schools to set targets in the continuing quest to raise standards and they offer a range of examples where partnership with parents is actually helping in achieving this. Many of their examples are with children older than the Early Years but nonetheless their examples make thought-provoking reading;

- being a valuable experience for the parents themselves. Nurseries have been described as outposts of adult education and indeed for some parents/carers contact with their children's nursery or infant class can be the first positive experience of schooling that they have had for some time. Once a trust has been established parents/carers may find that working in the Early Years setting as a volunteer could lead to growing confidence and to developing a career in Early Years. Certainly this has been the case in **Pen Green** and the impact of the centre on the lives of parents/carers is described in **Chapter 7 of Whalley et al (2001).**

It is also useful to recognise that parents/carers working alongside staff will allow:

- the children to witness their parents/carers working alongside the Early Years staff and this could help in terms of their security and behaviour management;

- more children to have more time with an adult and thus we need to ensure that this is time of a high quality;

- staff to model a range of positive behaviour management techniques, questioning skills and general talking with children, in a non-patronising way that parents/carers might find useful;

- wider experiences to be offered to the children.

Also the guidelines provided for schools preparing for an OFSTED inspection highlight the need for schools to form good working relationships with parents and the community. These guidelines appear to promote the need for schools to actively involve parents/carers in their child's education more than simply communicating with parents/carers about their child's education.

What roles might parents/carers play?

The roles that parents/carers can play vary considerably between the statutory and the non-statutory sectors. Further there are huge variations *within* sectors. If you would like to read more about this you will find the work of Pugh and the National Children's Bureau (1987 and 1989) to be helpful. They have suggested that there is a fivefold dimension to working with parents/carers in terms of their relationships with the Early Years setting. This ranges from:

non-participation ➞ support ➞ participation ➞ partnership ➞ control

This illustrates that parents/carers will take on different roles in the Early Years setting. Some parents/carers, for a variety of reasons that will be discussed later, may decide not to participate. Others may support the setting, perhaps by buying raffle tickets, and others take more of a participatory role, for example by attending parents/carers assembly. In some settings parents/

carers will be working alongside staff in a partnership role and in other settings parents/carers could serve on the governing body.

Practical task

Consider an Early Years setting that you know and think how each of the roles of non-participation, support, participation, partnership and control might exist there. Think about what the parents/carers might do in each role?

In order to promote the partnership between educational settings and parents/carers there needs to be open communication between the two groups and effective home/school links established. We are fortunate in the Early Years since it is likely that we will have regular contact with parents/carers when they deliver and collect their children. However, this is not always the case and we need to ensure that **all** parents/carers are kept equally informed of their children's progress. Written communication is therefore essential in the development of positive home/school links and this could be in a variety of forms, largely determined by the reason for the communication.

The most common forms of written communication are:

- **written reports, summarising the children's achievement and progress over a given period of time;**
- **end of year profiles/record of achievement;**
- **weekly bulletins describing the activities that have taken place and those planned for the following week;**
- **day books which provide a means of daily liaison between staff and individual parents/carers, each writing in the booklet what they want the other to know (with older children this includes homework requirements).**

But note that all of these assume a level of functional literacy in English which may not exist. It is therefore essential for you to sensitively discover where this is not the case and to develop alternative strategies to deal with this.

Written communication also needs to go alongside verbal communication. Again this will vary with its purpose and will range from informal discussion on the children's arrival and departure to formalised meetings arranged by prior appointment. The tone of all of these interactions is important and all staff involved in the education of the children should play a part in them.

In this section we are particularly concerned with parents/carers working alongside you in the Early Years setting. This is what is commonly referred to as parental involvement and as with any commonly used term there is an assumption that we all know what it means: that we all have a shared understanding of that meaning, that it is unproblematic and is viewed unquestioningly. The reality of parental involvement, however, is highly complex and not least since the skills and abilities needed by Early Years staff to work successfully with parents/carers do not necessarily come naturally or by accident.

Practical task

Make a list of all of the possible activities where parents/carers can be involved in the Early Years setting.

Your list could well be very long. It will no doubt include those activities that are:

- **curriculum-based, such as listening to children reading or sharing a book with them;**
- **practical activities such as baking with a small group or working on the computer;**
- **helping with outdoor activities, remembering the importance of the outdoor environment to the needs of Early Years children;**
- **accompanying the children on visits or days out;**
- **housekeeping tasks, including washing out the paintpots;**
- **involvement in the Parent Staff Association or the Friends of the setting/ organisation.**

It would be a real waste of opportunity for your list not to also include activities where parents/ carers feel that they have a special skill to contribute. As was indicated earlier, we do have to be mindful not to perpetuate simplistic sex stereotyped images and expectations. So if you do have a mother/female carer who can support children using the computer you have extra help **and** are providing a positive role model for girls and ICT.

But we need to remember that parents/carers have their own lives too and they do not exist purely as parents/carers. If you would like to read of further ways that parents/carers have been involved in a range of Early Years settings then see Chapter 9 in Smidt (1998).

Also the work taking place at the Pen Green Centre may be of interest to you. This centre, set up in 1983 for the under fives and their families is a multifunction service, staffed by a multi-disciplinary team. It has a fascinating history and central to its philosophy are the local community and the parents/carers. In 1983 there were 6 staff at Pen Green, working with 50 children. By 2001 there are more than 35 staff involved with working with more than 500 families.

To find out more about Pen Green and its relationships with parents/carers see Whalley (1997).

Practical task

Consider some of the reasons why parents/carers might not become involved in the Early Years setting.

This might include practical reasons such as:

- parents/carers may be geographically remote from the Early Years setting with children being bussed to and from school;
- children may spend only a short time in the setting, for example, two to three hours a day in a nursery school or unit;
- parents/carers may be in paid work;
- parents/carers may have other pressing family commitments;
- parents/carers may not wish to become involved. They may wish to use their time in different ways, yet feel guilty if they are not at the beck and call of the staff in the Early Years setting. Thus an invitation to involvement can easily become another pressure on already pressured parents/carers.

In contrast there is the possibility that so many parents/carers may wish to be involved that this too becomes a problem. For example, what is the optimum number of parents/carers in any one session? Who decides this? If there are too many volunteers, who selects and what selection criteria are used? How do 'rejected' parents/carers feel? A rota system could be an option but who organises it? Who has the power to dictate who attends and when?

Further there might be other reasons, including those parents/carers who are not confident in speaking English and who may belong to a culture where such involvement would be discouraged.

We also need to guard against the possibility of cliques being developed where those parents/carers who do become regulars in the Early Years setting appear to have access and insight which other parents/carers do not have, creating resentment and barriers. Further it has been found that barriers can be created if staff are seen to be over friendly or 'intimate' with certain parents/carers.

The following classroom story illustrates how the development of cliques can actually mitigate against the successful involvement of parents/carers.

Classroom story

In a nursery attached to a primary school the staff were committed to the involvement of parents/carers. They were proud of the quality relationships that they had with parents/carers. Each year they held a successful Autumn Fayre, where money was raised for school funds. Each Thursday afternoon was 'open house' where parents/carers were welcome to pop in, for a few minutes or for the whole session, to their children's nursery. There was a rota when parents/carers volunteered to come to nursery to work alongside staff and children and there were always parents willing to accompany children on the various school trips taking place throughout the year. Indeed such was the nature of the relationships that in the privacy of the staff room (i.e. not in front of the children) parents/carers referred to staff by their given names. However, over the years it was clear that, although there was a group of dedicated parents/carers who were involved with the school, despite numerous initiatives, new parents/carers were simply not becoming involved in the life of the school.

Some years later it was discovered that the group of parents/carers who were involved did all in their power to maintain their exclusivity and actually discouraged other parents/carers from becoming involved in the school. They fiercely guarded their relationship with the staff and ensured that no parents/carers from outside their group were allowed entry. The staff were oblivious to this state of affairs and as they became increasingly reliant on the group of involved parents/carers (because there were no alternatives) so the power and status of this group was enhanced. Thus the situation self-perpetuated.

What are the advantages of involving parents/carers in your Early Years setting?

Clearly an extra pair of hands is always useful in Early Years settings, but how useful is it to view parents/carers in this limited way? Also how legitimate is it to ask unpaid parents/carers to carry out the menial tasks where there is unlikely to be little satisfaction for them? Also is it not problematic to exploit parents/carers as unpaid volunteers at the expense of failing to recruit trained and paid staff? Certainly professional associations and the staff unions have considered this and have concluded that new guidelines need to be drawn up to clarify parents' roles and responsibilities in school. Their major concern is that parents should not 'be enlisted to paper over the cracks in educational provision' (Caudrey, 1985).

If we invite parents/carers into our Early Years settings to take part in the activities that are taking place there, what might be the advantages, for them, for their children and for the staff?

Practical task

List the advantages of inviting parents/carers into the Early Years setting, bearing in mind the following sub-categories:

- *advantages for the staff;*
- *advantages for the children;*
- *advantages for the school/staff.*

Nursery staff have indicated the following advantages of mothers becoming involved in their nursery units:

- **a positive impact on the self-esteem of the mothers taking part;**
- **increased self-esteem of the children;**
- **giving mothers an insight into the importance of early education;**
- **allowing the nursery children to go on trips and visit places of interest;**
- **improving relations with school staff;**
- **providing help in a range of areas where adult supervision is required. This included ICT, art and craft, baking and story sharing;**

- helping the children to settle into the nursery routine;
- supporting children experiencing difficulties, the implication here being that the child's mother would stay with her child if s/he was finding it difficult to settle.

What are the disadvantages of involving parents/carers in Early Years settings?

Of course nothing is ever so simple that there are benefits without costs and so we need to think about potential disadvantages to involving parents/carers in Early Years settings.

Practical task

List what the disadvantages might be of parent/carer's involvement in the Early Years setting, for the parents/carers, their children and for the staff?

Much of the research about parental involvement indicates that there are two major concerns for staff, that of confidentiality and of reliability.

- In some staff rooms, mention that you are thinking of inviting parents/carers into your Early Years setting and you will be regaled with horror tales of parents/carers repeating overheard staff discussions, commenting on the progress (or lack of it) of children with whom they have worked and other apocryphal stories, which may or may not be grounded in reality. Clearly confidentiality is something that can become a concern but below we discuss how this can be dealt with simply by ensuring that it never becomes a problem in the first place.
- Similarly there will be those who will regale you with tales of hours spent preparing activities for parents/carers to carry out, only to be let down by them not arriving for the session. Again below we will discuss how this can be managed.

OTHER CONCERNS
- Boundary problems for staff, including uncertainties of what to say, when and how to address or be addressed.
- Staff have also indicated that their valuable time can be taken up planning for parents/carers, taking this finite resource away from meeting the needs of the children. This potential for an increased workload as a result of parents/carers in your Early Years setting has to be carefully managed. Staff have indicated a concern about neglecting their proper professional role to keep parents 'happy' and 'useful'. Edwards and Knight have used the term 'needy parents' to indicate those parents 'whose own economic, emotional and/or educational deficiencies potentially inhibit the educational support that they might give their children and can consume enormous amounts of teacher time' (1994: 114). They suggest that parents who fall into this category should be regarded as clients rather than as potential partners, with the need for whole school commitment and multidisciplinary liaison across all of the caring services.
- Children's behaviour can deteriorate when parents/carers are present and some children can be inhibited by their parents/carers' presence, not mixing with the

other children as usual but tending to cling to their parent/carer. Furthermore, staff can feel inhibited in their relationships with the children when their parents/carers are present, particularly if this involves staff disciplining the children.

- We cannot assume that all parents/carers have the time available to become involved with their children's Early Years setting. As indicated earlier, both men and women are economically active or in paid employment. However, it is also important to remember that even if parents/carers are not in paid employment, it may not be possible for them to become involved, they may have other responsibilities of which the Early Years staff are unaware. Also, parents/carers may have available time but may *choose* not to become involved and it is important for staff not to misinterpret this as a lack of interest in their children or as an example of poor parenting.

- Where parents/carers are unable to become involved for whatever reason, this can easily lead to feelings of guilt on their part. Insensitive staff who see parents/carers as a ready, willing and able unpaid labour force can perpetuate this.

- Unsureness about what it is suitable to ask parents/carers to do. Involving them in the process of correcting children or introducing new techniques, according to Stacey (1991), is not acceptable to most teachers. This fine line between mentoring and teaching creates anxieties for both the teacher and the parents/carers. Therefore, both the teacher and the parent/carer need to make explicit the expectations and requirements related to each activity.

We also need to take care not to patronise parents/carers or to see schemes designed to involve parents/carers in nursery and infant classrooms as a means by which parents/carers can be educated into improved parenting/caring. This certainly was the case in the 1970s, for example, when in particular working class parents/carers were seen as deficient and schools were identified as the means of remedying this. So rather than valuing parents, programmes of parental involvement actually served to fuel theories of parental incompetence. The seminal work by Tizard and Hughes (1984) helped destroy this image in that they showed how the children in their study received a greater cognitive challenge at home than in the school setting. But it is important to be vigilant to avoid the trap of staff believing that they have the monopoly of knowledge and experience.

How can I manage the involvement of parents/carers?

One of the most difficult aspects to face is that of our attitudes to parents/carers. It is all too easy to fall into the trap of labelling concerned parents/carers as over-concerned, apparently confident parents/carers as 'pushy' and those parents/carers who for whatever reason do not build working relationships with staff in the Early Years setting, as uninterested. If this is the case it is a useful exercise for you to examine your own attitudes to discover why a parent/carer makes you feel uncomfortable. What we need to remember is that all parents/carers want what is best for their children. Clark (in Tizard, 1974) believes that changes in parental attitudes towards school and changes in teacher attitudes towards parents are the **major** (my emphasis) benefits of any programme of school-based parental involvement. But any changes of attitudes need to be shared by everyone involved.

From the above, it is clear that inviting parents/carers into the Early Years setting is not necessarily without potential difficulties. However, this is not to argue that it should not take place. Rather, the advice offered here is that it is vital that all of the staff concerned understand and share the rationale for involving parents/carers and that this is discussed, made explicit and owned by all of the staff. New members of staff usually accept the status quo, and in particular the taken for granted practice that goes on in the school. But as one becomes more experienced it is important to question this and to take on board only that which is good practice.

Many of the concerns expressed above could be avoided by providing a set of agreed guidelines for parents/carers involved in the Early Years setting. These guidelines need to be drawn up by a wide degree of consultation and will need regular and thorough review. But it is preferable to think about how difficult situations can be avoided before they ever arise.

You might decide that there is a need for a set of guidelines to explain in detail what the expectations are of parents/carers working alongside staff in Early Years settings. In order to produce these you might find it useful to think through all of the possible scenarios for things going wrong! For example, the anxieties of some staff about confidentiality issues were mentioned earlier. In order to avoid this you might produce a booklet for parents/carers containing details not only of the need to respect confidences in school, but also making explicit why this is the case. For example, you could point out that when parents/carers work alongside Early Years workers, they might have to be provided with sensitive information about specific children. Consequently, it is essential that all participants respect the confidentiality of such information. If this is not made explicit and understood, it could become problematic and everyone therefore needs to be fully aware of this potentially damaging situation. Alternatively, or in addition, you might want to run a short training session for parents/carers where you could offer a role-play situation of an Early Years setting where problems of confidentiality have occurred. If you do decide to offer training for parents/carers, however informal this might be, do contact your local College of Further Education which might be able to offer accreditation for this kind of work.

Where children respond badly to having their parents/carers present, why not discuss this with the parent/carer and, where size of setting allows, suggest that they continue to come into the Early Years setting but to work alongside another group of children in another room.

To avoid parents/carers' generosity of help being undermined, the Early Years setting should display respect for the helpers and ensure the children do not see time spent with a parent/carer helper as a relaxation of school discipline. Most children enjoy working with parent/carer helpers. However, some children will play one adult off against another, including the Early Years workers against the parents/carers, particularly the child's own parent/carer. This again may lead to an uncomfortable situation, which could easily be avoided by clear guidelines on standards and general procedures being articulated to the parent/carer before they begin work with the children. Thus you might include in the booklet information on what is and what is not expected in terms of behaviour from the children ... and so much the better if the children and their parents/carers have helped in the production of this Code of Behaviour!

The first step: inviting parents/carers in

The initial meeting with parents/carers is important to all parties. The parent/carer may be looking around a nursery establishment with a view to their child starting to attend, or they may visit the infant school, perhaps the only infant school in their area, and thus have very limited choice about their child's attendance. Whatever the situation, parents/carers will be seeking reassurance that their children will be cared for and provided with appropriate educational experiences. Even at this initial stage it is suggested that you share your commitment to a partnership with parents to the benefit of their children. You might want to provide them with a short booklet (remembering that not all parents/carers will be literate or literate in English) explaining your philosophy since much of what is said in situations such as these will be forgotten. But what of existing parents/carers? If you decide that you would like to develop more of a partnership with parents/carers by inviting them to spend time in the setting, how might you go about this?

Before you do anything, you need to think through carefully, as a team, why you are doing this, what are the reasons and whether this commitment is shared by all of the staff team members. It would be unfortunate, for example, if not all of the staff wanted parents/carers working in the establishment and by their behaviour made this clear to those parents/carers who do attend.

Conclusion

Whatever the Early Years setting, statutory or non-statutory, staff and parents/carers will have some kind of working relationship. The nature and depth of this relationship will vary with individuals and individual settings. It might take the form of staff welcoming the children and parent/carer to each session and returning the children to the parent/carer at the end of the session. But even with a limited relationship such as this, the parents/ carers will need to feel secure that the children are being cared for and that their educational needs are being met. The trust that is needed for a parent/carer to leave their child develops from the very first visit of the nursery staff to the child's home, or from the day that the parent/carer visits the establishment to put their child's name on the waiting list. From this initial and sometimes brief contact, parents/carers will be making decisions about the establishment – were they made to feel welcome, did they feel that their contributions to the development of their children would be valued? Early Years staff need to be particularly careful to explain and to demonstrate by their actions that they seek a partnership with parents/carers. The exact nature of this partnership will vary from individual to individual and may indeed change over time. As has been indicated above, we cannot assume that all parents/carers will be able to have or indeed will want to have the same depth of partnership. Furthermore, if parents/carers are invited into the setting to work alongside staff it is vital that there are clear, shared aims and well-thought out objectives.

Working with parents and other carers:
a summary of key points

In this chapter we have hopefully alerted you to the importance of not only establishing effective working relationships with parents/carers but also to have gone beyond superficial and uncritical understandings of what is commonly referred to as parental involvement.

The key points are:

⎯⎯ *parents/carers have a key part to play in the educational experiences of their children;*

    the need for effective communication and liaison between home and setting is paramount;

    Early Years settings are particularly appropriate as venues for involving parents/carers where they can play a variety of roles;

    there needs to be a thought out and shared rationale for this involvement;

    managing the relationships with parents/carers is a skilled and important aspect of the role of Early Years staff.

Further reading

Cameron, C., Moss, P. and Owen, C. (1999) *Men in the Nursery: Gender and Caring Work*. London. Paul Chapman Publishing. Addresses the gendered nature of working with young children in a range of Early Years settings.

Edwards, A. and Knight, P. (1994) *Effective Early Years Education: Teaching Young Children*. Buckingham. Open University Press. Discusses the needs of parents/carers and how a whole school approach may be needed to met these needs.

Pugh, G., Aplin, G., De'Ath, E. and Moxon, M. (1987) *Partnership in Action: Working with Parents in Preschool Centres*, Volumes 1 and 2. London. National Children's Bureau.

Pugh, G. and De'Ath, E. (1989) *Working Towards Partnership in the Early Years*, London, National Children's Bureau. The roles that parents/carers can take vary considerably between the statutory and the non-statutory sectors. Furthermore there are huge variations *within* sectors. Gillian Pugh and the National Children's Bureau have examined this in detail.

Pugh, G. (ed) (1996) *Contemporary Issues in the Early Years: Working Collaboratively for Children*. 2nd ed. London. National Children's Bureau. Discusses the background to parental involvement in Early Years settings, in particular see the chapter written by John Rennie entitled 'Working with Parents'.

Reay, D. (1998) *Class Work: Mothers' Involvement in their Children's Primary Schools*. London. UCL Press. Discusses in detail why we use the term parental involvement instead of mothers' involvement and gives a fascinating account of a group of women and their involvement with their children's schools.

Smidt, S. (1998) *A Guide to Early Years Practice*. London. Routledge. For further ways that parents/carers have been involved in a range of Early Years settings see Chapter 9.

Vincent, C. (2000) *Including Parents? Education, Citizenship and Parental Agency*. Buckingham. Open University Press. Discusses the experiences and motivations of parents. Wider issues such as citizenship and public participation are then highlighted, and the experiences of different ethnic groups and social class groups are also addressed.

Whalley, M. (ed) (1997) *Working with Parents*. London. Hodder and Stoughton and

Whalley, M. and the Pen Green Centre Team (2001) *Involving Parents in their Children's Learning*. London. Paul Chapman Publishing. Here you can find out more about Pen Green and the relationships with parents/carers.

Wolfendale, S. and Bastiani, J. (eds) (2000) *The Contribution of Parents to School Effectiveness*. London. David Fulton. Discusses the roles that parents/carers might play in the quest to raise standards in schools.

Professional Standards for QTS

→ 1.6

This Standard states that in order to gain QTS, teachers must understand the contribution that support staff and other professionals make to teaching and learning. You may find it helpful to refer to the appropriate section of the Handbook that accompanies the Standards for the award for QTS for further clarification and support.

By the end of this chapter you will have:

- *discovered why it is necessary for you to know about other professionals that have a responsibility for children;*
- *increased your knowledge of other professionals with responsibility for the care of young children;*
- *understood that there are some other professionals whom you will work closely with on a regular and sometimes daily basis;*
- *understood that there are some other professionals whom you will need to call upon for assistance and who will collaborate with you in meeting the needs of the children for whom you have responsibility;*
- *understood that there are other professionals with a responsibility for children who you should be aware of, even though it is unlikely that you will work with them directly.*

Introduction

This chapter will give you knowledge of a wide range of professionals who have responsibility for children. In some cases they are people with whom you will have direct contact – sometimes working alongside them (e.g. **support teacher** for children for whom English is a second language) and sometimes calling upon them for specific assistance (e.g. **educational psychologist**). Some professionals are included because you need to be aware of them but you may not work with them directly (e.g. **play therapist**). In this chapter you will be asked to imagine situations that might occur in your setting and you will be advised of the correct form of action. You will be told who to contact to help you and how that contact should be made. You will be asked to carry out some practical tasks in order to help you to understand your wider role in caring for children.

The holistic nature of working with young children

The Early Years worker needs to take a holistic view of children. More and more it is being recognised that an approach which aims to bring all services together for the benefit of children and their families is by far the best way of addressing children's needs. To this effect the government has recognised centres of excellence where all of the children's needs can be met on the same premises, and developments such as *Sure Start* are included to meet the needs of the whole family. Nevertheless you will find that in working with children and in addressing their varied needs you will need to call upon the services of many others who have specialist abilities. The more that you can work closely with other professionals the better the holistic approach will be. In all these cases the need to work closely with parents is paramount.

There are times of particular need such as key transitions from home to care/education setting and from nursery to school. At times such as this it is particularly important that support for the child is well co-ordinated to help the child settle into a new environment. It hardly needs saying that the child's parents or primary carers are the first and most important partner for those who will take over the care and education of the child whilst they are in the setting.

As a teacher you will need to call upon other professionals to help you with the specific needs of children as well as to help you provide for the children generally. The professionals discussed in this chapter can directly help you in a variety of ways.

The following classroom stories should be borne in mind when reading about the professionals presented in this chapter.

Classroom stories

1. *Susan is five years old. She has been absent from school on numerous occasions. She does not talk much and hasn't made friends in class. When you try to engage with her she is very reluctant to talk to you. When you tell stories to the whole group of children you notice that Susan has a faraway expression and doesn't seem to be listening to the story. One day she is getting ready for PE and you notice unusual marks on her skin, they are regular and do not look like bruises children usually get from the rough and tumble of childhood.*

2. *Samina is four years old. She is a happy child who plays with her friends in a lively way. She and her parents speak Punjabi at home and Samina speaks a little English. She talks very readily in Punjabi when playing with her friends and makes up stories in Punjabi when sitting with a storybook.*

3. *Paul is three years old. His articulation is poor and he has difficulty making himself understood. He gets very frustrated with you and the other children. His concentration is poor and he rarely spends more than a few minutes engaged in any activity. He frequently snatches toys from other children and has occasionally hurt other children.*

4. *Susan is three and has a nut allergy. Her mother brings food for her to the nursery and asks you not to give her any biscuits or other food that the other*

children have. You are concerned that she might eat something that contains nuts when you are not looking.

5. *Gillian is five. She is a happy child and gets on well with the other children. She enjoys playing in the role-play area. Her speech is less mature than her peers and her manipulative control is poor. Her baseline assessment shows that she has little phonographical awareness and that she is unable to count to ten.*

We will return to these classroom stories later.

Behavioural and learning difficulties

You may find that a child for whom you are responsible is not achieving as well as you would expect. Perhaps you have noticed that they are unable to read simple texts or to spell common words, and despite trying the strategies that you have learned and that work with other children they do not make progress. You may have a child who has very poor concentration and who cannot persist with a task such as doing a jigsaw or playing with Lego for more than a few minutes. You may even have a child who persistently hurts other children or who is very withdrawn and appears unhappy a lot of the time. What do you do in these cases? The starting point is observation. You need to clearly identify what concerns you by collecting data about the child's behaviour. You need to involve the Special Education Needs Co-ordinator (SENCO) at this point. (All schools must appoint a member of staff who is responsible for special educational needs – the SENCO.) At some point you may need to call on the educational psychologist. This will be when it is clear that the child needs to be assessed by a psychologist so that their particular difficulties can be identified and their needs can be met more specifically. The SENCO will advise you when this is necessary. Normally the SENCO will arrange for the educational psychologist to visit the setting and assess the child's special needs. The educational psychologist will offer help and advice and may recommend that special arrangements be made to help the child as appropriate.

ROLE OF THE SENCO IN MAINSTREAM PRIMARY SCHOOLS
The SENCO is responsible for:

- **overseeing the day-to-day operation of the school's SEN policy;**
- **co-ordinating provision for children with special educational needs;**
- **liaising with and advising fellow teachers;**
- **managing learning support assistants;**
- **overseeing the records of all children with special educational needs;**
- **liaising with parents of children with special educational needs;**
- **contributing to the in-service training of staff;**
- **liaising with external agencies including the LEA's support and education psychology services, health and social services, and voluntary bodies.**

EDUCATIONAL PSYCHOLOGIST
Education psychologists work with children and young people, mainly under 19 years of age, experiencing difficulties (e.g. learning, emotional, behavioural) to promote their educational

and psychological development. Most are employed by Local Education Authorities, but some are self-employed and work as consultants for Social Services departments, voluntary bodies, parents and others. They work mainly in consultation with parents, teachers, social workers, education officers and other people involved in the education and care of children and young people.

The Association of Educational Psychologists (2001) identifies involvement with teachers as follows:

- **helping teachers to gain a greater understanding of and insights into the nature of the pupils' difficulties;**
- **examining positive and negative features of teacher/pupil interactions and classroom management;**
- **advising on targets, Individual Action Plans and features of planned interventions;**
- **evaluating planned interventions and reviewing progress with teachers;**
- **introducing new techniques or learning materials that have been successful elsewhere;**
- **empowering teachers to be confident and to develop their own solutions.**

Co-operation with schools as institutions might include help with:

- **positive behaviour management;**
- **anti-bullying policies and practices;**
- **early intervention systems to minimise the cost of learning failure;**
- **review of current systems and evaluation of any changes;**
- **professional development of staff, both teaching and non-teaching;**
- **support networks for staff at all levels within the school;**
- **planning, development and evaluation of SEN systems;**
- **critical incident support for staff.**

Interventions with other professional groups involve a multidisciplinary approach to dealing with the learning or behavioural difficulties of the child or young person. These might involve:

- **pre-school work with child development clinics;**
- **family therapy in child and family guidance centres;**
- **joint working with health and social services teams;**
- **being able to communicate with a wide range of different professional groups.**

Educational psychologists are involved in assessing children with special educational needs and in providing advice for writing the statement of special educational needs. The statement of special educational needs is a legal document that sets out the child's individual needs precisely, and aims to identify areas of need, and define the way in which these areas will be addressed. The local education authority is responsible for writing and issuing the statement of special educational needs. The process of preparing the statement is known as statementing, and the DfES

Special Educational Needs Code of Practice (2001) outlines the steps towards statementing. If statementing is required before the age of four it is undertaken by the health authority. It is estimated that 20 per cent of school children may need special educational help at some time but only two per cent will need a statement of special educational needs.

DEFINITION OF LEARNING DIFFICULTY
The DfES Code of Practice on Special Educational Needs (2001) defines learning difficulty in section 1:3

Children have a learning difficulty if they:
a) have a significantly greater difficulty in learning than the majority of the children of the same age; or

b) have a disability which prevents or hinders them from making use of educational facilities of a kind generally provided for children of the same age in schools within the area of the local education authority;

c) are under compulsory school age and fall within the definition at a or b above or would so do if special educational provision was not made for them.

(DfES, 2001)

Causes of learning difficulties

Learning difficulties can be caused by:

- **emotional and behavioural problems – these may relate to social, psychological and environmental factors;**
- **mental disability – this may refer to medical, physical, physiological and neurological factors;**
- **sight, hearing or speech disorder;**
- **physical disability;**
- **medical or health problems.**

Clearly, learning and behavioural difficulties can be interrelated.

You will also need to consider children who are considered to be gifted/talented.

How do you work with the SENCO and the educational psychologist?

A vital part of the process is ensuring that the child has an Individual Education Plan which addresses their particular needs. You will be involved in drawing this up. It is a plan which sets achievable targets for learning or behaviour for the child.

The SEN Code of Practice implemented in January 2002 sets out the gradual response you must make when you suspect that a child has special educational needs. It emphasises parent partnership and considering the views of pupils. Multi-agency working is also emphasised.

Chapter 4 of the code sets out the identification, assessment and provision in early education settings including the criteria for statutory assessment of children over two and less than statutory school age and statutory assessment of under twos. It describes *Early Years' action* where you must devise intervention, which is different from the normal provision for delivering the curriculum. It emphasises the importance of parental involvement in assessing and deciding upon intervention. It goes on to describe *Early Years' action plus*. This is when you involve external support services. When you decide to do this you must first ask the following questions following the *Early Years' action* which has been taken.

- **Has progress been made?**
- **What are the parent's views?**
- **Is there need for more information and advice about the child?**

If a child presents considerable cause for concern you must request a *statutory multidisciplinary assessment* (which will involve the educational psychologist and others) from the LEA. Before you do this you must demonstrate that you have adopted a strategy or programme for a reasonable period. After the *multidisciplinary assessment* has taken place a statement of special educational needs may be drawn up.

Chapter 5 of the code deals with identification assessment and provision in the primary phase.

OBSERVATION

Whether or not you need to call upon the help of the educational psychologist you do need to be sure that you are providing the best possible care and education for the children for whom you are responsible. The best way for you to make a start is to be a good observer. It is vital that you make detailed observations of children's behaviour. These observations might cover:

- **physical activities;**
- **intellectual activities such as problem solving;**
- **working with shape, space and number;**
- **speaking and listening;**
- **reading and writing;**
- **social activities such as co-operating with others, negotiating, and self-care;**
- **emotional behaviour such as coping with separation.**

The notes you make will allow you to draw up plans for individual children but they will also aid the educational psychologist in their assessments. Working closely with parents is also vital. In order to get a full picture of a child's development it is essential that you understand their full life. Parents will be able to communicate knowledge of the child that you do not have access to, and can share with you fears they have for their development.

The information you gather should start by describing what the child can do or understand. It should then identify what the child cannot do or understand – but not why at this stage. Once you have collected evidence from every source you can then draw up an action plan. The action plan will set out the following:

1. Nature of the difficulty.
2. Targets for learning.

3. Activities and resources.
4. A review date.

Working as a team with the SENCO, the educational psychologist and the child's parents ensures that the child in your care receives the best possible care and education and exemplifies how various agencies working together with those closest to the child can bring about positive effects.

Practical task

Plan an observation for a given period, say ten minutes. Decide how you will keep a record. You may devise a table to show the type of activity a child chooses to do and the length of time the activity is sustained.

Draw up a schedule for observing one or more of the following:

• a child's ability to use manipulative skills;
• a child's social interactions;
• a child's ability to follow instructions;
• a child's verbal interactions.

The following observation lasts for half an hour and is intended to discover something about the child's interests and how well they are settling into a new situation.

Name of child	10.00	10.05	10.07	10. 11	10.30
Jonathan Age 4 years Date: 10/10/02	J is playing with Lego. He is trying to make a box. He throws Lego to floor and goes to sand tray.	There are no other children playing with the sand. A support worker joins him and asks him what he is going to do. He doesn't respond and walks away to the painting area. (After J left three children play together with the sand using the containers available and chat with one another.)	J stands by group of children who are painting using sponges, printing blocks etc. He tries one. Support worker gives him an apron. He says 'no' and walks to book corner.	J goes to book corner and looks at Rosie's Walk. He turns pages one at a time. Aimee joins him. He turns away from her. She tries again to look at book. J walks off.	J goes to toilet.

Of course this is only slight evidence and needs to be supported by other observations. Given the evidence of this observation how well do you think Jonathan is settling in? What activities does he like best? What might you say about his social relationships?

Attending to children's health needs

As a professional concerned with the education of children you will be aware of the need to consider the whole child. Part of your role as an educator is to ensure that the children develop in an all round way, understand themselves and their bodies and know how to look after themselves. You will also be aware that children cannot learn effectively if they are not healthy. Your concern for children's health is matched by that of health professionals, and these can be called upon very specifically in your setting.

WHEN WILL YOU CALL ON THE HELP OF A HEALTH PROFESSIONAL?

Some health professionals − such as the dentist − visit regularly to make routine checks. The whole staff may wish to increase their knowledge of the management of children with certain conditions − such as nut allergy − and so can invite the school nurse to give a talk. You may have a child with a specific condition such as asthma − in this case the school nurse can give specific help and advice. You may wish to involve the school nurse in planning a health curriculum. The school health service should be seen as a vital part of the life of the setting and should be called upon to be part of that community in a positive and active way.

School health service

The school nurse is part of a broader heath service for children in school. Finch (1984) has given three reasons for a school health service:

- *efficiency* **– children's health problems need to be addressed so that they can benefit from education,**
- *convenience* **– it is appropriate to have a service which can reach all children and school is a place where this can happen,**
- *complementarity* **– in requiring children to leave the care of their parents the state has a duty to care for their health and welfare at school.**

As well as the school nurse the school health service provides doctors and dentists.

ROLE OF THE SCHOOL NURSE

School nurses are responsible for a number of schools in their area.

- **They carry out routine health assessment such as weight, height, eyesight and hearing.**
- **They might be involved in giving immunisation when this is called for.**
- **They may be involved in drawing up a health education policy and may become involved in the sex education policy.**
- **They might be involved in delivering sex education.**
- **They can be called upon for general health advice and will talk to children on topics of interest to them.**
- **They can be called upon to talk to the staff about the management of certain pupils, e.g. those with asthma and those with nut allergy.**
- **They can give instruction on how to keep asthma sprays available to children.**

- They can give instructions on how to administer a life-saving injection for children with anaphylactic shock.
- They can also give advice about head lice, although they no longer carry out inspections.
- They give advice to parents about enuresis (bed-wetting).
- They play a role in child protection surveillance.

It is well worth forming a close relationship with the school nurse, who may well be willing to take on a much fuller role than has traditionally been assumed. Your manager/head teacher will arrange for visits but you can contact the school nurse yourself if you wish for help with the curriculum.

Practical task

What do you think a school nurse should provide? What children could be particularly helped by a school nurse? How could the school nurse be involved in health education?

Draw up a collaborative programme that a teacher and a school nurse could work on together.

Children who give cause for concern

As well as being concerned about children's learning, behaviour and health there will be times in your professional life when you have concern for children because they are not attending your school or setting or because you suspect that they are being abused – either physically or sexually.

If a child is persistently and unaccountably absent from school you should alert your superiors (usually in a school the head teacher), who will call on the **Education Welfare Officer** who is responsible for investigating persistent unaccountable absence from school. If you suspect abuse, you will have to follow procedures set out below.

Child protection

Some information and procedures in this section have been summarised from Chapter 16 of Bruce and Meggitt (1999). You are recommended to read this chapter for a fuller account of legal issues in childcare provision.

When children start nursery or school or are already doing so, social services are required to notify the head teacher if a child's name is put on the child protection register. This should state:

- **whether the child is subject to a care order;**
- **the name of the key worker in the case;**
- **what information the parents may know.**

The nursery or school must carefully monitor how the child is progressing – particularly in the area of the child's development. Any concerns must be shared with the social services department.

You may feel nervous about finding that there are children in your care who are being abused or neglected. This is understandable. But your responsibility is quite clear. You must report any suspicions to your senior manager, who will ensure that proper procedures are followed.

You may find that children:

- **are withdrawn or aggressive;**
- **have bruising to the body (in cases of non-accidental injury they are likely to be in a regular pattern of various ages and may reflect the shape of the object used, such as a belt);**
- **do not look as if they are being well cared for, e.g. do not look well nourished or their clothing is inadequate.**

Children may confide in you. The procedures which are followed in cases of suspected abuse or neglect are set out below but, before moving to this, you need advice on what to do if children confide in you. It is important to reassure the child and make it clear that you will help them by informing others. You must not promise to keep a secret. You must take what they say seriously. Listen sensitively to what they say but do not ask questions. Tell your senior manager what has been said. This leads us to the procedure you must follow in all cases of suspected abuse or neglect.

If you suspect child abuse there are procedures which must be followed – the Department of Health published guidance in 1991.

PROCEDURES FOR REPORTING SUSPECTED ABUSE

- **Each school must appoint a teacher responsible for linking with the Social Service department.**
- **Each school must have a written policy in child protection and line of reporting to social services and sometimes to the NSPCC.**
- **Registers of named staff taking this role must be kept by the Local Education Authority.**
- **Schools and care settings are encouraged to develop plans which help children to develop skills and practices that protect them from abuse.**

When you have reported your suspicions to your seniors, the police, social services and possibly the NSPCC will be involved. Written evidence is required within 24 hours. The police and social services will consult with each other to ascertain whether there is evidence, and to decide whether a police protection order and emergency protection order or a child assessment order is issued.

POLICE PROTECTION ORDER
If the child's safety is in question the child can be removed to foster care for 72 hours by specially trained police officers who must then inform the parent or carer and the local authority.

EMERGENCY PROTECTION ORDER

If the situation is considered to be an emergency the teacher or other concerned adult can apply to a court or magistrate for an emergency protection order for up to eight days. In this case the child is taken to a safe place such as a foster home. This can be extended for a further seven days.

CHILD ASSESSMENT ORDER

In situations which are not an emergency but where parents do not co-operate the local authority can apply for a child assessment order. The child can then be assessed over a period of seven days.

CHILD PROTECTION CONFERENCE

When evidence of abuse or neglect has been established a child protection conference is arranged. Professionals involved with the family – possibly the early childhood worker – attend. Sometimes the parents attend but if this is not felt to be appropriate by the chair of the conference the parents must at least be informed that a conference is arranged. Local authorities have an obligation to work towards involving parents at some stage attending at least part of a conference. After discussion of the evidence an action plan is made. The child may be placed on the child protection register

CHILD PROTECTION PLAN

The child protection plan following a conference might involve further assessment of the child and the family. A care order might be issued in which case the child will be taken into care of the social service department (in a foster home or children's home) or a supervision order might be issued, in which case the local authority will support and supervise the family and the child in the home setting for one year.

REVIEW

The child protection plan is reviewed every six months in a review conference. The child is de-registered if the situation changes and the child no longer needs support and supervision.

Practical task

Research the ways in which professionals build up trust with children and raise their self-esteem, e.g. circle time. What ideas do you have of your own? Maybe in your own schooldays you found some teachers particularly trustworthy – what was it about them that made this so? Did they do anything of note that would account for this?

Children who need special support

As mentioned earlier there may be children in your class or setting who have a special educational need. This need may be such that in order for them to gain fully from the education you offer they need additional support from other adults. As well as children with special educational needs there are other children who benefit from support of other adults within the setting. For example, you may have a child who has hearing or visual impairment, or you may have a child for whom English is a second language. Who can you call on to help? There are a number of support teachers and assistants who can be called on. Normally the head teacher would decide who to deploy, sometimes calling on the Local Education Authority to provide help. Each school and education authority has its own policy about what support can be given.

SUPPORT TEACHER FOR CHILDREN FOR WHOM ENGLISH IS A SECOND LANGUAGE

If you have children in your class or setting for whom English is a second language you may have a **support teacher** who can work with the children in their first language and who can translate the talk between you and the children. You will work very closely with this teacher, carrying out joint planning and discussing any difficulties these pupils are facing. There may be cultural as well as language considerations to take into account when planning their learning. It is always essential to be aware of cultural differences within your class or setting – for example, not all the children in your class or setting will use the same kitchen equipment as you at home, which could be very significant in learning activities that you provide. Even something as simple as identifying the beginning letter of something that you may think is a common object can be difficult for some children, not because of poor visual or auditory skill but because they do not recognise the object. Having a support teacher with wider knowledge than your own is a great asset and invaluable to the children.

LEARNING SUPPORT ADVISORY TEACHER

Learning support advisory teachers are specialist teachers who have experience in working in locally maintained schools with children who have a range of learning difficulties. They will advise schools on how to plan and carry out work programmes for children. The learning support advisory teacher can also offer training for teachers and classroom assistants.

SPECIAL ADVISORY TEACHER

The **special advisory teacher** has special knowledge about different types of difficulties and conditions, for example, hearing or sight impairment. In some areas there are specialist advisory teachers for pre-school children.

SPECIAL NEEDS TEACHER

Special needs teachers have had additional training to work with children with special needs. They are often peripatetic and might specialise in working with children with disability, visual or hearing impairment or learning difficulties.

Special needs support assistants may be qualified nursery nurses who work with children with a statement for SEN.

BEHAVIOUR SUPPORT TEACHER SERVICE

The **behaviour support teacher** service provides support to settings that require suggestions and help with children with behavioural difficulties. They observe the children, suggest appropriate activities to improve the child's behaviour, and suggest where the child can be referred, if necessary, for further help and advice.

SPEECH AND LANGUAGE THERAPIST

The **speech and language therapist** is a specialist who works with parents and school staff as well as with the individual children, to help them overcome speech, language and communication difficulties.

EDUCATION SERVICE FOR VISUALLY IMPAIRED CHILDREN

The **Education Service for Visually Impaired Children** is responsible for the assessment and monitoring of the needs of visually impaired children – it contributes to assessment of special educational needs.

It provides:

- **sessions for pre-school children and parents;**
- **advice and training to schools and settings on the management of children with visual impairment;**
- **individual specialist teaching, including mobility training and Braille and keyboard skills;**
- **specialist equipment and adaptations for materials for use by visually impaired children.**

EDUCATION SERVICE FOR HEARING-IMPAIRED CHILDREN

The **Education Service for Hearing-Impaired Children** is responsible for diagnosis of children with hearing impairment, and counselling and supporting parents with hearing difficulties. It fits hearing aids, arranges for nursery provision for hearing impaired children and offers appropriate support.

Professionals who are called upon for specific purposes

As well as working with other professionals on a regular basis there are some who can be called upon now and again to fulfil a particular role at various times.

The police

As well as playing a major role in child protection, the police can help with road safety and give advice to teachers and children on avoiding danger from child molesters. The police will work with you in school, giving advice and information and will also give special talks and presentations to children appropriate to their age.

Rail companies

Employees of rail companies will visit schools to talk to the children about the dangers of playing on and near to railways. This is particularly important when settings are close to a railway.

Road safety officers

Local authorities may provide officers to visit schools to give children specific guidance on how to keep safe when walking in areas where there is traffic (most places these days).

Fire service

Fire Prevention Officers can be called upon to give advice about fire prevention and to give presentations to the children. It is particularly important for them to visit prior to Guy Fawkes Night.

Traffic patrol officer

Colloquially known as the lollipop lady or man this officer sees the children safely across the road. They need to be informed if the school day is altered for any reason. They are also a valuable resource when engaging children in topics such as 'people who help us' or topics exploring employment in the area surrounding the school or setting.

Professionals who may be involved in voluntary activities undertaken by children

Sometimes professionals visit schools to help on a voluntary basis. Here is one who visits schools for specific purposes. You may think of others who you would like to visit your setting.

Football training

Sometimes high profile football teams provide team members to come to school to train youngsters in footballing skills.

Professionals with specific roles with children but whom you may not meet

So far you have been introduced to professionals whom you may work with directly, or whose help you can call upon. There are other professionals whom you need to be aware of, but you may not have direct contact with them.

General practitioner

The **general practitioner** is a doctor with whom the family registers. They are responsible for the health of the child and also carry out developmental checks at six months and three years. They also administer immunisations.

Health visitor

A **health visitor** is a member of the primary health care team attached to the doctor's surgery. They are qualified nurses who have undertaken further training, including midwifery experience. As well as routinely visiting the newly born and carrying out developmental checks (including a hearing check at seven months) they also visit families where children are in need. They give health education, support and advice within the home. They work with children up until the age of five years. They can be approached directly or through the family doctor.

Hospital play specialist

The **play specialist** working in a hospital has a number of roles. The play specialist may help children come to terms with medical procedures they are going to encounter by talking through in the play situation or by reading appropriate books. They may also use play to help relax children and take their minds off their illness. They may use play as education for children who are long-term patients and are missing out on formal education. The play specialist may be an NNEB and/or have a qualification in play specialism.

Play therapist

Play therapy is a form of psychotherapy. A psychotherapist may use play therapy to help children talk through difficult problems such as abuse or bereavement or for children who are exhibiting behavioural difficulties.

Portage

Portage is a service which helps meet the special educational needs of pre school children whose development is delayed. It helps parents teach at home under the direction of the **portage home visitor**. The scheme specifies particular teaching techniques and a curriculum of skills to be learnt.

The parent and home visitor decide one or two skills the child is to learn during the following week. The home visitor designs appropriate teaching activities. Skills that are difficult or take a long time to learn are broken down into easy steps which can be practised daily. The parent teaches the child daily and records progress for the home visitor to see on the next visit. The need to give praise and rewards to the child as the child strives to succeed is emphasised.

Clinical psychologist

Clinical psychologists normally work in hospitals. They assess children's emotional, social and intellectual development. They sometimes advise special programmes for children with severe difficulties and can arrange for children to receive therapy, e.g. children suffering bereavement. They can also advise on activities to promote development.

Occupational therapist

The **occupational therapist** works in hospitals and schools. They make an assessment of a children's practical abilities and can advise accordingly. They can advise on equipment to help children to lead a fuller and more independent life. They can also give advice about appropriate activities for children with specific difficulties.

Physiotherapist

The **physiotherapist** is a specialist who works with children who have movement difficulties. They can advise parents on suitable exercises for their children.

Social worker

Social workers are employed by social services departments. They assess the needs of children. They sometimes act as an advocate for children, ensuring that they have all the facilities that they require. In cases of child abuse there must be a named contact person within the school. If child abuse is suspected the named person has to contact the social services department, and a social worker will visit.

Voluntary agencies

As a professional working with young children you should be aware of the major voluntary agencies that take up the cause of children in difficulty. Here are just a few.

NSPCC

The National Society for the Prevention of Cruelty to Children (NSPCC) is the UK's leading charity specialising in child protection and the prevention of cruelty to children. It is the only children's charity in the UK with statutory powers enabling it to act to safeguard children at risk.

Childline

Childline is a 24 hour free helpline for children in danger. Children can ring in confidence and receive advice.

Kidscape

Kidscape aims to keep children safe from abuse. It produces materials for teachers on topics such as bullying.

Other organisations which you may find helpful

National Deaf Children's Society

Scope – the association for children with cerebral palsy

Royal National Institute for the Blind

Downs Syndrome Association

How do I contact other professionals?

SENCO	Approach them directly.
Educational psychologist	The SENCO will approach them.
School nurse	Your manager/head will arrange visits but you may approach them (at the local health authority) for curriculum help, having talked it over with senior managers.
Social services	The named person responsible in cases of suspected child abuse will contact them but you must tell the named person of suspected abuse.
Support workers	Your manager/head will arrange for these in liaison with the local education authority.
Other visitors	Depending on the purpose either you or your managers can arrange for visitors for specific purposes – e.g. police for child safety work – but be sure to talk over any visits you have in mind with your senior managers.

Practical task

Return to the case studies at the beginning of the chapter. Address each one in turn, suggesting which other professionals you would call upon in each case.

Roles and responsibilities of other professionals:
a summary of key points

In this chapter you have been introduced to the roles and responsibilities of other professionals with responsibility for the care of young children. You should now have a clear idea of whom you can call on to help you in specific circumstances and how to contact them.

Knowledge of other professionals with responsibility for children helps you:

- *to see your role as a teacher in a holistic way;*
- *recognise that teachers are not alone in providing for the needs of children in their setting;*
- *recognise that the needs of children go beyond the educational;*
- *recognise that other professionals can enhance the role of the teacher;*
- *recognise that other professionals can play a part in enriching the experience for children.*

4 PLANNING TO MEET THE PHYSICAL AND CREATIVE DEVELOPMENT NEEDS OF YOUNG CHILDREN

Elaine Hodson

Professional Standards for QTS

(→) 2.4

This Standard states that in order to gain QTS, teachers must understand how children's learning is affected by their physical and cultural development. The Curriculum Guidance for the Foundation Stage refers to planning for physical development on page 100, and creative development on page 116. You may find it helpful to refer to the appropriate section of the Handbook that accompanies the Standards for the award of QTS, for further clarification and support.

By the end of this chapter you should:

- *be aware of the physical and creative needs of young children;*
- *recognise the Early Learning Goals for physical and creative development as stated in the Foundation Stage curriculum;*
- *understand the role of the adult in these areas of development;*
- *be aware of appropriate teaching strategies.*

Introduction

This chapter seeks to address the requirements of the Professional Standards for the award of QTS within the areas of the Foundation Stage curriculum which deal with physical and creative development. It will examine both the theoretical background and the practical issues that you will need to consider when planning for these curriculum areas.

Planning to meet the physical needs of young children

Why is it important to plan for physical development?

Psychologists, building on the work of Piaget, argue that young children have an innate desire to investigate and make sense of their environment. In order to do this they need to gain increasing control over their physical skills – for example, as in the following classroom story.

Classroom story

Grace is a new-born baby. At present her physical development is limited. However, as Grace learns to control her head and neck, she becomes able to direct her gaze more effectively at the objects around her. As she becomes able to support her spine, she can reach out for favourite toys placed within her reach. Once she crawls, she is no longer dependent on objects being brought to her, but is able to move towards them. Standing and walking, she gains the ability to move freely around her environment, investigating cupboards, chasing the cat, answering the telephone, and so forth, restricted only either by the deliberate restraints imposed by carers, such as stair gates and playpens, or by the natural limits which she has not yet gained sufficient confidence to challenge. When she learns to ride a tricycle, Grace becomes able, as far as safety allows, to move beyond the confines of her own home and begin to familiarise herself with the immediate neighbourhood. In a relatively short space of time, physical development has changed a totally dependent babe in arms into a dextrous young child about to become part of a neighbourhood community. As her access to new experiences develops so her ability to learn is extended.

When she arrives in your Early Years setting it becomes your responsibility to ensure that you continue to offer Grace learning experiences that will build on and extend these skills. Experts differ in their view of the extent to which Grace's ability to learn physical skills is determined by her biological growth, but there is general agreement that all practitioners need to be careful observers in order to spot individuals as they become biologically ready to attain a new skill. It is unlikely, for example that Grace will have a mature enough sense of balance to be able to hop on one leg much before her fourth birthday. However, if you as her teacher present her with an environment that motivates her, for example by providing attractive playground markings and an adult model, she will become much more likely to practise, experiment and refine her developing skills. You will not be surprised, therefore, that opportunities to meet Grace's physical development needs will have a high priority in her early learning. This contrasts with their more restricted position in the primary curriculum. The Y1 child has her opportunities limited to a timetabled PE lesson and the teacher-free periods of play time and lunchtime. The three to five year old will have much greater opportunity for physical play. At the present time, the introduction of the Foundation Stage curriculum into Reception classes has highlighted the challenges for the teacher in providing an appropriate environment for physical activity in a more formal setting.

Practical task

Spend a few moments considering what the restrictions and challenges might be for the teacher working in the Reception class.

Planning for physical development and its relationship to the rest of the curriculum

By now you will be aware that the holistic nature of Early Years education means that you will need to give equal attention to all areas of the young child's development. If Grace is to meet her optimum level of development, opportunities must be available for physical, intellectual, social and emotional growth. You will already be aware that each of these areas is linked and each mutually dependent. For example consider the following classroom story.

Classroom story

As Grace, in her first weeks in your nursery school, becomes proficient in climbing to the top of the climbing frame, she will not only improve her ability to balance and support her own weight, but she will also gain a new view of her surroundings which will add to her appreciation of spatial relationships, attach new meaning to language such as 'on top of' and 'beneath' as well as adding to her self-esteem as she succeeds at a new challenge. From Grace's viewpoint, learning is not compartmentalised. She may practise a new song or rhyme as she climbs, recognise part of the climbing frame as a red triangle, like the one she saw in the Logiblocs game last week, and finally negotiate with a friend her turn on the slide as she returns to ground level. At the same time, she will experience the sensation of the cold wind whipping her cheeks, and the exhilaration of strenuous effort. The excitement and success of her venture may subsequently become the subject she brings to a discussion in group time later in the day, so giving her further opportunity for learning as she refines her communication skills.

Aside from this philosophical justification, you will be aware that opportunities for large movement and boisterous play are often lacking in our modern society. Homes may have inadequate space and carers may be reluctant to allow young children to play in outdoor areas where supervision is more difficult. You will know already that young children need opportunities to let off steam and to move spontaneously as and when energy bursts occur. They then need to be free to withdraw and to rest. This is not a requirement which sits easily with a rigorously timetabled day and needs careful thought. Finally, as an Early Years teacher you will be planning to develop the vital positive attitude to physical activity that Grace will need in order to become a healthy and active adult.

What are the key issues in planning for physical development?

Your plans will need to include opportunities for both fine and gross motor development. Usually a young child develops control over large movements before control over fine movements. This is not always the case. QCA state that high quality teaching should plan to develop physical control, mobility, awareness of space and manipulative skills, and indicate that this learning should take place in both the indoor and outdoor environments. At the same time, children need to establish positive attitudes to a healthy lifestyle.

By the end of the Reception year most children should be able to:

- **move with confidence, imagination and safety;**
- **move with control and co-ordination;**
- **show an awareness of space of themselves and of others;**
- **recognise the importance of keeping healthy and those things that contribute to this;**
- **recognise the changes that happen to their bodies when they are active;**
- **use a range of small and large equipment;**
- **travel around, under, over and through balancing and climbing equipment;**

- handle tools, objects, construction and malleable materials safely and with increasing control.

(DfEE/QCA, 2000:11)

Planning for physical activity outdoors

Access to a high quality outdoor environment, whilst most generally available in nursery settings, is a recent requirement for many Reception classes and this may present challenges for you. This difficulty may call for inventive planning on your part until more adults and better facilities become available. Teachers in Reception classes often plan as a team to ensure sufficient supervision is available over an extended period, or they may restrict outdoor access to particular parts of the day, or to targeted groups. Ideally, all children between three and five should have continuous opportunities for gross motor activities throughout the school day in order to ensure that they have sufficient opportunity to practise, develop and refine their emerging skills. If a child is gaining confidence and the necessary balancing skills to move across a plank raised a metre from the ground for example, he or she needs to be able to practise this procedure several times over a few days. You will need to plan activities for children to work individually, to work in small groups and to work as part of the whole class group. You will also need to balance adult initiated activities with opportunities for child initiated activities, and ensure that children have the chance to experience both planning physical activity in advance and later reviewing their own performance.

Practical task

Plan an activity that will enable Grace to practise catching a large ball between extended arms. Make notes on the way this may impact on her:

- *self-confidence;*
- *ability to learn independently;*
- *willingness to meet new challenges;*
- *ability to gain equal access to the whole curriculum;*
- *increasing mobility;*
- *developing spatial awareness;*
- *co-operating with others;*
- *understanding how to keep healthy.*

Creating an appropriate learning environment

Good practice, then, indicates clearly the need for opportunities for physical activity to be available both indoors and out. Elsewhere in this book you will find discussion on using the outdoor area for delivering all curriculum areas. At this point, discussion will be restricted to promoting physical development. It is important that you do not fall into the trap of planning for gross motor activities outside and fine motor activities inside.

ORGANISATION OF THE OUTDOOR AREA

Most LEA nursery schools and classes have been built with an outdoor area which is easily accessible and visible indoors. This is not always the case. Some Early Years providers, housed in old Victorian buildings may have to find ways of helping children walk a distance and negotiate steps to an outside area which is out of sight of those working indoors. A good outdoor area would incorporate several different areas. Brown et al (1997) (in Wetton, 1997) identify four separate environments:

1. An open space which allows for play with bats, balls, ropes and other small equipment, as well as space for running and playing organised games such as 'What time is it Mr Wolf?'.

2. A challenge area for bikes and trikes. This might be a hard surface which would include changes of surface, humps and dips, junctions, corners and so forth, all allowing children to negotiate access, take turns, and make decisions. This area might incorporate road markings and signs. Working in this area children would be encouraged to develop the skills associated with pushing, pulling, pedalling, passing, and also working together in order to propel a large vehicle.

3. A natural area with trees and shrubs where children might hunt for mini-beasts or plant seeds.

4. A climbing area. This would include both fixed and portable equipment, such as a climbing frame, tunnels, balancing planks and bars, and large colourful hollow shapes that can be easily moved by the children to create a 'Krypton Factor' style obstacle course. Ideally, a fixed sand and water area might be available, as well as an area of seating and shade where children might sit quietly and draw, complete a puzzle or read a book.

Practical task

Using the table below, consider how you might plan a series of activities that would develop balancing skills.

Learning intention, knowledge skills and attitudes	Areas and resources	Activities	Teaching points and key vocabulary
To plan and carry out a sequence of activities which involve balancing at ground level	Ropes on the ground to balance along	'Who can help to build an obstacle course using these ropes?'	Remind children to use their arms to help balance.

INDOOR AREA

This needs to include a climbing frame with planks or bars for balancing, large building blocks, space to move wheeled toys, and an open space for dance games and adult-directed activities.

What is the role of the teacher in meeting the physical development needs of young children?

We have already talked about the need for you to observe each child carefully during physical activity in order to move individuals on in their learning. It will also be important that you bring your knowledge of each child's home background and experiences to bear when planning and interacting in physical activities. Opportunities for individualised treatment are much easier to provide in an Early Years setting than in a primary setting. Wetton (1997) argues that it is for this reason especially that high quality learning opportunities be offered in the Early Years so that children can benefit from this and become physically confident and competent before they move into Key Stage I. It will be your responsibility to ensure that this takes place.

In order to do this you will need to have some idea of the average ability of normal three year olds. Wetton (1997) offers the following guidance on possible levels of achievement.

GROSS MOTOR AND LOCOMOTOR SKILLS

- **Walk backwards forwards and sideways.**
- **Walk on tiptoes.**
- **Show a basic running style.**
- **Climb up steps or ladder with one foot leading, maximum step depth 21 cm.**
- **Climb down a ladder with one foot leading, with hand support.**
- **Pivot round and round on feet.**
- **Walk up and down mounds.**
- **Jump up and down on the spot on two feet.**
- **Jump a distance of 36 cm.**
- **Jump down one foot to two feet from a height of 45 cm.**
- **Balance walk along a plank at a height of 18 cm from the ground.**
- **Balance on one (preferred) leg for four seconds.**
- **Crawl through a barrel or drainpipe.**
- **Climb through three lowest rungs of the climbing frame.**

FINE MOTOR SKILLS

- **Place three blocks (2.5–5 cm) on top of each other.**
- **Make a straight road with ten building blocks having been shown an exact replica.**
- **Affix a piece of construction apparatus to a hole in another piece.**
- **Assemble a six-piece jigsaw.**
- **Paint a person with a head and two other parts identifiable.**
- **Grip and make marks on paper with a thick soft pencil.**

- Hammer shapes into a pegboard.
- Make a ball with clay or playdough.
- Pour water from a jug with a spout into a large container.
- Thread large beads onto a lace.

EYE–HAND EYE–FOOT CO-ORDINATION

- Catch a large ball thrown by an adult between their extended arms.
- Catch a small ball thrown by an adult between extended arms.
- Kick a standing ball forcibly.
- Pedal tricycle along a wide chalked line.
- Push a ball away from self across the floor surface.
- Pull an empty truck around obstacles.

It will be an important part of your role to ensure that children who are not able to perform these tasks are targeted for extra help. It has been a common fault in the Early Years setting to treat physical activity as though there were no need for active teaching and that the provision of an appropriate environment is enough to ensure learning takes place (Bruner, 1980, reporting on the Oxford Preschool Research). It will be vital that you build in time for careful observation when you assess children's learning which you then use to inform future provision. Working closely as a team with other staff will be important here. Other features of your role will be to demonstrate skills, for example completing a hopscotch sequence, and becoming involved in imaginative physical play, for example on a large wheeled toy which is being used as a coach taking children to the seaside, in order to ensure it is extended and developed.

Challenging stereotypes

If all the children in your care are to reach their full potential, you will need to be aware of likely difficulties they might encounter. Some children may come to school in inappropriate clothing. Parents will need information about activities in your setting if you want them to appreciate that a frilly dress might create difficulties on the climbing frame, or that wellingtons are a necessary additional item on a wet or snowy day. You will need to deal sensitively with the child whose cultural background means she has had little opportunity, for example, to experience ball play before. Children who are overweight or less agile than others in the class will also need extra support. Involving children with mobility difficulties will require both detailed planning and discussion with the other children. Finally, you will need to be prepared to challenge the stereotypical views some children will have already developed, such as 'You can't play football, you're a girl', or 'Girls aren't strong enough to carry big blocks'. You may also be confronted with parents who object to some activities, such as boys skipping or being asked to dance.

Health and Safety

As a student you will always be accompanied by a qualified teacher when supervising physical activities. Nevertheless, you will be expected to be aware of the need for attention to safety and to take some, though not ultimate, responsibility. Once qualified you will of course have complete responsibility. Whilst it is the nature of young children to have accidents, you will be expected to be aware of the school's Health and Safety policy and to apply it – for example, concerning the movement and erection of portable equipment, supervision of children moving in large numbers between areas and so forth.

Practical task

On your next visit to school ask to see the school Health and Safety policy and make a list of issues to consider when taking a group of children outdoors for a focused activity on balancing.

Planning to meet the creative development needs of young children

Defining what is meant in curriculum terms by creativity is in itself a challenge. In the DfEE document *All Our Futures: Creativity, Culture and Education* (1999), it is defined as, 'Imaginative activity fashioned so as to produce outcomes that are both original and of value'.

Within the Early Years curriculum, it has generally been used to cover the elements of learning and teaching connected with art and technology, and those linked to communication. However, a wider interpretation is clear from the Foundation Stage guidance, which describes creativity as 'fundamental to successful learning'. Creativity is part of every subject area. It can be found in the study of patterns in maths, in problem solving in science, and it is also evident in imaginative responses to communication.

Creativity has long been valued as a central aspect of Early Years education. You will be aware already that many of the early pioneers placed creativity at the centre of their philosophy; Froebel, Montessori and Steiner speak of the inner life of the child. Froebel saw children as taking knowledge into themselves from their experiences, transforming it, then storing it in their imagination. Play, the imagination, and the ability of the mind, were seen to be vital in making the 'inner outer', that is, allowing the outward expression of the unique nature of each individual. He believed that the child's knowledge could be shared with others through the use of paint, clay, music, drama, the written word, conversation, mathematics and so forth. Both Steiner and Froebel held that through imagination the child strove to make links between new experiences and previous knowledge.

You will also know that Early Years practitioners have long championed the need for children to develop positive self-esteem by having the opportunity to make creative responses in their learning. This emphasis has contributed greatly to the overall ethos of early learning. Developmental Psychologists argue that the desire to learn about and contribute to a culture is innate (Trevarthan, 1995) and highlight this as the explanation for even the youngest child's predisposition to making a creative response. For example, Trevarthan argues that the ability displayed by carer and baby dyads to strike up communication through song and rhyme is striking in its cultural universality.

In your work you will find that the young child entering an Early Years setting is highly predisposed towards the many and varied opportunities available for her to make a creative response. She has an innate desire to make sense of the world around her and is happy to immerse herself in a learning environment which is attractive and stimulating and which, in presenting opportunities for active learning, allows her to begin to make new connections and to represent her developing ideas.

Bruner (1981) has argued that the symbolic mode of representation, together with iconic and enactive modes, contribute to the child's developing ability to represent their world. It is the creative area of learning that particularly facilitates the symbolic area of representation.

At this point in the history of Early Years education in this country, it is difficult to visualise an early learning environment devoid of opportunities for art, imaginative play, music or movement. In fact much of the parody of early learning which takes place is often based on our apparent obsession with this, for example the late Joyce Grenfell's exhortation to her invisible children to 'stand like a tree', followed by the comic addendum 'No, David, trees do not kick their friends as they pass'. Sometimes, however, it is disappointing to witness that opportunities planned in the name of creative development are linked more closely to the adult's creativity than the child's. The walls in many settings are decorated with friezes based on the seasons or on a shared book. Children will undoubtedly have been enthusiastically involved in such a production. Their role may have been to paint a large piece of corrugated card brown to form the trunk of a tree, or use sponges to produce a pattern, which was then painstakingly cut by an adult into the shape of a butterfly, or a cloud. In these situations young children take on the role of miniature labourers contributing to the production of an end product which is largely meaningless to them. How can we expect them to recognise that the newly created cloud began life as their rectangular piece of work? What happens to their ownership? How would you feel if someone cut up one of your assignments and made a public display of odd words and phrases? And, ironically, all carried out in the name of creativity. Compare the following two classroom stories.

Classroom story

1 *As part of a topic on transport the practitioner has set up a creative activity. She has set out on the table pre-cut bus shapes complete with cut out windows, a supply of green paint (the buses in this area have green livery) and a selection of implements for printing in a variety of shapes – circle, oblong, star etc. The children are then invited to 'do some printing on a bus'. The adult then interacts with the children by questioning them on their preferred printing shape and on their experiences of travelling by bus with their families.*

2 *As part of a topic on transport a practitioner has set up a painting table. The children are provided with a range of paints they have assisted in mixing, and a selection of brushes. Pencils and marker pens are also provided. The children are invited to select paper from a range of textures, colours and sizes. Around the area are displayed drawings and photographs of buses and some model buses. Included are some particular photographs taken on a recent visit to the local bus depot. As the children arrive at the table, the adult reminds them about the recent visit. They discuss what they saw in terms of size, shape, and colour. She reminds them as well of the slippery, shiny surface of the bodywork and of the smell of the engines. She talks to them about the photographs, paintings and models set out around the area.*

Practical task

Spend a few moments analysing which of these classroom stories presents the child with the principles enshrined in **All Our Futures** *(DfEE, 1999).*

It is important that you spend time considering how far learning can be described as creative when children are encouraged to produce rows of identical buses differentiated only by the shape of the print with which they are decorated. No wonder practitioners stress the importance of naming work, how else would these finished products be reclaimed at the end of the session!

By the end of their time in the Reception class children are expected to have had opportunities to:

- **respond in a variety of ways to what they see, hear, touch and feel;**
- **use their imagination in art and design, music, dance drama, stories and play;**
- **express and communicate their ideas, thoughts and feelings by using a widening range of materials, suitable tools, drama, movement, designing and making, and a variety of songs and instruments.**

The *Curriculum Guidance for the Foundation Stage* also describes creativity as 'fundamental to successful learning', then goes on to consider its significance in helping children develop links between separate areas of learning. Duffy (1998) divides the creative curriculum into four aspects:

- **two- and three-dimensional representation;**
- **imaginative play;**
- **music;**
- **dance.**

Two- and three-dimensional activities

Three-dimensional experiences are designed to encourage children to employ all their senses as they explore a range of surfaces and materials. You may encourage them to use clay, sand, cones and conkers or manufactured products like cardboard, shaving cream, playdough or modroc. You will be teaching them to use a variety of tools, ranging from fingers and sand equipment, to household implements such as hammers and saws. You will also provide a wide variety of construction equipment. Working on three-dimensional representation will allow the child to investigate shape and space, texture, colour and pattern. The two-dimensional experiences you provide will add further opportunities for children to investigate colour, line and tone.

In planning these experiences it is important that you ensure children are offered a wide range of materials since different children are attracted by a whole variety of stimuli at different times in their development, and all have individual preferences. Whilst one child might be appalled by an invitation to work at a table covered in brown slip, another child will be excited and mesmerised by it. Consider the following classroom stories.

Classroom story

1. *John arrived at nursery school one morning to the said table of slip. His eyes lit up and he hastily dismissed his mother as he struggled to pull the requisite apron over his head. Without hesitation he spread his fingers onto the table and stood delightedly examining his wet brown hands. He then rushed around the table making a circular five-fingered track. He erased this and went on to make a series of wriggly lines and swooping curves, all at great speed. Finally, slowly, with his index finger, he drew a large capital J in the slip and with a flourish added a full stop. 'There you are', he said to the adult at the table, 'J for John' at which point he went off to investigate further. His rapid and enthusiastic activity had lasted less than three minutes. John was a child who concerned nursery staff with his reluctance to join in adult-led activities and with his particular aversion to writing, which had led subsequently to his refusal to handle pens or pencils.*

2. *Hannah arrived at a table set with palettes of paint, mixing trays, jars of water and a selection of brushes varying in thickness. In the middle of the table was the figure of a dragon, cast in metal, sitting on a nest of opalescent eggs. Hannah sat for three quarters of an hour discussing the colours, line and tone and creating the dragon's story as she painstakingly painted her picture.*

Practical task

How far do you think the two children could be said to be responding creatively? How important was the planning and presentation of the activities on offer? As a practitioner what might you offer next to each of these children?

Imaginative play

The opportunities you offer to children for imaginative play will present them with the chance to explore personal relationships, develop empathy, explore emotions, investigate causality and develop their ability to communicate. You will need to include amongst other things, a role-play area, the use of puppets, the provision of small world and construction equipment, as well as access to a natural environment with places to hide, climb and test skills such as balancing. Imaginative play can provide a meaningful context for learning, for example by incorporating literacy events such as consulting a telephone directory or television guide, taking note of an appointment, or presenting a mathematical problem in the need to decide how best to fit packets of food onto the shelves in the shop.

Many Early Years practitioners struggle with the concept of planning for imaginative play and with the role of the adult in that play. Whilst it is important that children experience opportunities for spontaneous play, you will have a responsibility for ensuring that the equipment provided is stimulating and of high quality. Many home corners are depressing areas resourced with dirty, naked dolls and a random collection of unattractive pots, pans and plates. Is it any wonder that in such areas babies are to be found wedged in microwaves and the telephone directory is stored in the fridge? What can such areas have to offer as a basis for learning? Besides being a facilitator, you have an important role helping the child to make links between her own life experiences, her prior learning, and the new situation you are making available for investigation and manipulation. Many practitioners become impatient when children appear to lack the skills to play appropriately in the newly provided shop or hairdressers and ignore the fact that some children will be unaware of the appropriate behaviour as it is not part of their previous experience. Children need to see you and the other adults modelling that behaviour for them. Ideally, a visit into the local community should be planned so that children can bring back first hand experience to their play. Or you might be able to organise a visit to the setting by a relevant adult. You will then, by joining in the play, be able to scaffold the children's imaginative responses by helping them recall and repeat what they have learnt. For example, a willing adult can act as a parent bringing her baby to the clinic, modelling for the children a conversation with the receptionist, the careful undressing and reassurance of the baby and so on. Children will also benefit from adult challenges which structure their play. Consider the following.

Classroom story

Practitioners in one setting had identified that the construction area was often dominated by boys. Where girls attempted to join in the play, they were ignored and marginalised. With careful observation, the adults became aware that girls fared better when an adult joined the play and when the equipment provided included figures. An activity was planned as a girls' only session when girls were invited to help make a playground for the Play People using junk materials. The practitioners were highly gratified by both the sustained involvement of the girls and the high quality work they produced.

Learning in the Early Years needs to be organised to ensure that children have a broad and balanced curriculum which allows them to have access to adult directed and self-initiated activities. Play is the most worthwhile self-initiated activity. However, if all children are to reach their full creative potential in your care, it is important that as an Early Years practitioner you challenge prevailing stereotypes which might place obstacles in the way of development.

Music

You will need to plan opportunities for children to listen to and respond to music. They also need to have time to create their own music with the use of everyday objects, purpose-made instruments and the use of voices. They need to learn how music can be written down and returned to later, and to experience both adult-led music sessions and periods when they are able to extend their understanding through self-initiated activities. Children need opportunities to develop such concepts as sound, rhythm, pitch, tempo, and to become familiar with a range of instruments.

Dance

Clearly dance and music will be closely associated. It is vital that you provide opportunities for children to investigate moving to music. They need to experience a wide variety of different music including that from a variety of cultures. They need opportunities to respond both to recorded music and to that which they produce themselves. Dance in the Early Years should explore rhythm, space, direction and height as well as the concepts of speed and duration. Once again children will need opportunities to be involved in adult-led activities as well as self-initiated activities, and to work individually as well as in large and small groups.

As the curriculum in our schools becomes more and more crowded and prescriptive, it is vital that teachers continue to nurture individual creativity. Busy home lives and fears about health and safety may mean that it is only in educational settings that children have sufficient space and time to explore their creative abilities. Early Years practitioners ignore these factors at their peril.

Planning to meet the physical and creative development needs of young children:

a summary of key points

Planning for physical and creative development should be:

- *based on a firm philosophical and ideological foundation;*
- *linked to the rest of the Early Years curriculum;*
- *mindful of the significant role of the teacher and the importance of effective management;*
- *designed to promote equal opportunities and challenge sterotypes.*

5 DEVELOPING CHILDREN AS INDEPENDENT AND CONFIDENT LEARNERS: PERSONAL, SOCIAL AND EMOTIONAL DEVELOPMENT

Angela Harnett

Professional Standards for QTS

→ 2.2, 2.4, 2.7, 3.1.3, 3.3.9

These Standards state that in order to gain QTS, teachers must be familiar with the National Curriculum Framework for Personal, Social and Health Education. They should understand how children's learning can be affected by their physical, social and emotional development, be familiar with a range of strategies that promote good behaviour, and take account of children's interests and backgrounds when preparing and organising resources. Teachers should have high expectations for classroom behaviour, promote self-control and independence, and establish a clear framework for discipline. You may find it helpful to refer to the appropriate section of the Handbook that accompanies the Standards for the award of QTS, for further clarification and support.

By the end of this chapter, you should be able to:

- *recognise the Early Learning Goals relevant for personal, social and emotional development;*
- *be aware of the need to encourage children to be independent and confident learners;*
- *be aware of the meaning of independent and confident learners;*
- *identify ways of encouraging confident and independent learning within your own classroom practice;*
- *understand the need to provide an environment that develops children personally, socially and emotionally.*

Introduction

This chapter looks at the requirements of the Professional Standards for the award of QTS within the context of the area of personal, social and emotional development in the Foundation Stage curriculum. It will address issues such as:

- **the importance of personal, social and emotional development;**
- **why we need to encourage children to be independent and confident;**
- **the practical implications to practitioners.**

Personal, social and emotional development of children requires a secure knowledge of both child development and how children learn and think. This is not an easy task and many aspects of this are learnt through experience, asking more experienced colleagues, observation and research such as reading relevant literature. Personal, social and emotional development is part of all curriculum areas. It could, however, be argued that without comprehensive development in this area, learning is made more difficult.

The importance of developing children in this area is well documented from Piaget (1896–1980, quoted in Barnes 1997) through to writers such as Rogers (1983) and the High Scope Educational Research Foundation (Hohmann and Weikart, 1995). Reports such as Plowden (1967) and Gulbenkian (1982) also highlighted the need for children to have a broad and balanced curriculum that developed the whole child. This has been further refined within the Early Learning Goals by providing explicit guidance on the opportunities that enhance this area of learning.

The Early Learning Goals are:

- **dispositions and attitudes;**
- **self-confidence and self-esteem;**
- **making relationships;**
- **behaviour and self-control;**
- **self-care;**
- **sense of community.**

Foundation Curriculum (DfEE/QCA, 2000:28).

Although there are only six goals within this section, analysis of the areas shows that this is a complex and vast area of work. Personal, social and emotional development is about feelings and relationships. Here we should ask ourselves: can you teach this or do you provide an environment, opportunities and discussions to develop this? If we look at these goals as being the backbone to all other goals the task does not seem so onerous. The six Early Learning Goals within this section have many aspects within each one and these will be investigated throughout this chapter.

Importance of developing children personally, emotionally and socially

In order to address the QTS standards you will need a clear understanding of what personal, social and emotional development means.

This area of learning requires an understanding of values, beliefs and attitudes. What are you trying to develop in these children? Perhaps the starting point for you is to know yourself. Part of your own development is to know your own values, beliefs and attitudes. Do you bring anything in your own life that you need to challenge? How can you foster personal, social and emotional growth if you have not challenged yourself and your own assumptions regarding life personally, socially and emotionally? This is a daunting task but we need to understand how to establish relationships, address difficult subjects such as death and provide a secure, understanding environment. We all have individual perceptions of the world around us. As adults it is a far more difficult task to understand the perceptions young children have of their world.

Practical task

It would be useful to complete this task with a group of friends.

Brainstorm the factors that helped you develop

- *personally;*
- *socially;*
- *emotionally.*

Are there people or events that have been crucial in your maturity in these areas?

Within this task did you challenge yourself? Words that might have appeared are trust, friendships, feelings, relationships, and belonging but also hurt, loneliness, guilt. These are all part of progressing in these areas. If children do not have experiences of areas such as hurt they will not foster an understanding of how this feels.

Children begin to develop relationships from birth. Each child's experience is unique. Your task is dependent on how these relationships have developed and how well the child understands the world around them. This is your starting point, the building blocks for the future.

Providing a supportive environment means knowing your group/class of children well. This is particularly difficult when training and early in your career. It is, however, important to get to know your children well so that you don't make mistakes that might have long-reaching effects on the child.

The responsibility placed on all educators is enormous. Even writing this chapter gives me the responsibility of knowing that I might challenge some people more than others about themselves. However, the joy of teaching is seeing children who are quiet and shy become confident and independent.

Practical task

What would you like to achieve in your own setting?

Analyse your own views of classroom environment/ethos using the following headings:

- *children's attitudes;*
- *children's self-confidence and self-esteem;*
- *relationships between children and children;*
- *relationships between children and adults;*
- *relationships between adults and adults;*
- *behaviour and self-control;*
- *independence;*
- *classroom as a community.*

When you have completed the task compare them with the goals above.

Now you have analysed your own ideas about how you see your classroom we need to look at how we go about producing an environment that expands children personally, socially and emotionally.

We have explored some of the issues related to what is personal, social and emotional development. This is only a brief visit in order to remind us of what we have learnt through initial teacher training, classroom experience and personal experience.

As with any area of education it must always be remembered that we are dealing with people. There are no quick fix answers. Many of the ideas might not work in your particular setting. It is hoped that the ideas will develop your own creativity in how to promote personal, social and emotional development in young children.

Why develop children personally, socially and emotionally?

Preparing children for adult life and the needs of society is an important area for debate. Through this chapter it is hoped that you will have challenged your own ideas related to how you can advance children in this area of their learning.

Practical task

If you were asked to draw a picture of a child who is well developed personally, socially and emotionally, what might your pictures look like?

Can you identify a child from recent experience who you think is well developed in one or more of these areas? What are the things that have made you identify this child?

What are the assumptions we might make when thinking about these children? It is similar to asking older children what a thief looks like? They often describe a person who is scruffy and has a face that is frightening. The problem with assumptions is that life is not always like that. We as teachers have to be very sensitive and aware of the children in our care. They might look all right on the surface but knowing them well will enable you to pick out small changes in their behaviour and body language.

The ultimate aim of developing children personally, socially and emotionally is to help them to become secure, happy children who are independent and confident. In order to do this they need to grow in their knowledge of themselves as individuals. We need to enable children to explore where they fit within this micro society, how they as individuals relate to others and how groups function.

Developing independence and confidence needs to be balanced with the children's safety. Children are learning about their environment; they need to take risks to explore their social, physical and emotional environments. However, these risks need to be managed in such a way that children are safe. Teachers need to be aware that children are progressing at different rates and some might need more support than others.

Independence could be defined as needing little or no help, being able to make one's own decisions. Confidence could be defined as being secure in one's own abilities. Children will be at different levels in these areas. Your perception of independence has possibly changed during your experiences in the classroom. Children who are seen as independent or confident in one school might not be the same in another school. Again this may be due to the classroom environment, school environment or even the social environment. Some children can be too independent or confident and not wish to ask for help. Part of developing independence and confidence is related to knowing your own capabilities and what you can and cannot do. This is where children need to understand consequences of actions and words.

The High/Scope Educational Research Foundation (Hohmann and Weikart, 1995:46) defines this as a sense of self. They see this as developing:

- *trust* – the confident belief in oneself and in others;
- *initiative* – the capacity for children to begin and then follow through on a task;
- *empathy* – the capacity that allows children to understand the feelings of others by relating them to feelings that they themselves have had;
- *self-confidence* – the capacity to believe in one's own ability.

Classroom story

A Reception class has settled to work with various activities. The teacher has noticed that Nichola is not very responsive today. When the teacher talks to Nichola she discovers that her hamster died last night. The teacher comforts Nichola and says, 'Never mind' – perhaps getting on with her work will help take her mind off this. Nichola tries to play with the Lego but all she wants to do is cry.

The teacher assessed correctly that Nichola had a problem, she comforted Nichola and gave a solution to the problem. However, was this the correct solution? Did the teacher perceive how important the hamster was to Nichola? This pet could have been one of the most important things in her life. How might the teacher have provided a different solution?

How do we encourage children to be independent and confident individuals?

Classroom management

The environment and ethos of the setting you are in needs to embrace a philosophy that supports and encourages children to be independent and confident. Does your setting provide a directed, supported or totally free environment? Or does the setting require movement between these different ways of working?

> Well-planned and purposeful activity and appropriate intervention by practitioners will engage children in the learning process.

Curriculum Guidance for the Foundation Stage (DfEE/QCA 2000:11)

Issues that you need to consider are:

- **routines;**
- **behaviour management;**
- **layout of the classroom;**
- **relationships with children;**
- **relationships with adults;**
- **access to equipment.**

Routines

Young children benefit from knowing what is going to happen. Knowing there is some routine to the day allows children to be able to make choices. This is not to say that the day is rigidly set out or that the children are not made aware when the normal routine is different. It might be only that the children know when outside play will happen and that if it is raining and there is no covered area this will change.

Practical task

Using the Early Learning Goals for self-care identify the routines that might support and encourage independence and confidence in both nursery and Reception classes. Do these routines allow the children to engage in tasks and complete them?

To support independence and confidence, the routines need to be arranged around the children's needs not the adults'. Routines can develop shared control of the Early Years environment. Children can take responsibility for their own actions and develop a sense of culture that everyone is part of. This culture gives children the security they need to be able to make sense of their surroundings.

RECEPTION CLASSROOM ROUTINE

A reception classroom routine might look like this:

- *children welcomed at the door;*
- *informal gathering allowing children to communicate anything that has occurred;*
- *working/playing;*
- *outside play;*
- *lunchtime;*
- *reading in the book corner;*
- *working/playing;*
- *story;*
- *home.*

How would you plan for this day? Would you have a weekly plan, daily plan or session plan? Within your planning you need to show evidence of making provision for these areas of development. Some might be formal, as in 'circle time'; others might be how the children take turns in the sand, for example. This is related to your classroom management that is crucial to how the children respond to being confident and independent. Planning also has to be related to the children's experiences. (See Chapter 4 on planning.)

Classroom story

A group of nursery children are working with paints. They are choosing what they paint and the colours they want to mix. Amy decides she wants to use some chalk on her painting. She finds the colour she wants from the box and uses the chalk to define the outlines of the picture. The adult helper comes over to look at the paintings. She looks at Amy's painting and remarks that it is very nice but we are only using paints today.

There are a number of issues here. The children were being allowed to make choices and decisions. However, when they wanted to choose other equipment this was not seen as being independent but wrong.

The questions that need to be asked here are:

• **What are the messages that this group of children receives?**
• **Do all the adults within the environment have the same understanding about how to develop confidence?**

Planning for personal, social and emotional development is not only about long-, medium- and short-term plans, it is also about managing your environment, the adults you work with and having a structure to some of the elements of the Early Learning Goals. How do you manage incidental events, e.g. an argument in the sand? Although you cannot plan for these you do, however, need to know how you will deal with these incidents and how long you are prepared to spend dealing with them.

Teaching children to become independent and confident learners

Developing children personally, socially and emotionally, as we have described, is about feelings, attitudes and relationships. Whilst supporting children in this area of learning we also see it in the context of the child's own experiences personally, socially and emotionally. Children need to develop self-awareness, self-control and knowledge of others and the world around them. This is quite an awesome task; however, as with other areas of growth it takes place in small steps. A word of warning here. You need to be aware that you are encouraging this development without denigrating the society the children live in. The perception they bring from home might not be the same as your perception of the values and standards you need to encourage. Your role is to ensure that children are aware that there are different standards, values and beliefs.

By looking at the Early Learning Goals and seeing how we develop these areas we can begin to advance our understanding of personal, social and emotional learning. The Early Learning Goals give a very comprehensive breakdown for each area of learning and can be used to develop your children from their own personal starting point. You will become aware as you read this section that there is a lot of overlap between the areas.

Early learning goals

CONCENTRATION AND MOTIVATION

- **Continue to be interested, excited and motivated to learn.**
- **Be confident to try new activities, initiate ideas and speak in a familiar group.**
- **Maintain attention, concentrate, and sit quietly when appropriate.**

We have all had experience of finding some events or tasks motivating. Reflect on what has motivated you.

Practical task

Think about yourself. How are you motivated:

- *at home;*
- *in your day-to-day work or study;*
- *in your leisure time?*

Can you list the moments or events in your life that you found particularly exciting or interesting? What are the factors that contribute to these feelings?

Having considered the practical task you will have a clearer view of how you are motivated. Individual motivation is an interaction of needs, incentives and perception. Perhaps the task helped you identify the intrinsic and extrinsic needs you have. For example, you might be motivated to work because you enjoy it or you might have a need to socialise with people. So how do you motivate children, particularly young children?

There are a number of factors that can be pinpointed. These include:

- **appropriate level of work;**
- **interesting topics;**
- **good quality equipment;**
- **variety of equipment;**
- **high quality and interesting displays;**
- **engaging with the children;**
- **playing with them;**
- **being prepared to work at the children's level;**
- **rewarding by praise or other means.**

You could make your own list and add many more items to this. However, I feel that one of the most important factors with Early Years children is something I call the WOW factor. Think of the teachers/lecturers who have enthralled you during your education. These people perhaps did not provide different information from other teachers but they usually had a presence that made you want to listen or learn.

Charles Handy (1985), an eminent management guru, describes this as the 'E Factor': 'Things that trigger energy, excitement, enthusiasm, effort, effervescence, even expenditure.'

Young children are engaged when teachers make everything larger than life. Teachers of Early Years children show an intense interest in the smallest thing.

Classroom story

Lucy, a Reception child, took a small coloured stone into school. As she showed it to the teacher another child commented that it was a piece of broken bottle and what was special about that. Further investigation by the teacher ascertained that this was a special stone to Lucy and she wanted to share it with the rest of the class. As Lucy showed the class the teacher asked the children if the stone might be magic. After much discussion the children decided they would draw pictures and/or write about a magic adventure they had with the stone.

The whole class became enthralled in this activity for the whole day. Lucy was excited all day because for the first time she had joined in with class activities. Lucy brought her mum in to show her the stories at the end of the day. Lucy felt she now belonged to the class and the magic stone became a subject of discussion that re-occurred throughout the year.

Some interesting discussion points related to this incident might be:

- **How can we develop children's individual interests?**
- **How does this individual learning fit into the learning of other children?**
- **Can we address this within our planning?**

Some of you will have discovered that teaching in the Early Years can be exhausting. All teaching is exhausting for different reasons, but Early Years is particularly exhausting because you enter stage left in the morning and exit stage left in the evening. I have always compared Early Years teaching with acting. Teachers need to know how to get the children excited and how to bring them back to order. Movements have to vary from being very small to extremely large. The use of your voice changes how the children behave and react to a situation. If you have ever lost your voice you will know that young children often whisper to you all day.

This is one area that new teachers are often very nervous of. What will happen if the children get excited and I cannot get them to listen again? This is where experience and support from your colleges helps. You need to try out different techniques and develop your own style. There are no definitive answers.

Practical task

- *What techniques have you observed teachers using to excite Early Years children?*
- *What techniques have you observed teachers using to bring the children back together?*

Next time you are in school observe the different techniques one teacher uses during a day.

If young children have a thirst for enquiry they will want to try things out. New activities can be initiated by the teacher or initiated by the child. (See Chapter I for a further discussion of this area.) This is where they need to have access to a variety of equipment. Does the environment provide children with an ethos that encourages them to try things out? Remember the class-room story about paints – will that group of children be prepared to make their own choices or will they feel that this is wrong?

For many children it is difficult to develop confidence. The world from their perception is a very frightening place. Things that we as adults take for granted are daunting for young children. How many times have we seen young children in school plays begin to cry? This is not to say we should not take part in such activities. It does, however, mean that teachers have to be sensitive to the feelings of all their children. Often just giving children the choice can alleviate their fears. (Chapter 6 on language helps to address the question of confidence of speaking in-groups.)

The world of today is full of noises. It is very difficult to find anywhere that is silent. Many young children might come from homes where there is constant noise from television, radio, other siblings and general living noise. These children might not be aware that there can be quiet. Being quiet might also be intimidating for some children. How do we help children to be quiet, and concentrate? This is a skill that often has to be taught. Children in Early Years need to be allowed to sit for short sessions and gradually build up to longer sessions. Many schools now recognise that asking Reception children to sit through whole school assemblies can be difficult at the beginning of the year.

Practical task

Investigate how children are encouraged to concentrate. How do colleagues foster concentration? What are the techniques they use?

This task could be by observing in different settings, talking to colleagues or by brainstorming with friends.

Is there a pattern to your findings? Are there any factors that might make some children less able to listen and concentrate? From this section you can see that developing children's concentration takes time and experience helps you as teachers to develop this area.

SELF-CONFIDENCE AND SELF-ESTEEM

- **Respond to significant experiences, showing a range of feelings when appropriate.**
- **Have a developing awareness of their own needs, views and feelings and be sensitive to the needs, views and feelings of others.**
- **Have a developing respect for their own cultures and beliefs and those of other people.**

Work on self-confidence, self-esteem and feelings can take place formally during sessions such as circle time. Children can be encouraged to recognise how facial expressions, body language and changes in voice can tell them how a person might be feeling. Emotions, however, are a very complex area of study even for adults. Again this is an area that relies on your own knowledge of how feelings develop and sensitivity to the world of young children.

All teachers of young children experience the time when children first enter education. That first morning when children are leaving their carer. It's always a good idea to have a box of tissues ready! This is a time when feelings are running high not only from the children but also the adults. Leaving your carer for maybe the first time can be traumatic. Both carer and child observe how you deal with this situation. Do you deal sensitively with them or do you disregard their feelings and believe that they must be independent on the first day?

Many schools now have great flexibility to the start of nursery or school. Parents are more welcome to stay in many schools. This, as you might be aware, has positive and negative sides, it can also put more pressure on you as an Early Years teacher. However, if children are to work together, value others and be sensitive to people's feelings, we as teachers have to be seen to do the same. It is not only the children who have problems with their feelings.

The ethos/culture/environment of your classroom needs to take every opportunity to develop this area. You are responsible for ensuring that your classroom reflects society and the divergence within that society. There needs to be equality of opportunity and everyone should feel respected. Children need to develop an awareness that members of their school family do not necessarily have the same beliefs and culture as they do. There is a wealth of opportunities to investigate areas such as:

- **different weddings;**
- **different foods;**
- **different religions;**
- **different countries and climates;**
- **different accents;**
- **different nursery rhyme words across the country.**

Many teachers discuss classroom rules at the beginning of the year. What are the expectations within this small society? Although for young children these will be very small rules the area of individuals' rights needs to be addressed. This is all part of your behaviour management strategy. There is a wealth of materials that develop behaviour management strategies and self-esteem; (Roffey et al; 1998; DfES, 2002). When you have your own class the school will have their own behaviour policy; this will also include a section on bullying and might have some guidance on how they develop children's self-esteem.

Praise is a vital part of building self-confidence and self-esteem. We are all aware of how we feel when someone has praised us for our work. We also know how it feels when someone criticises what we have done. Praise needs to be used appropriately and children need to become aware that you praise different children for different reasons.

Classroom story

Lee, who has Downs Syndrome, has finished his painting and is showing it to the teacher. This is the first time Lee has finished a painting on his own. He has managed to concentrate for three minutes without intervention from an adult. The teacher is talking to Lee and telling him how wonderful his painting is and how well he has done to concentrate so hard. Lee shows how pleased he is with himself by his smile and wanting to show the other children.

Sarah is also at the painting table and she also takes about three minutes to complete her picture. When she shows the teacher she is told that she needs to take more time and be more careful with her colours. Sarah is totally confused because she thinks her picture is better than Lee's. She goes back to the table and paints the whole page blue.

What would you have done in this situation? Perhaps the children have not been made aware of the difficulties Lee has. As teachers we constantly have to encourage children who are working at different levels. You need to develop techniques that enable you to do this but also ensure that children are aware that you have different expectations for different children.

RELATIONSHIPS

- Form good relationships with adults and peers.
- Work as part of a group or class, taking turns and sharing fairly, understanding that there need to be agreed values and codes of behaviour for groups of people, including adults and children, to work together harmoniously.

As you can see from these goals there is an overlap with the above section. Developing children's understanding of other people's feelings and values is all part of working together. As teachers you need to develop a perception of when to intervene, when to observe and when to draw the whole group/class together. Children need to experience conflict and find resolutions to conflict in order to learn and understand how to develop relationships that respect others.

Classroom story

A nursery class is taking part in outdoor play. There is a variety of equipment for the children to use and they are able to make a free choice. Two children are playing with large wheeled vehicles. Tony has decided that he would prefer the vehicle Jane is using. Tony goes up to Jane and asks her if he can have her vehicle. Jane replies that she is still using it and he has his own vehicle. Tony then turns back to his own vehicle and discovers that someone else is now using it. Tony goes up to the vehicle and begins to physically pull this other child out. Whilst he is doing this he is shouting, 'I was here first'.

What would you do in this situation? Would you intervene or observe? Tony asked Jane nicely and he understood her reply and accepted it. However, he had then lost his own vehicle. Perhaps in his mind he felt let down that although he had done the right thing and not insisted on Jane's vehicle he had now lost his own vehicle. Maybe he felt he would have been better to have insisted on Jane getting out. How do you deal with these complexities of feelings? Tony needs to be praised for his actions with Jane. He does, however, need to understand that the other child perhaps did not realise Tony had left his vehicle to ask Jane. This is the type of situation you will be constantly facing and there is a need for you to know how you will deal with these situations and also how you might develop your class/group so that these situations do not develop too often.

Developing the skills of sharing can be very difficult for some children. They may have a number of siblings and have to constantly assert themselves in order to do things. Passing an object around at circle time is a good way of children physically seeing what taking turns means. Giving children a turn when explaining a problem that has taken place also gives them insight into the fact that their opinions are valued.

Conflict often arises in Early Years groups in relation to taking turns in areas such as the sand, water or the play area. There are ways to lessen these conflicts. You as a teacher need to set out the ground rules for such areas. For example, are there four children in the sand and six children in the play area? You might tell the children this but what happens if someone has had to go to the toilet? As you observe different teachers you will realise that there are a variety of ideas that can help.

Classroom story

The Reception play area was a building site. All the large bricks and Lego were placed in this area. There were also plastic spades, a small wheelbarrow and numerous hats.

So that the children knew how many children were playing in this area the teacher had devised a system where they had to clock in. Each child had a name card and there were six pockets for these cards. By the pockets were the words foreman, secretary, bricklayer, labourer, architect and plasterer. The class all knew what these jobs were as they were doing a topic about houses. As the children entered the area they found their name and placed it by one of the jobs.

All the children knew how the system worked. They all knew they had to clock in and out. The children were quite diligent about returning their cards. There were however, occasions when you would hear someone shout 'the last architect didn't clock out'.

In this one small area it can be seen that the children were developing co-operation, relationships and responsibility. In Early Years settings there are usually a number of adults working together. There is a need for you as a teacher to ensure that all adults are working together and understand the expectations you want from your environment. This can be very difficult for new teachers and teachers during school practice. Having said that, you can do this through your planning. It might be that you plan together with these adults and this is an opportunity to ensure they know what you expect out of a certain activity. You need to be explicit if you want children to have a free choice. You also need to be explicit about the language that is appropriate with this age of children.

BEHAVIOUR
Again we can see the links between relationships and behaviour:

- **Understand what is right, what is wrong and why.**
- **Consider the consequences of their words and actions for themselves and others.**

As teachers we need to ensure that children learn in a safe environment that enables them to reach their potential as individuals. Within this structure we need to develop their understanding that there are certain ways of behaving so that your class/group environment can co-exist.

Sometimes we have to behave in certain ways in order to enable the greater number of people be satisfied. Unfortunately rules and laws are usually made for the minority with the majority suffering. I previously mentioned class rules or guidance. In Early Years this could be called 'Getting on together'.

Practical task

Imagine you are starting with your first class/group. How would you develop your class/group guidance? These headings might be useful to use:

- *being kind to each other;*
- *being helpful;*
- *taking care of our classroom;*
- *taking care of one another.*

How might you as a teacher discuss these issues with a group of children? For example, what is meant by being kind and helpful? It is often useful to use practical examples of these concepts in your day-to-day teaching – for example, praising a child for being helpful. During this activity did you consider how you might allow all the children to take part? Would you find the list of guidance helpful when working with children on this?

It is often useful to have guidance of broad headings without too much detail. This not only helps the children remember them – it also means that if something unusual happens you can fit it into one of these headings.

Behaviour management is something that you will change and develop throughout your career. Each class is different and will need different issues addressed. There are, however, some generic areas to focus on such as the ones mentioned above and also praising positive behaviour – for example 'Amy and John are sitting so nicely'.

SELF-CARE

- **Dress and undress independently and manage their own personal hygiene.**
- **Select and use activities independently.**

Early Years children enter nursery or school with different levels of self-care. Some children will be able to dress themselves and use the toilet properly, some will not. Unfortunately people are not always aware that these skills have to be taught or modelled. Children have different levels of dexterity. As teachers you need to be aware of what your children can and cannot do. Some children are independent and want to try; others might be quite willing to let someone else do it for them.

Your classroom needs to have an ethos that 'trying' is all right and help is at hand if needed. You need to give children the time to try things. They need to experiment and help each other. One of your management issues here is giving the children enough time. There is nothing more frustrating than getting children changed after PE just before break. Young children need to know they have time to try to do things themselves and not feel under pressure to hurry up. These are the times when frustration and anger can surface.

Part of the day will be spent getting children to wash their hands. Discussions about why we need to wash our hands are important. This can also lead to discussions related to having a bath, washing your hair and germs in general.

In order for children to be independent they need to have access to the resources. For example, can the children reach the paper towels in the toilets?

Practical task

List the items of equipment you would expect children to have access to in an Early Years setting under the following headings:

- *play;*
- *drawing/painting;*
- *creative activities.*

During your next visit into school list areas that are not accessible to Early Years children.

One of the most important aspects of children being independent learners is health and safety. All the children need to know where they are allowed access, there might be areas that are not appropriate for them to go and they need to be aware of the dangers around them. Some people might feel that we should keep all dangerous items away from Early Years children. However, all items are potentially dangerous – even a book when thrown. Children will only learn about dangers and consequences if they use items such as scissors first in a controlled manner and later with less supervision. There is a great element of trust in allowing children to be independent, children need to have the security of knowing they can make mistakes but need to learn from these mistakes.

From a teacher's perspective health and safety is a vital issue. You as a trainee teacher need to know what is allowed and what is not. You need to make every effort to maintain your classroom as a safe environment where the children will not be at risk.

CULTURES AND RESPECT
This section reiterates the work in the section under self-confidence and self-esteem.

- **Understand that people have different needs, views, cultures and beliefs, that need to be treated with respect.**
- **Understand that they can expect others to treat their needs, views, cultures and beliefs with respect.**

There is a lot of valuable and enjoyable work to be gained from looking at differences within not only your classroom culture but also the wider community. Early Years settings lend themselves to having a nursery or Reception class granny or granddad. This is a valuable experience for both the children and the adults who might be willing to take on this role.

PLANNING

Personal, social and emotional development needs to be in all your areas of planning. However, it is also a day-to-day culture within your classroom and perhaps long-term planning is the most important. What are your expectations and values for this particular class?

EVIDENCE

You need to begin to think how you can show your competence in this area of teaching. If someone asked you to prove that you can develop a child personally, socially and emotionally, how might you do this?

Your planning is one factor that will show the intention to develop this area. Other things such as photographs and recordings of events are useful. An activity that Early Years children enjoy and that also produces a ready source of evidence is a 'Class Book'. In this you can record all the major events that have happened, social activities the children have taken part in – even any work surrounding circle times.

Developing children as independent and confident learners:

a summary of key points

Whilst reading this chapter you should have:

- *begun to develop or build on your own philosophy of working with Early Years children;*
- *considered your own opinions and assumptions of values, attitudes and beliefs;*
- *have a greater understanding of children's attitudes to values, attitudes and beliefs;*
- *a greater understanding of what you might teach, how you might teach and how you can build on your knowledge;*
- *developed an understanding of the non-statutory, extra-curricular activities that take place within the classroom;*
- *begun to analyse the importance of relationships and ethos/culture within the classroom setting.*

As you have read this chapter you will have realised how complex this area of development is. See this as an exciting journey that you take with the children. You will need to use all your creative abilities to keep up with the different children, different classes and different schools you may encounter during your career. However, the smile on the child's face when they have achieved tying their shoelace is a reward in itself.

Further reading

DfEE/QCE (1999) *Non-statutory Frameworks for Personal, Social and Health Education and Citizenship at Key Stages 1 and 2*. London. QCA. This sets out the expectation of pupils in the primary years.

Goncu, A. (ed) (1999) *Children's Engagement in the World. Sociocultural Perspectives*. Cambridge. Cambridge University Press. Concerned with children's development in its cultural context. The contributors reflect on how the activities and interactions of children vary across cultures.

Schaffer, H. R. (1998) *Social Development*. Oxford. Blackwell. Looks at recent developments in thinking of how children develop socially. Reflects on the theory of social development, self-awareness and relationships in developing socially.

6 COMMUNICATION, LANGUAGE AND LITERACY
Rosemary Boys

Professional Standards for QTS

→ **2.1a, 2.4**

These Standards state that in order to gain QTS, teachers must have a secure knowledge and understanding of communication, language and literacy in the Foundation Stage, and must be able to understand how learning is affected by linguistic, social, cultural and emotional development.

You may find it helpful to refer to the appropriate section of the Handbook that accompanies the Standards for the award of QTS, for further clarification and support.

By the end of this chapter you should:

- *be aware of the influence of language on social, emotional and academic development;*
- *recognise the Early Learning Goals for communication, language and literacy as stated in the Foundation Stage curriculum;*
- *understand the adult/child relationship necessary for language and literacy acquisition;*
- *understand the relationship between oracy and literacy development;*
- *be aware of the teaching strategies appropriate to language and literacy acquisition.*

Introduction

This chapter will address the professional standards required for the area of learning identified as Communication, Language and Literacy in the Foundation Stage curriculum. It will examine theoretical and pedagogical issues related to oracy (speaking and listening) and literacy (reading and writing), and make explicit their importance for the child's social and emotional development.

There is an important interrelationship between oracy and literacy. This is not only because the knowledge and understandings of one informs the other, but also because of the way in which acquisition takes place. Both literacy and oracy should be learned within a purposeful and social context. Both rely upon other more competent users to model and provide encouragement, and both require opportunities to practise developing skills.

Examining the Early Learning Goals for this area of learning shows that the first five of these are explicitly related to oracy development. Further reading will show that these goals recognise the need for direct learning about the social nature of oral communication. These same goals also have implications for all future learning. Consequently the establishment of effective language and the ability to use this language for such interpersonal processes as questioning, retelling, negotiating and justifying is a priority for early childhood practitioners.

Early Learning Goals 1–5

1. Interact with others, negotiating plans and activities and taking turns in conversations.

2. Enjoy listening to and using spoken and written language, and readily turn to it in their play and learning.
   Sustain attentive listening, responding to what they have heard by relevant comments, questions or actions.
   Listen with enjoyment, and respond to stories, songs and other music, rhymes and poems and make up their own stories, songs, rhymes and poems.

3. Extend their vocabulary, exploring the meaning and sounds of new words.

4. Speak clearly and audibly with confidence and control and show awareness of the listener, for example by their use of conventions such as greetings, 'please' and 'thank you'.

5. Use language to imagine and recreate roles and experiences.
   Use talk to organise, sequence and clarify thinking, ideas, feelings and events.

Learning Goals six to nine are concerned with literacy acquisition, but still have relevance to oracy skills, particularly the development of the young child's auditory skills. These goals are the **outcomes** of the Foundation Stage. It is the role of the practitioner to identify each child's developmental needs, continuously monitor children's progress, and provide appropriate learning opportunities for children to move towards these goals.

Early Learning Goals 6–9

6. Hear and say initial and final sounds in words, and short vowels within words.
   Link sounds to letters, naming and sounding the letters of the alphabet.
   Use their phonic knowledge to write simple regular words and make phonetically plausible attempts at more complex words.*

7. Explore and experiment with sounds, words and texts.
   Retell narratives in the correct sequence, drawing on language patterns of stories.
   Read a range of familiar and common words and simple sentences independently.
   Know that print carries meaning and, in English, is read from left to right and top to bottom.
   Show an understanding of the elements of stories, such as the main character, sequence of events, and openings, and how information can be found in non-fiction texts to answer questions about where, who, why and how.

8. Use their phonic knowledge to write simple regular words and make phonetically plausible attempts at more complex words.*
   Attempt writing for different purposes, using features of different forms such as lists, stories and instructions.
   Write their own names and other things such as labels and captions, and begin to form simple sentences, sometimes using punctuation.

9. Use a pencil and hold it effectively to form recognisable letters, most of which are correctly formed.

(*This goal appears twice within the documentation.)

Oracy development

The importance of effective communication skills

In the education of young children the teaching of language skills is far more than a preparation for becoming literate. It is our responsibility to work in partnership with parents to prepare children to become functioning members of our society. It would seem that from birth children are active participants in their own social integration. Trevarthen (1995) holds the view that 'being part of a culture is a need human beings are born with'. The initial stage in the development of social competence is the attainment of intersubjectivity or mutual understanding. This begins in the mother/child interaction starting at birth, and develops as the child's communication and language skills become increasingly sophisticated. It is now recognised that effective language acquisition is essential for both social/emotional and cognitive development. Unless both of these are recognised and addressed the child will not thrive.

Classroom story

Consider a child called Joel. Joel began nursery for three mornings a week when he was three years three months old. Joel's speech and behaviour soon gave cause for concern. His only form of oral communication was through grunts and gesture. Frustration at not being understood or being thwarted would result in screams and tantrums. He found interaction with his peers and adults difficult and was often withdrawn and socially isolated. He frequently took toys from his peers and would respond with aggression if they tried to retrieve them. He was unable to participate in story time, group activities or role-play situations, and was unable to concentrate on any task for any length of time. He found it difficult to establish trust with his key worker.

The practitioners in the nursery were concerned for this little boy and were aware that his main problem was an inability to communicate. But why was this child so behind his peers? From their experiences with young children the reasons could have ranged from a hearing loss to autism. However, a talk with the child's mother gave a quite different story. After Joel's birth she had suffered with severe post natal depression and found it difficult to respond to her child, so apart from feeding and changing him there was little interaction between mother and son. As the baby became more distressed the mother became more anxious. Throughout this time the relationship between Joel's parents was deteriorating. Joel's father was convinced his son had brain damage and left the family when Joel was 19 months old. Joel had never been to any kind of playgroup because his mother was embarrassed by her son's behaviour and poor development.

Careful assessment of this little boy showed that his communication and language problems were the consequence of his lack of nurturing and interaction with a caring adult rather than a clinical problem. There is now evidence indicating that children are born with a predisposition to engage and communicate with others (Schaffer, 1996). In Joel's early life his need to interact and participate in constructing meanings with a caregiver was not addressed.

The development of language and communication skills

Learning to communicate and use your own language is the most difficult learning task ever undertaken, but for most children in an appropriate child/caregiver relationship the task is one of mutual satisfaction. Bruner (1983) argues that children are 'geared to respond to the human voice, to the human face, to human action and gesture'. They are also strongly motivated if the reward is a sense of belonging, being able to communicate, and having supportive adults with whom to interact.

Figure 6.1 on page 82 provides a brief guide to the order in which language and communication behaviours develop in many children. This is not, however, a prescriptive sequence and it is now recognised by practitioners that all children are individuals and that the majority of children will become competent communicators in their own time, and via their own route.

Initial assessment

Children's successful integration into their pre-school community can permanently influence their attitude to school and education. To provide the optimum learning opportunities for each child it is essential that an accurate assessment of a child's ability to use language and communicate is made as soon as possible after their admission. As the purpose of assessment is to become aware of a child's skills and competences, and to establish an accurate profile of the child, assessments should:

- **be unintrusive and non-threatening for the child;**
- **be done within the context of familiar and purposeful tasks;**
- **be based upon observations during interactions with peers or familiar adults;**
- **include observations of language use and communication with familiar people;**
- **focus on the positive aspects and achievements of the child's language use and communication skills.**

What is actually assessed will depend on the focus of assessment observations. This could be based upon a perceived need, or to monitor progress or to gauge the success of learning, and will be decided upon by the practitioner. Figure 6.2 on page 83 categorises and lists some aspects that can be observed, but this is **not** a finite list, nor should more than two or three items be assessed at a time. The level at which these will be assessed will also depend on the age, experience and competence of the child.

The adult/child relationship in the classroom

Language acquisition is as much a social process as one of cognition, and children's development depends largely on their interactions with others. From birth the child and primary carer are both participants in the generation of mutual understanding. Although a very young child has little competence as a communicator and language user, there is the expectation that the child will become adept.

Age	Language skills	Communication behaviours
Birth – I mth	The child can hear sounds before birth, and at birth can recognise its mother's voice. Verbal communication is through crying.	The child is addressed continually and directly by adults from birth. New babies have been found to be attuned to the visual patterns common to faces, and begin to imitate the facial expressions of others. Different cries have different meanings and range from distress to contentment, these are responded to and reinforced by caregivers.
2–3 mths	The child maintains the sensitivity to sound. They can tell the difference between several pairs of consonants and vowels. The child listens more carefully and responds to the voices of others. Cooing becomes more varied and extended as the child gains control of vocal organs and breath.	They respond to adult tones of voice e.g. anger, soothing tones. They will listen before responding with own interjections. They are becoming interested in objects.
4 mths	The child is beginning to use vocal play in which they produce a wide range of noises which are more controlled and often repeated.	The child begins to engage in protoconversations with caregiver, and will practise these alone. They enjoys joining in musical songs and rhymes e.g. 'This little piggy'. The child still very self-oriented.
6 mths	Babbling develops with inflections in the flow of sound as the child becomes aware of the rhythm of language. Turns head to whoever is speaking and responds to the tone and inflection in a voice.	Ready to play lively games with familiar people e.g. peek-a-boo, active nursery rhymes. Becoming aware that their actions will cause different responses from adults. Becoming aware of utterances with social conventions e.g. bye-bye. Beginning to develop an awareness of others e.g. will follow a finger pointing at something a caregiver has seen.
9 mths	Babbling becomes more sophisticated with greater variety in the consonants and vowels. The inflection in continuous babble is beginning to resemble the adult form. Protowords –where the sound is clear, but not the meaning – are common.	The child understands many adult gestures and will use them in simple contexts e.g. waving, clapping.
12 mths	Beginning to say first words but will continue to babble. The first words are familiar words used to express needs. The child is able to understand individual words. Hearing is acute and the child enjoys rhymes and songs, trying to join in. They can hear and understand a simple requests or command e.g. 'Put it down.'	The child uses protolanguage to engage others in conversation. Conversation includes vocalisation, gestures and facial expression. Conversations rehearsed as the child plays. Words are acquired during purposeful shared activities.
18 mths	The ratio of words understood to words used is 5:1. They are beginning to put words together, these are mainly names (nouns) and action words (verbs). Talk is in the present tense They can hear and understand simple instructions e.g. give the car to daddy.	Child is beginning to assert independence and use the word 'no'. Conversations include vocalisations with increased expression. The child responds to non-verbal communication. In play together children perform similar pretend actions but without negotiation. The child enjoys sharing and interacting with a book and adult.
2 yrs	The child can actively use about 200 words. They are beginning to use short, simple sentences. By 2½ there is evidence of language rules.	The child begins to use simple language to talk about people and things not present. Pretend play with peers still does not have a shared intention. Play includes enactments in which partners engage in sequenced pretend activities that require social exchanges but not negotiation.
3 yrs	There is a huge growth in vocabulary development to over 3000 words. Using longer sentences but will miss out less important words. Is using a wider range of words including adjectives and adverbs. Some developmental errors e.g. confusion of pronouns, I/me; she/her. Will use past tense verbs but make errors with their endings. Will listen to and follow favourite stories and join in the familiar parts.	The vocabulary explosion is related to the child's need to share ideas and experiences. Shared play includes imitative pretend activities in which children will have similar themes, but the actions of the partners are still not integrated. The number of questions children ask increases. The child will enjoy sharing tasks with a supportive, more competent person. They will initiate and maintain conversations.
4 yrs	The child's speech gives evidence of growing control over grammar, vocabulary and phonology. Verb endings are used with increasing accuracy, but generalisations are sometimes overused e.g. We wented to see nan.	In play children now negotiate play themes and intentions by arguing, talking and story telling. Play is represented with complementary pretend roles. The child enjoys sharing nursery rhymes, retelling stories and events and inventing their own stories.

Figure 6.1 The development of language and communication skill

Speaking	Listening	Communication skills
Articulation Can pronounce words that can be understood as approximate versions of the correct form. *Oral syntax* (grammar) Is combining words together to provide meaning. *Speaking for different purposes* Can use a range of oral genres e.g. to inform, to question, to describe, to inform, to imagine. *Vocabulary* Is able to use an increasing range of words in the right context. *Recounting and retelling* Can relate and retell events, experiences, stories in the right sequence of events.	*Auditory discrimination.* Can hear sounds such as initial sounds and rhymes as appropriate. *Auditory syntax* Can identify the type of sentence by its grammar and inflection e.g. question, instruction, command or statement. *Vocabulary* Is able to understand an increasing range of words. *Auditory memory* Is able to remember and recall events, experiences, songs, stories and rhymes.	Can be understood by others. Responds appropriately in conversations. Can follow and respond to instructions, question etc. *Semantics* (meaning) Can express need and wants. Understands when others express needs and wants. Can take turns in conversation. Is aware of the need for appropriate language in different contexts and with different people. Is able to understand the nuances of language i.e. does not take things literally.

Figure 6.2 Aspects of oracy that can be assessed

This collaboration extends beyond language acquisition, and also includes joint involvement in wider learning events. As the child grows and develops, collaboration will be with a wider range of supportive companions, but the quality of the learning event will be dependent on the quality of the language used in the interaction.

So, can the collaborative adult/child relationship be translated into the early childhood setting where the practitioner's role is to promote communication, language acquisition, and the use of language as the vehicle for learning?

In their analysis of interactional roles in early childhood settings Hughes and Westgate (1997) found that both during teaching tasks, and in more leisurely contexts, nursery nurses and community workers consistently used a more interactive and supportive style of communication with young children than did teachers. This was characterised by the reciprocal nature of the interactions during which children were given the opportunity to have some control of the discourse, and were given time to experience and use a wider range of functions.

Whilst the Foundation Stage Curriculum (2000) does not explicitly describe or recognise this relationship, it does identify some principles that should enable practitioners to practise collaborative learning. These include the recognition that effective teaching requires:

- **being aware of how children learn most effectively so that they can identify the range of needs and learning styles within their group (p13);**
- **enabling children to become involved by planning experiences which are mostly based on real life situations (p15);**
- **planning their time well, so that most of it is spent working directly with children (p16);**
- **helping to extend children's vocabulary and language (p16);**

- using language that is rich and using correct grammar. Recognising that what is said and how the practitioner speaks is the main way of teaching new vocabulary and helping children to develop linguistic structures for thinking (p23);
- using conversation and carefully framed questions because this is crucial in developing children's knowledge (p23);
- allowing children to teach each other (p23).

Interacting with young children

To elicit a wider range of responses from children will depend on the effectiveness of your own language. Consider some of the techniques found in the talk of teachers that have been found to enhance the quality and richness of children's responses. Consider also how some of the techniques can be used together, for example a confirmation and an elaboration.

TO ELICIT INFORMATION FROM CHILDREN

Direct elicitation	These are open and closed questions e.g. Why did he run away?
Cued elicitations	Providing strong visual clues and verbal hints e.g. How do birds fly? (flapping arms)
Reflective observation	e.g. I wonder why she is crying?

TO RESPOND TO WHAT CHILDREN SAY

Confirmations	Providing positive feedback e.g. Yes, I think you are right.
Elaborations	Encouraging children to extend their response, or extending it for them and modelling sentence structure and vocabulary. e.g. Could you tell us a bit more about it?
Repetitions	To restate what the child said to the child itself or to peers. e.g. Yes, he is climbing a very tall tree.
Reformulations	This can provide a positive way of providing a correct sentence structure for the child, or make a sentence comprehensible to peers.
Rejections	A wrong response is usually ignored, and the question or instruction reworded. e.g. Are you sure it goes next to the blue one?

TO DESCRIBE SIGNIFICANT ASPECTS OF SHARED EXPERIENCES

'We' statements	To encourage children to bring past knowledge and experiences to the present task. e.g. What did the baker we visited make as well as bread?
Recaps	To recap what has been done already in the lesson. e.g. Remember how Sammy sprinkled the glitter very gently so it doesn't get all lumpy.

Adapted from Mercer (1995)

Practical task

Look at these two conversations and consider the quality of the discourse. Why is one teacher able to elicit so much more discussion from the child?

Conversation 1

T: What's the hen doing?

P1: She's sitting on the floor.

T: Why is she sitting on the ground?

P1: 'Cos she's a bit tired?

T: No, look carefully, what is she sitting on?

P1: It's some grass.

T: It's called straw. Why do you think she is sitting on it?

P1: I don't know.

T1: Well, she's sitting on some eggs. Turn over and look at the picture. The hen has laid these eggs. What will happen next?

P1: I don't know.

Conversation 2

T2: Oh look at this hen sitting on this warm soft straw. I wonder what she's doing?

P2: I think she's very tired and she likes it 'cos it's warm and soft.

T2: You could be right. Let's turn over. Oh look at them.

P2: It's eggs. Look at this one it's got a hole

T2: I can see a little tiny beak poking out. Do you think it's trying to get out?

P1: It's a baby hen like what we had before.

T2: You mean when we had the eggs in the incubator and they hatched into little chicks.

P2: Yeah, but they didn't have a mum. We got them from a man, and put them in that, er, that (pointing at the incubator).

T2: Incubator.

P2: Yeah the incubator, to make them warm, to be little chicks ... You can eat eggs too you know.

Providing the appropriate conditions and environment for language acquisition

The learning conditions provided through the collaborative relationship were identified by Cambourne (1988). He maintained that children need to be immersed in meaningful and purposeful interactions, and given opportunities to practise their growing skills. The way in which adults accept the child's approximations, provide positive feedback and model the correct form of the language provides a supportive learning environment in which children can take risks and accept responsibility for their language.

For these conditions to be met careful thought needs to be given to the environment in which the learning will take place. If children are to be encouraged to take risks and practise their developing skills, their security within the learning environment also needs to be considered. The learning environment that practitioners should seek to provide for young children should therefore include:

- **a high child/adult ratio so that children have opportunities to practise their developing skills with competent users of standard English;**
- **a routine that includes opportunities for young children to use their language skills for a range of social functions, e.g. greeting people, engaging in conversation with a variety of people, negotiating with adults and peers, sharing and co-operating;**
- **a range of interactive activities and tasks that provide opportunities for explicit teaching, informal practice of skills and imaginative play;**
- **the availability of resources to promote speaking and listening, e.g. books, audio tapes, puppets, role-play areas, games for two or more children;**
- **a well planned and purposeful learning task that will engage children;**
- **differentiation of tasks to address the individual language needs of young children;**
- **positive and focused assessment based upon observation of children engaged in relevant tasks.**

Organising for oracy development

To be effective in the organisation of oracy development it is necessary to know precisely what needs to be addressed and the most appropriate way of providing learning opportunities. Oracy learning can be categorised into three main areas as shown in Figure 6.3. Each of these is purpose driven and therefore needs a context for the learning.

Language for communicating	Language for learning	Speaking and listening skills
• To express feelings and needs. • To be aware of the feelings and needs of others. • To make and maintain friends. • To negotiate and collaborate in play and group activities. • To initiate and participate in conversations. • To be aware of the need for appropriate language in different situations and with different people. • To share and take turns. • To be aware of non-verbal communication.	• To continue to extend vocabulary. • To consolidate and extend grammar usage. • To continue to develop articulation and pronunciation. • To promote auditory memory and discrimination. • To be aware of the rhythm, rhyme and intonations of language. • To enjoy listening to stories, rhymes and songs. • To enjoy participating in stories, rhymes and songs. • To participate in learning tasks involving listening and speaking. • To engage in collaborative play. • To take risks practising their developing competence.	• To ask and respond to questions. • To recall and recount. • To inform. • To make connections. • To formulate meanings. • To speculate. • To negotiate. • To justify. • To respond to suggestions. • To give and follow instructions.

Figure 6.3 Purposes for oracy development

In many cases this learning will not be within a specific language or literacy lesson, but will be embedded within other areas of the curriculum. It is the practitioner's role to recognise and plan for both the explicit and implicit teaching of oracy.

Practical task

Turn to the example of medium-term planning for Goldilocks and the Three Bears in Chapter 1 (Figure 1.1).

Read this carefully and identify:

- *where oracy is the explicit focus of the lesson;*
- *where it is an implicit but important aspect of the lesson.*

Literacy acquisition

Just as social relationships have been recognised as the foundation of oracy acquisition, so literacy acquisition can be described as a social process embedded in children's relationships with significant others who serve as models of literate behaviour.

Classroom story

Consider a child called Kate. Kate began pre-school for five mornings a week when she was four years one month old. On her first day she could recognise her name on her own coat-hook and tray. She was able to join in the nursery rhymes and most of the songs that were sung together. In story time she listened to the story with concentration and was willing to make predictions about the plot. As her first week progressed it was found that she could write her own name, read most of the environmental print in the room, 'write' a prescription for one of the patients in the role-play doctor's surgery and 'read' familiar books to herself and her new friend. Kate enjoyed word and sound games, and could make alliterative strings for the names of her peers (Sophie sits on Sarah's sofa), and recognise and identify rhyming words. She also recognised most letters and some words. It could seem that Kate's precocious ability was the result of ambitious parents and some serious tutoring. This, however, was not the case. Kate is the older of two children in a single parent family. Her mother is a nurse and, more importantly, an avid reader. She has been sharing books and stories with Kate since she was tiny. As Kate loves making up her own stories her mother has written these stories down, and made them into little books for Kate to illustrate and read for herself. Because Kate's mother works Kate and her sister have been cared for during the day by their maternal grandmother. This home confirms the literate behaviour that is evident in Kate's own home. Kate sees both her mother and grandmother writing shopping lists, cheques, letters and messages; using telephone directories and train timetables; reading books, newspapers, letters, messages and recipes. Because Kate is aware that print is meaningful and is encouraged to use it herself, she is aware of how other people also use it. She has been encouraged to find things in the supermarket, read environmental print and symbols, write her own shopping lists and visit the local library.

Just as babies are born ready and willing to communicate orally with their family, so Kate entered pre-school ready and willing to communicate through print. This readiness is evident in her awareness that print is meaningful, and that reading and writing are enjoyable and purposeful. Kate did not acquire her knowledge and skills through formal teaching, but through the same collaborative relationship as was evident for oracy acquisition. Within this relationship she was also provided with the appropriate conditions for becoming literate. She was immersed in enjoyable and purposeful print. Reading and writing were modelled for her by competent, literate adults. She was given opportunities to try reading and writing herself, and her efforts and approximations were supported and valued. She was encouraged to take risks with her reading and writing, and decide for herself what she would do.

The literacy process

It is now recognised that reading and writing are more than decoding and encoding symbols on a page, though these are an important and integral part of the literacy process. Reading and writing are complex processes during which the participant brings a wide range of knowledge and skills to the task, and actively interacts with the text. If you examine Figure 6.4 below you will see that it is the interaction between each level that will give coherence and understanding.

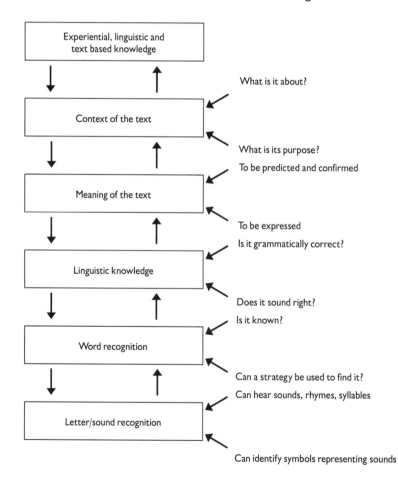

Figure 6.4 The interactive literacy model

Implementing the interactive literacy model

To beginning practitioners even the thought of teaching literacy skills to a group of children with different experiences and abilities can be daunting. The emphasis placed on phonological aware-ness and grapho-phonic knowledge in the Foundation Stage curriculum can also be unhelpful, as it can panic practitioners into adopting an inappropriately narrow and formal literacy pro-gramme. This form of teaching is inappropriate for young children for two main reasons. Firstly, it can damage children's perceptions of themselves as effective learners. Many children entering early childhood settings have had little experience with those rhymes, games and activities that promote phonemic awareness, so consequently they are still unable to discriminate between sounds. These children need both time and very context-based opportunities to develop their auditory skills. They should not be made to experience failure through being unable to complete decontextualised phonic task sheets, nor should they have to participate in inappropriate tasks that will confirm their lack of competence. Secondly, this form of teaching does not give children the understanding that print is meaningful, purposeful and satisfying to read and write. To become literate children need to engage with whole texts and be exposed to a wide range of different genres. They need tasks that integrate reading and writing.

It should also be recognised that a narrow and formal literacy programme can also have a negative effect on children who come from literacy rich homes. For these children the non-confirmation of their understandings about literacy will inhibit future progress. It will discourage their efforts as they will see no purpose to the decontextualised tasks.

For effective literacy teaching a practitioner needs to adopt a broad approach based on well written books and purposeful experiences. The practitioner's role is to plan, to model, to inspire, to enjoy and to interact with young children in exciting and interesting literacy events. To do this there are explicit aspects of literacy teaching that need to be considered and addressed. These include:

- **developing a rich literacy environment;**
- **developing opportunities to utilise play as a learning context;**
- **developing an awareness of books;**
- **developing metacognitive strategies;**
- **developing phonological awareness and graphophonic knowledge;**
- **developing fine motor skills (this is addressed in Chapter 4).**

The literacy environment

It is the practitioner's responsibility to consider the environment that will encourage and promote literacy. It has been suggested that children learn to become literate by being surrounded by print. If children are expected to learn to read, then the environment should be structured to support and encourage them. Young children need to be immersed in environ-mental print, books, games and writing materials. The home languages of all children should be evident. Neaum and Tallack (1997) recommend that several languages should be represented to accommodate children from non-English speaking backgrounds.

It is not only the physical environment that must be considered, people also constitute an important part of the literacy environment. It is essential that those working with children are confident and enthusiastic literacy users, and that they are willing to share their skills and experiences. As early childhood settings tend to have predominantly female staff members, practitioners must recognise the need of young boys to have literate male role models. Bilingual children also need to see and hear members of their own communities as proficient literacy users. The modelling can be in the home language or English as it is the behaviours and attitudes to texts that children need to be aware of. This can be done through the practical involvement of members of the whole community.

Practical task

Take this opportunity to reflect on the early childhood classrooms you have experienced.

- *How did these contribute to the literacy environment?*
- *How did the practitioners give evidence of their literate behaviour?*
- *How will you establish an exciting and relevant literacy environment in your own classroom?*

Developing opportunities to utilise play as a learning context

It is recognised that one of the most important aspects of the literacy environment is the way in which it facilitates play. The role of play in the education of young children and its recognition within the Foundation Stage curriculum (2000) is dealt with in Chapter 1. However, the relevant aspects identified here need to be considered.

- **Through play children are engaged in complex communication involving such oracy skills as recalling, recounting, negotiating, directing, sequencing, explaining, justifying and planning.**
- **Through play children have an opportunity to explore a range of non-fictional texts within an appropriate context, e.g. using cookery books in the home corner.**
- **Play provides a context for writing development. During play children have been found to write in a wide range of non-fictional genres, and write for a wide variety of purposes (Hall and Robinson, 1995).**
- **Books and stories provide a model for drama, role play and puppet work that has a clear benefit to reading (Williamson and Silvern, 1988). Through dramatic play children interpret character roles, develop an awareness of story sequence and plot, come to understand dialogue, and begin to generate their own stories from favourite and familiar texts.**
- **During free play children who use the book corner have the opportunity to practise reading familiar and favourite books. This often includes retelling the story from memory whilst pointing to the text and using the illustrations as a prompt.**
- **Play provides the opportunity for young children to integrate their literacy and oracy skills.**
- **Play situations can also provide rich assessment evidence of both literacy and oracy development.**

Developing an awareness of books

While many children arrive in an early childhood setting familiar with books, for some sharing a book and enjoying a story will be a new experience. Young children need the opportunity to listen to and enjoy as many stories as possible. Browne (1979) argues that the exposure of watching and listening to a skilled adult will demystify literacy. Barriere et al (2000) maintain that reading to children and modelling how enjoyable it can be from a person whom the children value can be beneficial.

During the more informal story-time books should therefore be read with enthusiasm, expression and sound effects. It is also important that all of the text is read in one sitting so that children can develop a concept for a story. During story-time the emphasis of the lesson should be placed on enjoyment and a sense of shared participation. When appropriate books are chosen story time can be an opportunity to engage children's concentration and listening skills. Favourite books need to be reread regularly. These are often the books children will attempt to read alone.

The more focused adult/child shared reading experience can be established in the classroom with the use of big books. These large texts ensure that all children have clear access to the text and illustrations, and enable both the practitioner and children to identify specific features of the book. For practitioners big books are excellent teaching tools as they enable them to imitate the shared intimacy with a book that is a feature of the child/carer literacy event.

For children to begin to interact with a book they need to understand how it is organised. To do this young children must develop concepts about print. Figure 6.5 lists the ones needed by children at the conclusion of the Foundation Stage.

Children need to be aware that:

- *print contains meaning and that the meaning is permanent;*
- *the title of the book is on the front cover;*
- *the book has a title page that also gives the title and the names of the author and illustrator;*
- *the book opens from right to left;*
- *you read the left page first on a double page;*
- *you begin at the top of the page;*
- *you make a return sweep at the end of a line;*
- *pictures contain (semantic) information;*
- *the words are in a familiar (syntactic) order;*
- *symbols (graphemes) represent sounds (phonemes);*
- *the symbols are grouped to make words;*
- *the words are grouped to make sentences.*

Figure 6.5 Print concepts (based on Clay, 1979)

These can be taught during shared reading through the context of the big book and reinforced each time a book is shared. When children are reading they should be encouraged to follow the text with their finger. Thorough understanding of these concepts will be evident in children's play writing. Although most young children can follow a text with their finger, it takes longer for them to use these conventions in their own writing. This is one reason why children need free and easy access to writing materials including small, blank, stapled books.

Developing metacognitive strategies

To be effective and fluent when interacting with a text, readers and writers need explicit knowledge which will enable them to work strategically using what is referred to as metacognition. Working in a thoughtful way through a deliberate selection of strategies gives the literacy user the opportunity to exploit all of their skills and knowledge.

By using big books it is possible to provide young children with enough strategies to function metacognitively. This is done initially through a combination of modelled and shared reading and writing. Modelling is when a teacher reads or writes alone in view of the children, and gives a commentary of what they are thinking and the strategies they will try using. During shared reading and writing the teacher and children work together and together employ the strategies previously 'modelled'. The strategies that can be modelled and shared with young children include:

Prediction	This strategy requires the reader to make an educated guess using their experiential knowledge and knowledge. Children should be asked 'What do you think will happen next?' They should also be encouraged to explain the reason for their prediction.
Picture cues	Illustrations are the first text-based semantic (meaning) cues a young child can access. They can be used for predicting and for decoding individual words.
Repetition	Both events and language can be repeated in stories. Once children recognise the repetition in a text they can predict what will happen next, and can join in the reading of the text, at first relying on their memory of the repeated text or refrain.
Intertextual skills	Children need to be aware that they can bring knowledge of the structure and content of one book to the reading of another.
Semantic cueing	Individual words such as nouns, verbs, adjectives and adverbs can be read from the context of their sentence. If these words are left out when the whole sentence is read and the children are asked 'What would make sense?' children can predict the word from the sentence meaning.
Syntactic cueing	Individual words such as different parts of a verb (e.g. jump/jumped) and adjectives (big/bigger/biggest) can be read from the grammar of the sentence. Young children have enough knowledge of sentence structure to be able to make a prediction. Even if the word is not correct it will probably be one from the same word group as the

deleted word. Children should be aware that you can read past a word, then go back and try a word that makes the sentence 'sound right'.

Grapho-phonic cueing Once children begin to develop an awareness of the sound–symbol relationship they will attempt to use it if they are encouraged and supported. It is usually first used to decode nouns in conjunction with picture cues. After seeing this strategy modelled young children will look at the illustrations for semantic information, then they will confirm their prediction using the initial letter of the word.

It is obvious that to promote and encourage the use of these strategies a practitioner needs access to good quality texts. Figure 6.6 identifies some of the characteristics that should be used to help in the selection of appropriate books.

A text appropriate for young children should include:

- *a meaningful and enjoyable text;*
- *a predictable story line;*
- *illustrations that support the text;*
- *language and grammar appropriate to young children;*
- *appropriate vocabulary;*
- *clear, bold, well spaced print;*
- *repetition (and in some texts rhyme);*
- *freedom from gender, ethnic and cultural bias;*
- *interactivity;*
- *ways to encourage children to draw on their own experiential and linguistic knowledge.*

Figure 6.6 Characteristics of a book

Practical task

Make a selection of four or five children's books. Using the criteria in Figure 6.6 assess the quality of these books.

Which strategies could you explicitly model or share with each book?

Developing phonological awareness and grapho-phonic knowledge

As well as an explicit knowledge of print concepts and strategies young children also need to be able to use the sound/symbol relationship and analogy. These are basic to both decoding and encoding (spelling) and develop through the establishment of phonological awareness in young children. The ability to categorise words develops naturally in children as a consequence of immersion in rich auditory experiences. Having the opportunity to share rhymes and focus explicitly on sounds sensitises children to alliteration and rhyme.

Phonological awareness is the metalinguistic ability that enables children to reflect on features of spoken language. Yopp (1988) argues that the goal of teaching phonological awareness is to enable children to understand that words can be separated into component *sounds*.

There is considerable evidence to indicate a strong predictive relationship between children's recognition and use of rhyme and alliteration and their reading and spelling ability. Bryant and Bradley, 1985, Goswami and Bryant, 1992, and Muter et al 1994 also argue that being able to recognise rhymes will help to develop a child's awareness of phonemes (the smallest units of sound). However, as has already been discussed, not all children enter early childhood settings aware of alliteration or rhyme, nor are they able to segment words. These three processes are basic to phonological awareness.

Within the classroom all children can participate in both formal and informal activities that will enhance these three processes. These *sound* activities could include:

- **matching objects and child by their initial sounds;**
- **saying and inventing tongue twisters;**
- **sorting groups of objects by their initial sounds;**
- **listening to, saying and learning poems, songs and rhymes;**
- **reading stories with rhyme;**
- **reading stories with alliteration;**
- **making up own versions of familiar rhymes and poems;**
- **games such as 'I hear with my little ear something rhyming with _____ ?'**
     'I spy with my little eye something beginning with _____ ';
- **clapping the rhythm to songs and rhymes;**
- **clapping the syllables of children's names.**

Practical task

See if you can generate three other activities young children could participate in for each of the three processes:

1. *Alliteration.*
2. *Rhyme.*
3. *Segmentation.*

Using analogy

Once young children are adept at using these three phonological skills, and are becoming aware of the sound–symbol relationship from their participation in shared reading events, they will be able to use analogy for both word recognition and spelling.

Onset and *rime*, the constituent parts of analogy, are the linguistic terms for the two sound segments within a syllable. With support children will find it easier to segment simple words into their onset (any consonants before the vowel) and rime (the vowel sound and any following consonants) than into the initial and final consonants and medial vowel expected in the learning goals of the Foundation Stage curriculum. Bielby (1994) argues that one of the earliest ways children develop phonological strategies to help word identification is by identifying the initial letter sound, or onset. It is therefore through experience of hearing the onset and developing recognition of its written symbol (grapheme) that the grapho-phonic relationship becomes explicit. In children's early writing this knowledge is evident when words are often written with only the initial letter indicating what the word might be.

According to Goswami (1993:313-14): 'A child who (is) good at rhyming might realise that shared sounds often mean shared spelling patterns, and that words like 'cat' and 'hat' not only rhymed, they also shared an orthographic unit (__ at).' Once this link is made children are able to use analogy to generate strings of words that share the same rime by changing the onset.

These understandings can be made explicit to children during modelled reading and writing. However, it is during interactive sessions in shared reading and writing that most children should have the opportunity to practise their growing skills. Within this context children can be supported and encouraged, while working on a real text. In these situations, by the use of differentiation, all children can participate in meaning making with text.

These skills can be reinforced through games that continue to develop and enhance children's auditory development in conjunction with written words exploring onset and rime.

Communication, language and literacy:
a summary of key points

This chapter has recognised that as practitioners we must:

- *acknowledge that competency in language and communication influences cognitive, social and emotional development;*
- *have an awareness of the development of language and communication skills in all of the children in our care, based upon careful observations and interaction with each child;*
- *plan explicit opportunities for children to use and extend their developing language skills with supportive adults;*
- *recognise the strong links between competence in oracy and the successful development of literacy skills;*
- *organise the learning environment so that children can be immersed in purposeful print, and engage in purposeful and appropriate literacy tasks;*
- *provide a model of literate behaviours for young children to emulate;*
- *recognise the role of the practitioner as central to children's development and the quality of provision.*

The role of parents/carers in literacy education has not been explicitly discussed in this chapter (see Chapter 2). However, their importance must be recognised.

7 DEVELOPING MATHEMATICAL UNDERSTANDING AND THE FOUNDATIONS OF NUMERACY

Norma Marsh with Wendy Baker

Professional Standards for QTS

(→) 2.1, 3.1.1

The first Standard states that in order to gain QTS, teachers must have a secure understanding of the aims and principles of the Foundation Stage areas of learning, the Early Learning Goals and, for Reception children, the relevant requirements of the National Numeracy Strategy; the second Standard relates to the provision of stimulating and challenging learning experiences underpinned by the knowledge of what is appropriate and relevant to the Foundation Stage.

You may find it helpful to refer to the appropriate section of the Handbook that accompanies the Standards for the award of QTS, for further clarification and support.

The Curriculum Guidance for the Foundation Stage (the Stepping Stones) (DfEE/ QCA, 2000) devotes a whole section to Mathematical Development (p68). This is informative and helpful in terms of progression towards the Early Learning Goals.

By the end of this chapter you should:

- *understand the ideas that underpin a relevant mathematical curriculum for children in the early years as embodied in the Early Learning Goals;*
- *be aware of ways in which you as a practitioner can best support children's mathematical development;*
- *have access to a range of appropriate starting points for activities that encourage development across the mathematical curriculum;*
- *understand some of the difficulties children may encounter and mistakes they may make;*
- *appreciate the contribution of play as the cornerstone of good provision;*
- *have insights into the planning process for mathematics.*

Introduction

The traditional view of children's mathematical development as a gradual and staged progression from a state of total ignorance to an acceptable level of competence was firmly rooted in the adult perception of competence. Children's earliest efforts at number mastery were therefore measured in terms of their failure to match up to adult expectations. More recent thinking based on developmental psychology and research has concentrated on examining what children can do rather than what they cannot, and this has led to the emergence of a very different picture. Carol

Aubrey's ongoing project at the University of Durham (1997) has highlighted the levels of mathematical knowledge that children can have on entry to the Reception class and supports earlier work by Gelman and Gallistel (1978), Starkey (1987) et al.

What we now have is the realisation that children, on entering the Foundation Stage, possess a wide range of mathematical abilities and competences based on their existing understanding. As practitioners, our role is to create the right environment, physically, mentally and emotionally, where all children's beliefs will be challenged, their opinions valued and their progress to the next stage of understanding supported.

This approach will lead to a very different kind of provision. Indeed to the untrained eye it may not appear to be mathematics at all!

Rather than teaching mathematics we need to think in terms of encouraging children to participate in activities that allow them to develop as mathematicians. What does that involve? What do mathematicians do?

The nature of mathematics

Calculation is a very important part of mathematics but it is by no means the whole story. Essentially, mathematicians can be seen as people who are striving to understand and make sense of the world and all that it contains. Nature is full of mathematical patterns and shapes and even the weather and other natural and social phenomena can be explained in terms of mathematical theories.

Teachers need to be confident in their own understanding of what constitutes mathematical behaviour – otherwise how will they recognise it in others?

Mathematical behaviour involves:

- **problem solving;**
- **investigating;**
- **collecting data;**
- **working systematically;**
- **searching for patterns and links;**
- **identifying possible cause and effect;**
- **thinking logically;**
- **developing explanations;**
- **convincing yourself and then others.**

Your task as the teacher is three-fold. The environment you provide, and that includes the personnel, has to be capable of:

- **scaffolding children's interpretation of the world through their own experiences, to illuminate mathematical ideas and concepts;**
- **allowing/encouraging the development of mathematical competence from a sound foundation of experience-based understanding;**

- supporting the development of mathematical language.

Play

Mathematical experience offered to children in the Foundation Stage must be relevant and appropriate to their emotional, physical, social and cultural needs as well as being challenging and absorbing. The most appropriate context for this is through play. Without pressure, they develop the very important attitudes that will influence their future approach to education.

Mathematical experiences

Whichever area of mathematics is the focus there are three main ways in which you can plan for children's learning.

1. You can plan a specific mathematical activity for a child to undertake either individually or in a small group under the direction of an adult.

2. You can set up/structure an area of the room – e.g. shop, model-making – so that play will expose children to mathematical ideas, where an adult can intervene to extend the learning.

3. You can provide equipment for freely chosen play that encourages certain mathematical concepts.

What you cannot plan for are those moments where the exact opportunity to intervene and extend the thinking of the children occurs! Such spontaneous learning occurs all the time and good Early Years teachers are ever alert to these opportunities.

Breadth of experience

All areas in the setting, from the outdoor play area to the book corner, have the potential to trigger mathematical learning. There are no subject boundaries for the young learner – the extent of your imagination as an innovative provider is the only limit on their experience.

Practical task

Think about the sand tray. When children are busy playing, what mathematical experiences are they encountering? How do these differ if the sand is wet/dry?

How would you intervene to encourage an understanding of positional language?

Scaffolding children's learning

As in all areas of Early Years provision, knowing what experiences to offer to which children, at what point in time, is crucial for effective learning. For this reason, careful observation and monitoring of children's achievement forms the foundation for informed and appropriate activities. All members of staff need time to observe children in order to keep formative records up to date for use in planning.

The Early Learning Goals

These set out clearly the learning objectives that children should have achieved by the time they transfer to the Key Stage I classroom. They are intended to be the end points and the *Curriculum Guidance for the Foundation Stage* ('The Stepping Stones') document breaks these down further to help teachers and other Early Years practitioners to keep track of progress up to this end point.

They are separated into three groups under the headings:

1. Number – number as labels and for counting.
2. Calculating.
3. Shape, space and measures.

Number

Number as labels and for counting

By the end of the Foundation Stage, children should be able to:

- **say and use number names in order in familiar contexts;**
- **count reliably up to ten everyday objects;**
- **recognise numerals I to 9;**
- **use developing mathematical ideas and methods to solve practical problems.**

As adults we are so accustomed to the notion of number and it fits so naturally into our lives that it is difficult to appreciate the enormity of the task facing young learners. Number is an abstract concept. It takes a vast range of experiences with, for example, two legs, two toys, two cakes, two shoes, two animals, two friends etc. to reach the realisation that there is a similarity between all of these very different groupings. What's more, this similarity has nothing to do with the objects you are handling but with the *quantity* of them that you have!

Only after this realisation can any number on its own begin to mean something to the young learner. In addition to this, children need time to acquire a range of skills and ideas that will help them to make sense of and manipulate numbers with confidence. They will need to:

- **hear, distinguish and remember the spoken number names;**
- **count confidently according to the principles (see below);**
- **recognise 'quantity' in a range of contexts;**
- **apply this knowledge to a range of situations;**
- **understand the conservation of number;**
- **understand the significance of the written symbol;**
- **write the symbols;**
- **understand, read and write the number word.**

GELMAN'S PRINCIPLES OF COUNTING
Research into the understanding of number led to the identification of a set of principles that govern successful mastery of counting. Of the five principles, the first three relate to the 'How' aspect of counting and the last two to the 'What' aspect.

1. **The stable order principle.** The recognition that there is a set order to the words that have to be used in the counting procedure.

2. **The one-one principle.** The procedure for 'tagging' each number word in turn to an object to be counted. In the early stages of counting, children physically move objects as they are counted. This develops through touching to pointing and then to nodding the head in order to keep track of the count.

3. **The cardinal principle.** The knowledge that the final number you say as you count a set of objects actually tells you how many there are in the set.

4. **The abstraction principle.** The understanding that counting is a skill that can be applied to any objects, seen or unseen, in any context.

5. **The order-irrelevance principle.** The order of counting objects in a set does not matter as long as the three 'how to count' principles are applied.

(Gelman and Gallistel, 1978)

COMMON DIFFICULTIES EXPERIENCED BY CHILDREN IN RELATION TO THESE PRINCIPLES

Gelman's principles	Common difficulties
The stable order principle	Children can adhere to this principle and still not arrive at an accurate count. The order of words they use may always be the same but it might not be the correct sequence. In other words their application of the knowledge is correct but the knowledge itself has flaws.
The one-one principle	Children may: • miss out an object; • tag an object twice; • tag as many objects as there are syllables in the number name e.g. se-ven
The cardinal principle	The situation often arises where a child is engaged in counting yet, if asked to say how many there are, will respond, not with a numerical answer, but by starting the count again.
The abstraction principle	Because of the way in which tasks are presented children sometimes gain the impression that only like things can be counted.
The order-irrelevance principle	Although this may seem self-evident, those who work with young children are aware of the difficulties children have with this aspect of counting. It is extremely difficult for them to keep a track of the tagging when they are not progressing in a logical way through the set of objects.

As teachers, your task will be to capitalise on all opportunities within the day to use the language of number and encourage children to take part in activities that help them to achieve the above.

Practical task

Although there are eight farm animals in front of him, Omar insists that there are seven. How will you find out what errors he is making? What will you ask him? If you watch his response to tasks you set, what will you be looking for? How will you help him to progress?

ISSUES TO CONSIDER

- Some number names are in general use within the language either as whole words e.g. 'to' (2), 'for' (4) or as parts of words e.g. 'tend' (10), 'once' (1) and children need to become aware of the particular mathematical significance of these.

- There is often a mismatch between the particular idea of counting (which is most usually 'saying the number names in order') and the notion of counting as a process that enables you to find the answer to the question 'how many'? The purpose of counting is often not recognised by young children (Munn, 1997).

- Children often have a knowledge of numbers used purely as labels – bus, house and telephone numbers for example.

Practical task

How many songs and rhymes that incorporate numbers or ideas of quantity do you know? Begin now to make a collection of these. Can you alter the words of well-known songs to include number words? Or write new words to familiar tunes?

Some ideas of activities that encourage children to acquire the necessary number sense

Linking the spoken/written number to the quantity

In response to a spoken/written number, children:

- show a number of fingers;
- place a number of objects on a plate;
- collect a number of small objects in a basket, bowl etc.;
- perform a number of actions (jumps, claps etc.).

Initially you will model these for children. Through repetition they will become able to respond independently.

Linking the sound to the symbol/numeral

- Use the symbol in conjunction with the spoken word so that children begin to associate the two.
- Discuss and describe the symbols with and to children.

- Use a variety of numerals (e.g. wooden, magnetic, tactile) to encourage children to handle and become familiar with the shapes. Always link to the number name.
- Use a washing line with the numbers pinned up in order. Refer to these when counting orally, singing number songs etc.
- Use a 'naughty' puppet to alter the numbers while children have their eyes closed. Turn numerals upside down, remove one, progressing to more complex tasks like swapping numerals as the children gain in expertise.
- Use digit cards so as you speak the number, children show the correct card.
- Use smiley/sad faces or thumbs up/thumbs down responses from the children to agree/disagree as you show a number card/speak the number word.

Practical task

Try to think of ways in which these activities can naturally be included within the routine activities of the nursery. What practical problems could you set for children that would encourage them to use number skills? How might you incorporate this into outdoor play?

The child who has had access to a range of experiences such as those detailed above, through adult-initiated, shared activities and in free and structured play contexts will be well on the way towards a sound understanding of numbers. But again, that is not the whole picture.

The number line

There is another aspect of number that contributes greatly to number awareness and that is ordinality. This hinges on knowing where numbers lie in relation to each other and work on the number line should form a significant part of children's experience once they recognise the number symbols.

The line can be thought of as the written equivalent of intransitive counting. This is the kind of counting where number names are said in order, but with no idea of a particular quantity attached, e.g. counting to 10 before you go and find someone in 'Hide and Seek'. Confidence and competence in using a number line underpins the development of many calculation strategies.

Early activities

Use a number track that is large enough for children to stand on and move along. Before children recognise the numerals a line with coloured spots or pictures can be used. Children become familiar with the format through taking part in activities where they are invited to:

- choose a particular spot/picture to start on;
- take a given number of steps;
- find out which other spot/picture they land on.

Once they begin to recognise the symbols, asking children to stand on a particular number and displaying that number on a card helps children match the symbol to the sound and to the position on the track. They could also use cards with spots on and match those to a 'spotty' track initially and later to the number track.

This can progress to giving the number cards to children and asking them to organise either numbers along a blank track or themselves into a line. Once they have mastered the problem of forming a line then there is the opportunity to ask questions and work on activities that will help children to acquire a mental image of the line that will help with calculations.

The development of visual imagery in mathematics is very important. It is the pictures formed inside your head that help to make sense of the information given. Children do need to practise this and games that involve closing eyes and thinking about something will all help, e.g. teacher asks children to think about two of something – then asks a child to say what he/she can see. All children are then encouraged to picture this.

Calculating

- **In practical activities and discussion begin to use the vocabulary involved in addition and subtraction.**
- **Use language such as 'more' or 'less' to compare two numbers.**
- **Find one more or one less than a number from 1 to 10.**
- **Begin to relate addition to combining two groups of objects and subtraction as 'taking away'.**

Calculating is a natural progression from counting and you should take every opportunity to provide children with practical challenges and problems that allow them to use their developing skills, whatever their level of expertise. The more purpose there is to acquiring skills, the more readily they are learnt!

Practical task

- *What is the language of addition and subtraction?*
- *How many words can you think of that could be included here?*

Check your list against that in the NNS vocabulary book for the Reception year.

Mathematical language

Children need to understand concepts in language that is meaningful to them. Once understanding has been established, then the mathematical terminology can be introduced. As an Early Years practitioner you will need to be a careful listener and skilful negotiator of the possible gaps between their understanding and your meaning, and vice versa!

Observation

The idea of 'less' as the inverse of 'more' is often alien to children. Within their experience the opposite of more as in 'Can I have some more?' is much more likely to be 'No' or 'No more' or 'None left'. The Early Learning Goals stress the need for practical activities and this is what you should aim for.

- **Within the context of games, free play and routines, initiate discussions where quantities are questioned. Use songs like 'Ten green bottles' and 'Five speckled frogs' to introduce ideas of 'one less' and 'taking away'.**

- Set up outdoor activities where children can throw bean bags into buckets, or knock down skittles and be required to work out their score.
- Use snack times to give experience of sharing and needing one more chair or two more pieces of apple etc.
- Play circle games like 'The farmer's in his den' to keep running totals and emphasise the idea of 'one more'.

Extending number line activities

Encourage the use of 'and one more step takes me to …?' as you or a chosen child move along the line (either a track on the floor, or children holding numbers).

Ask 'What happens if we move the other way along the line?' Once the line has been formed with children holding the number cards then you can begin to set the watching children challenges e.g. 'Can you swap with the person who is holding a number that is more than 5?' '…less than 8?' progressing to 'one more than / one less than' or even '2 / 3 more / less than' depending on the ability of the children. This is an activity that all children can take part in and achieve success.

Another line of questioning can be based on:

'If you start on ＿＿＿ and move on three more, where will you be?'

This forms a practical foundation for the strategy of 'counting-on' which comes later.

During activities with children it is tempting to stress words like 'altogether' when adding and 'left' when subtracting. Try to avoid using these words too often as they can become so inter-related with the processes in the children's minds that they listen exclusively for these triggers to identify the mathematics that is needed to solve a problem. This can be a difficulty when they encounter word problems later in their schooling.

Practical task

The outdoor area is set up as a garage/petrol station. How can you join in the play with a view to creating opportunities for the children to experience 'addition'?

Shape, space and measures

- Use language such as 'greater', 'smaller', 'heavier', 'lighter' to compare quantities.
- Talk about, recognise and recreate simple patterns.
- Use language such as 'circle' or 'bigger' to describe the shape and size of solids and flat shapes.
- Use everyday words to describe position.
- Use developing mathematical ideas and methods to solve practical problems.

Measuring experiences

At this stage, measurement is by direct comparison and it is through the refinement of this activity and the increasingly particular vocabulary used that you will extend children's knowledge.

Most children will enter the nursery with the basic measurement language of 'big' and 'small'. It will be your task to devise scenarios and challenges that will extend this to cover such attributes as length, height, width, weight, girth etc. and to encompass comparative language rather than simple classification.

Measuring activities should always take place in relevant contexts and be accompanied by the appropriate language. You will have to model this use of language for them.

Classroom story

Jade and Lauren, two four year olds, are busy using a set of large plastic bricks to make beds for various toys as part of a hospital. Jade informs the nursery nurse that the bed under construction is 'not big enough'. 'How can you make it longer?' asks the nursery nurse. 'Get more bricks' volunteers Lauren. The nursery nurse returns later to ask 'Did you manage to sort out the bed?'

'Yes it's big now' says Jade. 'Clever girls' says the nursery nurse. 'You have made a long bed for a tall teddy.'

Experiences with pattern

The identification of patterns is an important mathematical skill and one that contributes significantly to the problem solving process. Being able to recognise a pattern, a repetition of something familiar, depends on the skill of distinguishing between things that are the same in some kind of way and those that are different.

Early sorting experiences, many of which may occur prior to starting in the nursery, involve children in sorting objects according to particular criteria or shared attributes. In this way they learn to discriminate between objects and focus on particular features of the object.

ISSUES TO CONSIDER

- **Children will often ask 'Do you like my pattern?' when what they really have is a design. How will you respond?**
- **The notion of a 'repeating pattern' may be a new idea that you will have to introduce.**
- **Bead threading, whilst it can be based on pattern making, is not a particularly relevant or challenging *mathematical* activity.**

Contexts for pattern making include:

- **clapping games;**
- **action rhymes such as 'the hokey cokey';**

- *printing at the art table or in sand;*
- *follow my leader games;*
- *big shapes on the floor;*
- *'people' patterns e.g. stand, sit, stand, sit.*

Verbalise the patterns for the children so they can *hear* as well as see the repetition.
Plan for a progression from recognising the patterns in the early stages, through being able to follow on the pattern to being able to create patterns of increasing complexity.

Classroom story

Jen, aged four years two months, spent much of her time playing with the pattern blocks. She started with simple repeating patterns but quickly moved to patterns with bi-lateral symmetry and then on to designs with rotational symmetry. At the same time, Katie gained equal satisfaction from filling every hole in a pegboard with a coloured peg to make 'lovely patterns'.

Experiencing shapes

The focus here is on the properties of shapes rather than just learning to name any particular shape. Through building, stacking, rolling, sliding and handling shapes of all kinds children will begin to acquire a sense of what exactly constitutes any given shape.

Which comes first – 2-D or 3-D shapes? Since 2-D shapes only exist as faces on the 3-D shape or as drawings on a page, I would tend to introduce the language for the two at the same time but the practical and physical activity that the child will have will be through interaction with solid shapes during construction play and whilst playing on the large apparatus outdoors.

ISSUES TO CONSIDER

- Children often internalise irrelevant features as important, e.g. orientation.
- For this reason you should vary the way you present shapes to children.

Classroom story

During story time, I became aware that the children were whispering the names of various shapes that appeared on the cover of the book. I abandoned the story and we looked at the shapes. They identified the circle, the square, the oblong and the triangle that appeared as in Figure 7.1.

I turned the book through 180° and asked again about the shapes (see Figure 7.2). Square, circle and oblong were named immediately, but there was no further response. 'What about this?' I asked, indicating the remaining shape. Still no response; however, Stuart was looking uncomfortable. 'Yes, Stuart?' I inquired. 'Well, if it was the other way up it would be a triangle but ...' he shrugged.

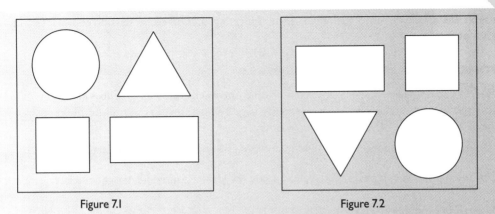

Figure 7.1   Figure 7.2

- **Children see shapes holistically, they do not understand that the properties define the shape.**

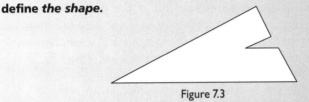

Figure 7.3

For this reason they see Figure 7.3 as a triangle with 'a bite out' (Josh 4y 1m) or 'with its mouth open' (Annie 3y 11m).

- **The thin plastic shapes that are often used as '2-D' are in fact 3-D. Use sticks/string etc. to outline the shapes on the floor.**

Children can be set challenges to make as many different shapes as they can using a box of straight sticks of different lengths. Children are much less likely to develop the misconception that a 'proper triangle' is the equilateral one (so often used in illustrations) if they have created a series of triangles for themselves as part of a game called 'Take Three Sticks'!

Use feelie-bags with shapes hidden inside to encourage children to talk about what they can feel.

Use language that the children will understand such as:

'point'   (you can put your finger on it);
'edge'   (you can take your finger for a walk along it);
'flat sides' (you can rub your hand over it);
'curved'   (you can curl your hand round it).

Use the inside and outside environment to set up 'shape' walks and do not forget to look at natural shapes as well as human-made ones.

Positional language

Many words are familiar to children on entry to the nursery, others less so. A good time to reinforce positional language is during physical activity, whether outside on the large apparatus or in the hall during movement lessons. Giving precise instructions to the children as part of the

F NUMERACY

:nable them to gain experience in locating themselves in relation to objects and

CTICAL AND MOTIVATING IDEAS

- Circle games where a teddy is passed around and each child has to follow an instruction as to where to place the teddy, e.g. 'Behind you', 'in the middle', 'next to your foot', 'on top of your head', 'in your lap' etc.
- Guessing games where a toy is hidden and questions as to its location are asked.

Within positional language we should also include the idea of a turn and of right and left.

A holistic curriculum

Although the Early Learning Goals have been described separately, each accompanied by suggestions of relevant activities, you must remember that in practical terms, within the Foundation Stage setting, such distinctions are neither necessary nor desirable. Most of the activities cover more than one area of mathematical development and when contextualised within the setting will give access to development across a range of areas of learning.

Recording

You will notice that there is no mention of children's recording of their mathematical experiences in the Early Learning Goals. This does not mean that **no** recording should take place but rather that there is no expectation that children **will** record in written form. This leaves you, the teacher, to exercise your professional judgement as to when and how it might be appropriate for individual children to take the first steps towards formal recording. Children should certainly be encouraged at all times to devise such recording as they feel necessary. The work of Martin Hughes (1986) indicates that children can record with meaning but that they have difficulties with standard representations for calculations. The introduction of formal symbols such as '+' and '−' and '=' should not be attempted until a sound understanding of the processes, based on considerable practical experience has been secured.

So far we have considered what might be termed the building blocks of an appropriate curriculum. How do you turn this into meaningful and enjoyable classroom activities and experiences?

Planning

The format for planning differs widely between settings as it must do in order to meet the specific needs of particular groups of children. However, there are common threads and the classroom story that follows gives insights into the ways that teachers approach planning.

Classroom story

Lisa teaches in an Early Years unit and describes for us how her team embark on planning.

'We find it useful to have an initial 'brainstorming' session to collect all our ideas

on a web chart (see Figure 7.4) and we then edit this into a final version for our medium-term plan. This shows all kind of experiences, teacher-led, teacher initiated (but then left to the discretion of the children) and just ways of setting out areas and resources in the learning base that will stimulate the children's enthusiasm and encourage them to extend their learning through play.'

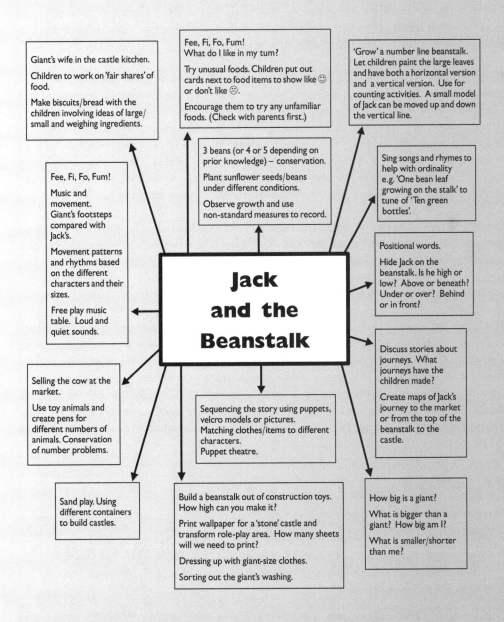

Giant's wife in the castle kitchen.

Children to work on 'fair shares' of food.

Make biscuits/bread with the children involving ideas of large/small and weighing ingredients.

Fee, Fi, Fo, Fum!
What do I like in my tum?

Try unusual foods. Children put out cards next to food items to show like ☺ or don't like ☹.

Encourage them to try any unfamiliar foods. (Check with parents first.)

'Grow' a number line beanstalk. Let children paint the large leaves and have both a horizontal version and a vertical version. Use for counting activities. A small model of Jack can be moved up and down the vertical line.

Fee, Fi, Fo, Fum!

Music and movement. Giant's footsteps compared with Jack's.

Movement patterns and rhythms based on the different characters and their sizes.

Free play music table. Loud and quiet sounds.

3 beans (or 4 or 5 depending on prior knowledge) – conservation.

Plant sunflower seeds/beans under different conditions.

Observe growth and use non-standard measures to record.

Sing songs and rhymes to help with ordinality e.g. 'One bean leaf growing on the stalk' to tune of 'Ten green bottles'.

Positional words.

Hide Jack on the beanstalk. Is he high or low? Above or beneath? Under or over? Behind or in front?

Jack and the Beanstalk

Discuss stories about journeys. What journeys have the children made?

Create maps of Jack's journey to the market or from the top of the beanstalk to the castle.

Selling the cow at the market.

Use toy animals and create pens for different numbers of animals. Conservation of number problems.

Sequencing the story using puppets, velcro models or pictures. Matching clothes/items to different characters. Puppet theatre.

Sand play. Using different containers to build castles.

Build a beanstalk out of construction toys. How high can you make it?

Print wallpaper for a 'stone' castle and transform role-play area. How many sheets will we need to print?

Dressing up with giant-size clothes.

Sorting out the giant's washing.

How big is a giant?

What is bigger than a giant? How big am I?

What is smaller/shorter than me?

Figure 7.4 Jack and the Beanstalk as a web chart

Practical task

Can you identify on the web chart which activities would best fit into the categories mentioned above?

Sometimes our themes last for some weeks. Other times we may have mini-topics that link together. We often use books or rhymes as a starting point. Children love listening to stories over and over again and we build this into the planning. This way we can use parts of the story to lead directly into the learning experiences we have planned. We make a conscious effort to consider which aspects of numeracy might be promoted through other areas of the curriculum and in this web there are clear links with other areas of learning.

Next, we begin to think about how the environment will promote and enhance the individual activities. What should the room look like? How can we include the outdoor environment? Have we got the right resources? Are they accessible? Is there a preferred order to the activities? What impact does this have on how we arrange the various sections of the room? An important question to resolve early on is 'Which activities could happen at the same time?' Is it possible to work with a small group on a 'quiet task' when there is a group of children enthusiastically acting out the 'Fi-Fi-Fo-Fum' part of the story complete with musical instruments? We try to 'trouble-shoot' classroom management issues such as this in order to avoid problems later on.

One theme rarely covers all aspects of mathematical development so we have to make sure, over the year, that we address all areas. 'Jack and the Beanstalk' allows the children access to quite a few of the Early Learning Goals and complements other themes during the year.

We display our web chart on the wall so that we can add other ideas as we go along.

This is vital because the children's free play often promotes learning that we had not considered. We observe their play as part of our role and are always ready and willing to make additions and alterations to our planning in order to make the most of their interests and enthusiasm. This observation also helps us to closely monitor the children's achievements so we actually know what to provide next. So our planning is flexible. We have to be led by the children to some extent. After all, teaching and learning is a two-way process. As teachers we have to decide what is appropriate and what is not but we do learn an incredible amount from observing and talking to the children as they go about their learning.

Practical task

Look at the web chart. Can you identify:

- *Which Early Learning Goals underpin the proposed experiences?*
- *Which experiences link with Knowledge and Understanding of the World?*
- *Which aspects of mathematical development does this theme favour?*
- *Which areas are neglected?*

Choose one of these areas and identify an appropriate learning objective from the Early Learning Goals. Can you think of experiences/activities that you could incorporate into this theme to address this?

Conclusion

In this chapter you have been introduced to many important issues related to supporting the development of children's mathematical thinking. With a sound understanding of these underlying principles and a good personal knowledge of the nature of mathematics you will have a firm foundation for creating the optimum learning environment for the children you teach. The big unknown is always what the particular concerns and interests of the children in the group might be. But, how you harness those concerns and interests to create absorbing and stimulating mathematical learning experiences is the constant challenge and ultimate satisfaction of the effective teacher.

Developing mathematical understanding and the foundations of numeracy

a summary of key points

- *Mathematics provision should build on and relate to life experiences.*
- *Activities should be practical, appropriate and enjoyable.*
- *Play provides the best medium for learning.*
- *Children should be encouraged to talk about their mathematical experiences.*
- *You are not just developing skills; you are encouraging a positive attitude and approach that will sustain the child throughout his/her mathematical education.*

Further reading

Atkinson, S. (1992) *Mathematics with Reason*. London. Hodder and Stoughton. An exploration of fundamental ideas in relation to helping children to 'emerge' as mathematicians. Includes case studies/teacher stories of such an approach in action.

Aubrey, C. (1997) *Mathematics Teaching in the Early Years*. London. Falmer Press. An examination of classroom practice in the light of teachers' pedagogical and subject knowledge. This book highlights significant issues for teachers within the foundation stage in terms of effective provision for optimum learning.

Montague-Smith, A. (1997) *Mathematics in Nursery Education*. London. David Fulton. A comprehensive, practical and easy to read guide that covers all aspects of mathematics from planning to assessment. A wealth of anecdotal evidence supports the ideas expressed and 'see at a glance' tables indicate which concepts can be developed through activities across all environments within the setting.

Nunes, T. and Bryant, P. (1996) *Children Doing Mathematics*. Oxford. Blackwell. Detailed examination of children's acquisition of competence across areas of mathematics. Includes international comparisons and research. The first two chapters give valuable insights into children's difficulties in the Early Years.

Pound, L. (1999) *Supporting Mathematical Development in the Early Years*. Buckingham. Open University Press. A clear rationale, linked to research and illustrated by example, gives a sound overview of all relevant aspects. A good starting point for further reading.

Thompson, I. (ed.) (1997) *Teaching and Learning Early Number*. Buckingham. Open University Press. A collection of writings covering recent thinking and research into the current structure of the mathematics curriculum in schools. Several chapters deal specifically with issues relevant to the Foundation Stage.

Professional Standards for QTS

→ 3.3.3, 3.3.8, 2.1a, 3.3.2

These Standards are concerned with: your ability to teach sequences of work which interest and motivate pupils, employ interactive teaching methods and promote active and independent learning; organising and managing the teaching space safely and effectively; and knowing, understanding and being able to teach the area of learning Knowledge and Understanding of the World in the DfEE/QCA Curriculum Guidance for the Foundation Stage (2000).

You may find it helpful to refer to the appropriate section of the Handbook that accompanies the Standards for further clarification and support.

By the end of this chapter you should:

- *have developed your understanding of how children learn in this area;*
- *know how to create opportunities for children to develop their Knowledge and Understanding of the World by:*
    - *adapting the learning environment;*
    - *selecting appropriate starting points;*
    - *using resources effectively;*
    - *considering your role as a teacher;*
    - *selecting appropriate teaching strategies;*
    - *involving other people;*
- *know how to make developing Knowledge and Understanding of the World manageable.*

Introduction

Knowledge and Understanding of the World is wide ranging, including aspects of learning such as:

- **exploration and investigation;**
- **designing and making;**
- **using ICT;**
- **sense of time;**
- **sense of place;**
- **cultures and beliefs.**

These interrelated areas enable children to develop the skills, attitudes, knowledge and under-standing that will support them in making sense of the world around them. They provide the basis for learning in science, design and technology, ICT, history, geography and religious education during Key Stage I.

Children's learning

> We all seem to be born with the miraculous capacity to extract from (early) experiences and begin the process of sorting our world into some sort of order.

(De Boo, 2000:2)

HOW DO CHILDREN GAIN KNOWLEDGE AND UNDERSTANDING OF THE WORLD?
Children's engagement in this area of learning shares many characteristics with learning in other areas of the Foundation Stage. The Rumbold Committee Report (DfEE, 1990) provides a helpful summary of the nature of learning in the Foundation Stage:

- **Learning should be primarily *first hand*, experiential and active. Young children need opportunities and space to explore and discover.**
- **Children's *independence* and autonomy need to be promoted. Children should be encouraged to take responsibility for their learning.**
- ***Talk* is central to the learning process. It should be reciprocal and often initiated and led by the child.**
- **Young children are social beings and learning should take place in a *social context*.**

To put it simply – children need to be **active** participants in all aspects of the learning process. An awareness of these principles for learning in the early years and of the range of contexts in which this learning might occur needs to underpin our planning and teaching of Knowledge and Understanding of the World. The answers to the questions we ask ourselves about the relationship between approaches and contexts help to identify what is *distinctive* about Knowledge and Understanding of the World so that we can teach it effectively. Specific questions for each of these principles support planning for children's learning in this area *and* highlight elements distinctive to developing knowledge and understanding of the world.

FIRST HAND EXPERIENCE
How can I provide close encounters with the world? What can the children touch, experience, observe, hear, see or smell? Will it be something from the past, from their immediate environment, from another place or culture? Will we be able to go out of the classroom to gain new experiences? Will the experience take children from the familiar world to the unfamiliar, to experience things in a way that they have never done before? Will computers, books or other media add to their understanding?

CHILDREN'S INDEPENDENCE
What can I do to help children to organise their own learning? What can they do without my support? (It may be more than you think!) Can they choose their own equipment to explore the world? Can they use computers and books to access information through illustration and simple text? Which play environments are the most appropriate? Can they interact with the play environment to take account of their own experience of the world? When should I leave them on their own to explore materials, artefacts or the environment? How can I work towards reducing the support they need?

TALK

How can I avoid talking too much? What interesting objects or experiences can I introduce to provide a context for children's talk? Can the children talk to each other about what they are exploring without my intervention? Which adults could they converse with to help them learn about the past, present and future world around them? How can I provide a focus for talk through helping children to observe, to notice things, to think about how, when, where and why, to raise questions and to seek answers? When should I talk?

SOCIAL INTERACTION

How can I create suitable opportunities for social encounters with other children and adults? How can children explore together? Can older children help? Which adults can help to create a sense of the place in which we live or the place in which others live? Which adults can provide views of the past, especially those related to the children's immediate environments? Who can help them to ask questions about and become more aware of different cultures? Who can help them to observe the world?

It is important to remember that:

- **learning about the world around the child cannot always be planned, controlled and systematic – the world changes and opportunities for learning change;**
- **gaining Knowledge and Understanding of the World may be coincidental, random and unsystematic;**
- **learning can be initiated by the child or by another child or adult;**
- **opportunities for learning cannot always be predicted;**
- **planning is helpful – being spontaneous does not imply lack of planning or preparation (see *Curriculum Guidance for the Foundation Stage*, DfEE/QCA, 2000: 15– 16).**

Practical task

It starts to snow. The forecast is for snow all week. Use the questions above and below to help you plan for children's learning.

- *Which aspects of Knowledge and Understanding of the World could you explore?*
- *What first hand experiences could you provide for the children?*
- *How could you encourage them to work independently and direct their own learning?*
- *What opportunities for talk could you create?*
- *What opportunities for social interaction could you provide?*

What should children's learning about the world be like?

In developing Knowledge and Understanding of the World children should experience learning as rewarding and challenging. Finding out about the world in which they live should motivate children to want to learn more. If you are enthusiastic and curious it is more likely that the children will be too. As Maxted (1999) noted, without motivation there can be no real learning.

When learning about the world children should have many opportunities to develop a wide range of skills and attitudes as well as knowledge and understanding (see DfEE/QCA, 2000, for details). They should encounter a range of resources – real objects (natural, made, old, new, everyday, unusual), the living world, the made world, books, computers and people. They should become more independent as learners and begin to learn about **how** they learn.

When learning about the world children should be finding out that:

- **curiosity is helpful;**
- **careful observation is helpful;**
- **good questions lead to answers and new ideas;**
- **sharing ideas with other people is helpful;**
- **being unsure is OK;**
- **having different ideas from other people is OK;**
- **being wrong is OK;**
- **there may be more than one answer;**
- **things change;**
- **they can change things;**
- **not everything is the same;**
- **variety and diversity are normal.**

Practical task

Are children aware of their own learning? Karina asked her four year old daughter Minelli what helped her to learn. Minelli replied that talking to her friend on the phone was best.

Talk to a pre-five child about learning about the world and find out more about children's awareness of their own learning.

Creating opportunities for developing Knowledge and Understanding of the World

1 THE LEARNING ENVIRONMENT

What can you do with the learning environment to support learning about the world?

The indoor setting should not be used as a substitute for the outdoor setting when developing knowledge and understanding of the world. A picture or painting of a building can never provide as good a learning experience as the real thing. An effective indoor learning environment should enhance what the children can experience and learn. It should stimulate interest, raise questions, encourage close observation and provide a wealth of opportunities to share new ideas and experiences. Your setting should feel like an exciting place to be.

A rich indoor learning environment:

- **invites observation – have you seen the old coins on the table that Jenny's great grandad brought in? Are they like the ones that we have today?;**
- **stimulates curiosity – there are some postcards on the wall. Can you work out where they are from?;**
- **poses problems – I've found a treasure chest but I don't know which key opens it;**
- **provides an opportunity to take learning forward – I've put some seeds and compost in the 'garden centre'. Can you make some plants grow like we did together before the holiday?;**
- **reflects the interests and achievements of the children – Tom and Khalida have collected some shiny conkers to put on our finding out table today. Look at Sam's wonderful drawing of the horse chestnut tree they came from!;**
- **involves children and other adults in deciding what to do where – Dani has asked Mrs Khan if we can put a sari in the dressing up area;**
- **is interactive where possible and includes questions and children's responses – what do you think will happen to the ice cubes? I will write your ideas in the speech bubbles and hang them from the ceiling.**

A rich learning environment can be created outside the setting by:

- **growing plants (in tubs if necessary);**
- **providing bird feeders;**
- **using an old log to create a habitat for insects and other small animals;**
- **marking out a time line;**
- **marking out compass directions and pointers to local landmarks;**
- **highlighting textures;**
- **creating a 'treasure' hunt;**
- **building a weather station.**

2 STARTING POINTS FOR LEARNING

Good starting points lead to a rich vein of enquiry in all aspects of developing knowledge and understanding of the world. You may be expected to work around a theme. You may find that developing Knowledge and Understanding of the World is treated as an area of learning on its own. You will need to decide what your starting point might be. It could be:

- **through display – have you seen the display of baby clothes? Have you ever worn any clothes as small as these?;**
- **through the focus for discussion – Paddington Bear has lost his hat. What do you think we should use to make a new one for him?;**
- **through a role-play area – let's make a cafe. What kind of food should we put in it?;**
- **through invited adults and artefacts – Mrs Bradbury went to this school as a little girl. She has brought some of her school books and photographs to share with you;**
- **through an unusual or interesting object – a sporran or Indonesian shadow puppet;**

- through programmes used on the computer, TV or radio;
- through incidental occurrences – a child brings in something to share, a rainbow appears in the sky.

As children learn in different ways it is important that you provide a variety of ways into learning for them. Table 8.1 shows a range of starting points for developing Knowledge and Understanding of the World around the theme of 'I am special'.

Person	Unusual object	Everyday object	Question	Book	Display	Visit/ outside	ICT
Health visitor	A child's special possession	Large mirror	What is special about you?	'Guess how much I love you'	Class/group photo. Poster of children from around the world	Photographers or camera shop	Tape record children singing. Computer program to create a simple data base

Table 8.1 'I am special' starting points

Practical task

Think of starting points under the following heading to help develop knowledge and understanding of the world within the theme of Homes.

Person	Unusual object	Everyday object	Question	Book	Display	Visit/ outside	ICT

How would you use the building of a new house next to the school/setting as a starting point?

3 RESOURCES

Learning environments vary in the type, quality and quantity of resources available. Effective Early Years teachers make the best use of the resources available and gradually build up a supply of materials to help to support the development of Knowledge and Understanding of the World. These will mainly be everyday objects. Parents and other friends of the school can often provide a surprising range of items. In this way a diverse range of resources can accumulate to reflect the diversity in society.

In order to make the best use of the resources available:

- invite adults to contribute resources (e.g. old toys, memorabilia, photos, travel documents, old phones);
- borrow resources from libraries, clinics, religious centres;
- foster links with local businesses (e.g. copies of old forms, travel brochures, leaflets);
- vary the nature of the resource and build progression into its use, e.g. dough → textured dough → coloured/scented dough → dough with tools → baked dough;
- change the problem or question related to the resource, e.g. can you make the car move? → can you make it move faster? → can you measure how far it has gone? → can you make a record to show how far it has gone? → can you compare that car with this car? → can you work out what makes a difference to how fast or slow the cars go?

Practical task

How can you make use of the following resources, with and without support, to help children of different ages or abilities to develop their Knowledge and Understanding of the World?

- *construction toys;*
- *sand tray;*
- *joining materials, e.g. glue, sellotape etc.*

Think about how you would build in progression

If children are to learn to work independently in developing knowledge and understanding of the world then they need to be able to access independently most of the resources that they need. In order to do this:

- children need to get to know what is available to them and how to take responsibility for resources;
- resources need to be clearly labelled – e.g. silhouettes of tools on the tool board or kitchen equipment, colour coding;
- focus on one set of resources at a time so that children build up their knowledge of what is available – offer lots of direction and support.

4 THE TEACHER'S ROLE
At the core of learning in this area there is a reciprocal relationship between children and adults.

Effective learning ⇐ Child's interest, enthusiasm, enjoyment   Teacher's interest, enthusiasm, enjoyment ⇒ Effective teaching

Figure 8.1 Reciprocal relationship between children and adults

It is the adults' role to be the catalyst for generating this relationship. This can be achieved through:

- modelling appropriate behaviours and responses – enthusiasm, curiosity, questioning, observing closely, showing surprise, showing wonder, using more technical vocabulary, responding positively to children's ideas, exploring ways of finding answers;
- working alongside children to illustrate an enthusiasm for learning – I'm really excited! I didn't know that we had two kinds of ladybirds in the garden until Thomas found them today;
- connecting learning to the outside world – look how we can make the Roamer work by pressing the buttons. What do you have at home that you can programme like this? A washing machine – what a good idea, Anjani!;
- valuing ideas of all people in the learning environment – Roisin said that the piece of wood is really big so it will sink. She has watched carefully and noticed that all the big things have sunk. Let's see what happens – what a surprise, it floats!;
- helping children to be aware of and reflect on their learning – who has learnt something new today? Sally? Sally's brick wall kept falling over and now she says that she has learnt how to make it stay up. How did you do that, Sally?;
- being flexible, willing to catch the moment, recognising that routines help young children but that surprise and spontaneity are also loved by children – Monika has just seen a rainbow outside – let's all look at it!

Classroom story

One afternoon, it began to hail. The Reception teacher quickly gathered the children in the 'home bay' where the windows slid open to allow enough room for 25 hands to reach outside. The children described the feel of the hail, watched it bouncing on the ground, made it melt in their hands and listened to the sound of it hitting the windows and roof. This prompted the teacher to fetch metal trays to hold outside and the class listened to 'hail music'. They later had opportunities to replicate the hail music with musical instruments.

Questioning is of particular significance in developing Knowledge and Understanding of the World. It helps to create a climate of enquiry in which raising questions and seeking answers are encouraged and promoted (see Harlen, 2000, for guidance).

To question effectively you need to:

- understand the difference between subject-centred questions (which appear to require a right answer – how do you fasten these two things together?) and a person-centred question (which invite opinion, are less threatening and can lead to exploration – how do you think we can fasten these two things together?);
- understand the difference between productive (which lead to further enquiry) and unproductive questions (which tend to close things down);

- encourage children to raise their own questions – what do you think we should ask the vicar when we go to the church? Can you think of a question to go on the question board by the side of the incubator?;
- use questions to model investigative behaviour – what do you think will happen if I put glue on this button and put it there? Can you tell me more about your visit to the Synagogue? How do you think I can draw this picture on the computer screen? Mr Singh brought in this interesting object this morning – what do you think it might be used for?;
- listen to children's answers and respond to them – Leon thinks if we go outside in the sunshine his shadow will be on the playground – let's go and look!;
- use strategies other than hands up if you know the answer – talk to your buddy next to you about what you think we might see when we go to the Post Office.

Classroom story

When asked why her children were always so keen to find things out and the setting was such an exciting place to be a nursery practitioner replied 'listen to the children – the magic comes from them'.

Practical task

You are planning to create a sensory trail in the setting and outdoor play area. What opportunities could you create and what kind of questions could you ask, or put on display, to encourage the children and adult helpers to make full use of it?

5 TEACHING STRATEGIES

Effective teaching for developing Knowledge and Understanding of the World encourages hands-on activity and talk. You have a central role in planning, supporting and effectively utilising talk and hands-on activity. You need to be aware that:

- children need to be allowed to talk to each other and discover things on their own at times without adult intervention – I am going to leave the three of you to work out how to put the toy together and you can show me when you have thought of some good ideas;
- children cannot discover everything themselves – If you want to make a hole in paper safely you shouldn't use scissors. You can use a hole punch like this – why not try it now?;
- you need to learn to wait longer than may feel comfortable for children to say or do something;
- children need opportunities to express ideas freely without being dominated by technical vocabulary;
- children need to talk to each other about their ideas in their first language as well as in English;

- the timing of interventions is important. Too early spoils discovery and interferes with child to child interaction; too late leads to frustration; too much gets in the way; too little may mean missed opportunities but may be the best option.

> 'Giving the game away too early' during an investigative activity may limit the depth of children's learning. For example, telling children that magnets attract and push away before they have had the chance to experience the 'eureka moment' provides information but prevents the development of investigative skills, including observation, testing and analysing.

(DfEE/QCA, 2000:83)

6 INVOLVING OTHER PEOPLE

People can be the greatest resource for developing Knowledge and Understanding of the World in the Foundation Stage, not just employed support staff but any adults and older pupils who are willing or able to spend time with the children. They bring the depth and breadth of experience needed in this very wide area of study. Principles for involving other adults effectively include:

- modelling good practice in interacting with children;
- ensuring all adults are fully aware of expectations and their specific role;
- involving all regular support staff in planning, target-setting, organising and managing the learning environment to encourage enquiry;
- encouraging colleagues to attend courses (in history, geography, ICT, design and technology, science ...) and to disseminate information/ideas afterwards;
- discovering the specialised knowledge and talents of staff so that you can make the most of their expertise – Mrs McDonnell makes china flowers. She is going to show us tomorrow and then we can try making some;
- discovering the specialised knowledge and talents of parents, relatives and adults in the community – Callum's daddy is a builder. He is going to come in to show us how he builds walls;
- briefing visitors carefully on the needs/abilities/interests of the children so that the content of their input is appropriate;
- creating a positive and supportive climate for people who are unused to working with children.

Classroom story

Joseph's grandad came regularly to help out in the nursery. Talking to the teacher one day he happened to mention that he had noticed how difficult the children found learning to hammer and how they never seemed able to produce anything interesting or creative. He had an idea that he would like to try out something that combined his love of gardening with his skills as a joiner. The next day he brought in a large bag full of fruit and vegetables from his allotment. With the help of the children he cut them into chunks. Now the children were able to use long nails to hammer the chunks together to make animals, trees, buildings, monsters, in fact anything that their imagination and skills would allow them to make!

Making developing Knowledge and Understanding of the World manageable

Manageability is a key challenge for an area as broad and disparate as Knowledge and Understanding of the World. It is necessary to make sure that the quality of the children's experience is not gained at the expense of your sanity. In order to keep a balance between what is the ideal and what is achievable it is important to plan so that you:

- **initially identify small activities which can be built on gradually as confidence in this area of learning grows;**
- **avoid being overambitious – young children bring lots of ideas with them, but so much in knowledge and understanding of the world is new to them and needs time to develop;**
- **take time to linger over experiences;**
- **value repetition – not all experiences have to be new;**
- **don't try to do everything yourself when others may have more knowledge and experience;**
- **make use of local resources;**
- **have experiences in reserve.**

And most of all do what you and the children enjoy doing together.

Knowledge and Understanding of the World: a summary of key points

- *Children develop knowledge and understanding of the world in active, not passive, ways.*
- *Learning about the world should happen in a social context with lots of talk and interaction.*
- *Variety is vital in starting points, resources, roles and teaching strategies.*
- *Manageability comes from starting small and working outwards, from the familiar to the unfamiliar, the everyday to the unusual, the local to the global.*

Further reading

Feasey, R. (1998) Effective questioning in science, in R. Sherrington (ed) *ASE Guide to Primary Science Education*. Hatfield: ASE. Concise yet thorough summary of question types, effective questioning and developing children's questioning. Practical advice for creating a questioning environment.

Harlen, W. (2000) *The Teaching of Science in Primary Schools*. 3rd edn. London. David Fulton. A comprehensive overview with much that is applicable to the wider curriculum and to teaching in the Foundation Stage.

Johnston, J. (1996) *Early Explorations in Science*. Buckingham: Open University Press. Useful examples, ideas, and strategies, all applicable in a broader context.

Moyles, J. (ed) (1995) *Beginning Teaching: Beginning Learning*. Buckingham: Open University Press. Very readable and comprehensive guide both to principles and practice, with effective ideas and clear examples.

O'Hara, M. (2000) *Teaching 3 – 8: Meeting the Standards for Initial Teacher Education*. London. Continuum. Reviews the standards for ITE, making clear links to Early Years practice and settings.

9 ICT IN THE FOUNDATION STAGE

Tony Poulter

Professional Standards for QTS

→ **2.5, 3.3.10**

These Standards state that in order to gain QTS, teachers must know how to use ICT effectively, both to support their wider professional role – for example, using software to develop resources for the children to use, using the computer as an electronic blackboard and using the Internet to download materials for both themselves and the children – and to teach their subject: for example, demonstrate the use of ICT skills, know how to provide for the development of ICT skills in Foundation Stage children and their use across the six areas of learning.

You may find it helpful to refer to the appropriate sections of the Handbook that accompanies the Standards for the award of QTS, for further clarification and support.

By the end of the chapter you should:

- **have an understanding of how ICT can enhance learning in the Foundation Stage across the six areas of learning;**
- **have an overview of the learning theories applicable to the use of various ICT tools;**
- **know the importance of promoting ICT so that pupils become confident users of it.**

Introduction

Well, can ICT provide genuine and long-lasting benefits to learning and teaching? The answer is an emphatic yes! (Munro and Smith, 2000).

This categorical conclusion was reached by the authors of an important document about the effect of ICT on teaching and learning and is, we believe, equally true of teaching and learning at the Foundation Stage. The often quoted motivational value of ICT is no less relevant to children in the Early Years. Its *potential* ability to enhance teaching and learning cannot be denied. ICT can make a large contribution in all six areas of learning, although the most overt references to Information and Communication Technology (ICT) can be found in the Knowledge and Understanding of the World section of the foundation stage guidance.

In the guidance (p93) practitioners are advised to:

- **give opportunities for the use of ICT to develop skills across the areas of learning;**
- **encourage children to observe and talk about the use of ICT in the environment;**
- **encourage children to show each other how to use ICT equipment.**

In this chapter we will be discussing how this might be done and offering some practical advice about resources that are available and how they might be used.

Upon their arrival in the nursery (or pre-Reception) class the development of basic ICT skills of the children should begin. Many children may already be confident users of the technologies but some will not be and this difference should be addressed quickly. The instillation of keyboard and mouse skills should be a top priority if children are to have access to learning opportunities right across the six areas. There are alternative input devices to help younger children, for example the concept keyboard, touch screens and switches. However, the ability to connect mouse move-ments to the pointer on-screen is a particularly important skill and many of the software packages mentioned in this chapter will promote the acquisition of this skill.

ICT in Knowledge and Understanding of the World

Although it is clear that ICT should be used 'to develop skills across the areas of learning' (Foundation Stage guidance, p93) it is the 'Knowledge and Understanding of the World' strand alone in the guidance that makes direct reference to ICT usage. Computers are seen as one amongst many 'tools' that can help the young child to learn. For instance, when gathering information children might utilise CD-ROMs or other ICT devices such as digital cameras, video cameras and audio equipment such as a tape recorder. ICT is seen as an invaluable tool to both teacher and learner.

Furthermore, the practitioner is responsible for planning and implementing equal access to ICT resources for both boys and girls, and those children with special needs. The computer is particularly good at giving the latter group access to the curriculum. The teacher should also address inequality with regard to home background and be aware of the 'digital divide'. Many homes today are ICT-rich environments that produce 'computer whizzkids'. As Marian Whitehead puts it:

> it is clear that young children are computer and TV/video literate at an early age, often outstripping their carers and teachers when it comes to reading visual narratives, images and icons. (In Blenkin and Kelly, 1996:132)

This is certainly true. However, some children will come from ICT-poor homes and practitioners should ensure various differentiation strategies are in place to develop their skills.

As well as ICT, Knowledge and Understanding of the World 'forms the foundation for later work science, design and technology, history, geography' (p82). ICT can assist the learner in all of these areas. One of the early learning goals in this section of the guidance (the ELG for ICT) stresses the importance of finding out about and identifying 'the uses of everyday technology' and of children using ICT 'to support their learning' (p92). The 'stepping stones' in achieving this ELG specify that children should:

- **show an interest in ICT;**
- **know how to operate simple equipment;**
- **complete a simple program on the computer and/or perform simple functions on ICT apparatus.**

The practitioner is given appropriate (if not in-depth) guidance in how to aid children in crossing the stepping stones to the achievement of this goal. The rest of this chapter will put some meat on the bones offered in the Foundation Stage document.

Many ICT devices are going to be of use in the development of skills in this area of learning. As well as the programmable robot (mentioned quite often in the guidance), the overlay keyboard, tape recorder, video and television, and the digital camera could prove to be very useful. John Stringer (2001) makes a good case for using ICT apparatus, other than the computer, in science. He suggests using cassette tape recorders to record observations of experiments, using the telephone to find out the latest local weather forecast and using the fax machine to contact another school and compare the progress of plants. Most Early Years settings will have access to a computer but it may not be a state of the art machine, or may not have appropriate software. Practitioners should be ready to take advantage of the huge variety of ICT-related devices around today and to stimulate their pupils' interest in them.

Certain types of content-free software packages could be of great benefit to the Early Years child in this particular area of learning. Talking word processors could be used in relation to various subject-based topics. They are not only to be used when focusing on literacy. There is a wide range of *My World* (Widgit Software) screens available on a variety of topics. *Clicker* grids, made up of text and/or pictures, can be found (or created) on many different topics and new ones can be downloaded for free from the *Clicker Grids for Learning (CGfL)* website (www.cricksoft.com/cgfl/index.htm). Content-specific CD-ROMs and websites will also be well worth utilising in every area of learning and these will be discussed later in the chapter.

Finally, opportunities for including ICT devices in a role-play situation should not be missed. The computer and other ICT equipment can be a part of various scenarios – the school office, the library, the shop and so on. Purposeful play is stressed in the foundation stage guidance and play seems more authentic to the children if real (not 'pretend') apparatus is used. The teacher as 'scene setter' has an important part to play too. By taking part in such activities children are not only learning *about* ICT but learning *through* ICT as well (Cook and Finlayson, 1999).

Practical task

Plan a lesson in which you design a role-play scenario of 'The Travel Agent'. The equipment you use could include a digital camera for passport photographs, a computer with word processing software to record customer details and an atlas on CD-ROM to explore the world looking for holiday destinations. Relate the lesson to objectives in the Knowledge and Understanding of the World section of the guidance. Other areas of learning may also be covered. Identify possible opportunities for assessment.

ICT in Communication, Language and Literacy

Multimedia computers can be used in this area of learning to:

- **develop reading through the use of talking stories (electronic books) on CD-ROM;**
- **develop early writing through the use of talking word processors with word bank facility;**
- **develop speaking and listening skills by playing adventure games.**

TALKING STORIES

Talking books are now commonplace in the Early Years classroom. Titles such as *Little Monster at School* (Broderbund Living Books), *Naughty Stories* (Sherston) and reading-scheme based CD-ROMs such as *Oxford Reading Tree* have become something of 'old chestnuts' nowadays but have lost none of their power to be instructive and engaging. Programs like this allow pupils to see and hear text being spoken in the context of colourful illustrations and also allow them to interact with the story through 'hotspots' that, when clicked, set off entertaining and engrossing animations. The benefits of using such packages with Early Years children are manifold. Here are just some of them.

- **They can be used like printed material to support a range of approaches to reading.**
- **They are fun and easy to use providing motivation.**
- **Interest in, and concentration on, the text is sustained and increased.**
- **They provide particular support to early readers and the less able.**
- **They give a simple introduction to the important skill of reading from the computer screen.**
- **The interactive nature of the screen enhances the story line and aids understanding of the text.**
- **They are an excellent precursor to reading the printed version of the book.**
- **They promote the increase of word accuracy and word recognition.**
- **They stimulate the all-important 'talk' about the story.**

Talking stories are actually designed to be used by young children without the assistance of an adult, whether it be the teacher, assistant or helper. Because the text can be spoken to them the program is in effect modelling the process of an adult reading aloud to the child thus negating the need for an adult to actually be there in person.

RESEARCH SUMMARY

Medwell (1996) found that gains in word accuracy were evident when pupils explored the talking story version of the book prior to reading the print-based version. However, the presence of a teacher/helper when children were using talking books was preferable. When talking stories were used with a teacher better use of semantic and contextual clues was apparent. Medwell concluded that the most of effective way of using these packages was to support reading with the teacher.

So, although talking stories can support the child's learning, the talk it promotes between teacher and learner is of greater value. Further support can be gained from the presence of another (perhaps more able) child at the computer. The teacher must get involved if young readers are to be active learners and not just passive recipients of text, no matter how 'edutaining' it is. It is as well to be aware that all the whistles and bells offered by this type of multimedia software (for example, eye-catching animations and noisy sound effects) can distract some children from the narrative.

TALKING WORD PROCESSORS

Word processors? For children who, perhaps, cannot even write their own name legibly? Surely not! Well, 'Yes indeed!' is our reply to that. The TTA exemplification material (2001), with regard to English, is clearly in favour of this giving the scenario whereby children are:

using simple word processing software, to communicate in images and writing and recognise the value of written communication, even before they have developed the fine motor skills required for legible handwriting. (p19)

Note the reference to 'a simple word processing software'. Use does not have to be made of the full-blown version of a program like *Microsoft Word* (though arguably it could). There are plenty of child-friendly word processing packages on the market with facilities to help the emergent writer along. Writing activities with word processors need to be well thought out by the teacher. They need to be short, simple, focused but meaningful exercises, especially in the beginning. More often than not they should be collaborative tasks with two, perhaps three, pupils involved. The intervention of the teacher or assistance of an adult helper is desirable and preferable.

There are many strategies that can be used to get the children writing, even if keyboard familiarity and mouse control are poor (although word processing programs will, as a by-product, assist in the development of these all-important ICT skills). An overlay keyboard (sometimes referred to as a 'concept keyboard') can be used in conjunction with the traditional QWERTY keyboard. By pressing an area of the overlay on the (usually) A3 tablet a word, phrase or even a sentence can appear on the screen and a substantial amount of text can soon be built up. The overlay has been previously created by the teacher (or perhaps purchased) on a given topic and may include pictures (perhaps drawn by the children) as well as text. So a simple overlay about the weather could contain an area with the words 'Today it is' and another area with a picture of the sun. Pressing these results in the sentence 'Today it is sunny'. The possibilities with the overlay keyboard, when used in the teaching of literacy skills to young children, really are only limited by the creativity and imagination of the teacher.

A program like *Clicker 4* (Crick Software) with its many 'grids' (essentially on-screen overlays) containing words and pictures is another way of getting children to build up sentences on-screen quickly. There are many topics to choose from and creation by teachers of their own grids is simplicity itself. Pictures can appear with text, which always provides extra motivation for young writers. Differentiation is easily incorporated into the grids according to the ability of the children. One nice feature of this package is that support for popular reading schemes such as *Oxford Reading Tree* is available, thus making the link between reading and writing clear.

The popular framework program *My World* is also very good for young writers. With 'screens' on a myriad of topics it can be used to create simple sentences for various scenes in popular stories, for example, 'Goldilocks and the Three Bears'. The scenes can be changed by simple 'drag and drop' techniques. The sentences that go with them can be discussed and edited before printing.

The vocabulary and spelling ability of early writers can often be quite limited and can put them off writing. The facilities of the programs mentioned above should help overcome this frailty. Another useful tool in the word processor's repertoire is the 'word bank'. The teacher can input words that are difficult to recall and/or to spell on a given topic before the children come to use the program. *Textease 2000* (Softease) is one such package. When the children need a certain word they can access the word bank and simply insert the word by clicking on it, a most useful facility that the Early Years practitioner would do well to emphasise.

Perhaps the most telling advantage of the word processor in early writing is the ability of some of them, *Textease 2000* and *Talking First Word* (RM) for example, to actually speak the text being composed as the children write. With these programs letters, words, sentences or whole paragraphs and texts can be read back to the children. Young writers get the benefit of immediate feedback. Words are highlighted as they are spoken enabling the children to follow the passage. Research evidence seems to show (Joy, 1994) that talking word processors, using synthesised speech feedback, leads to increased confidence and concentration, to improved punctuation and spelling, and to dramatic gains in reading ability. Joy's findings showed a sustained improvement in children's reading age by an average of over seven and a half months after structured use for one month of the program *Talking Pendown* (Logotron). The case for using such software packages with Early Years children would seem a compelling one.

When using any of the word processors mentioned, and the facilities they offer to the young writer, the activity should be a collaborative one. Once again the importance of the talk that goes on around the computer should not be underestimated. The writing being composed on-screen can be the focus for much quality discussion. Many argue (Scrimshaw, 1993, and Hardy, 2000) that computer usage is a social activity and through co-operative learning the greatest gains are made. This can be particularly true of collaborative writing with word processors. Composing text at the keyboard with a peer, and more importantly with the teacher or a helper, provides an excellent opportunity for talk and collaborative learning in what Vygotsky calls the Zone of Proximal Development (ZPD), the gap between a children's present knowledge and their future learning potential. The support given to children by the software, their peers and the teacher all provide what Bruner termed the 'scaffolding' needed to enable the children to bridge that gap.

ADVENTURE GAMES

One type of software designed specifically to promote discussion between pupils and the adults that inhabit the Early Years environment is the adventure game. This type of software is a simulation or model of (usually) an imaginary world, a *microworld*. As groups of children explore this world they have to discuss alternatives, solve problems and make decisions and predictions. They have to learn from mistakes and ultimately achieve their goal – escape the maze, find the treasure, rescue the princess and so on. Decisions are made based on reading simple text with picture clues and sound support. The sound aspect of multimedia programs like these (and indeed those mentioned above) should not be underestimated. *Aural* as well as *oral* skills are being developed.

These games have been around for 20 years now and have become more sophisticated, entertaining, engrossing and motivating since the advent of CD-ROM. A 'golden oldie' like *Granny's Garden* (4Mation) and adventures such as *Richard Scarry's Busytown* (Paramount), *Putt-Putt* (Humungous) and *Max* (Tivola) challenge and inspire children to think in creative and flexible ways. Here the literacy skills of speaking clearly, putting forward a point of view and justifying it are being developed. Listening to the perspectives of others and commenting sensibly is equally important.

Vygotsky's socio-cultural, communicative view of how young children learn through interaction with others (in this case their peers and their teacher/helper) and through objects in their learning environment (in this case the computer and its software) applies to the use of adventure games particularly well. According to this theory, language is paramount. The communicative aspect of teaching and learning is to the fore.

This has much in common with constructivist theorists such as Piaget and Bruner who espouse active interaction with the environment and the people within it to build up increasingly complex understandings over time. Adults provide support or scaffolding in the form of, for example, guided participation and purposeful intervention. The interactive, multimedia facilities of today's adventure games would no doubt gain their approval having, as they do, the potential to develop problem-solving skills, thinking skills and communication skills.

In using adventure programs individuals in the group see different aspects of a problem. Thus, together, the group comes up with the solution to that problem. They can then progress, perhaps with a little teacher prompting, to the next stage and ultimately the achievement of their goal. Studies seem to strongly suggest that computer usage has a great deal of potential to enhance collaborative learning. It provides the structure and direction needed to make collaborative learning effective. Fisher (1993) states that girls in particular found this mode of learning helpful, describing it as 'crucial to girls' effective use of the computer'. Boys tended to be more competitive and less co-operative around the computer, being less willing to listen to others' point of view and eager to impose their own. This is where the teacher's role as an active participant in the learning process becomes important. They must give guidance, offer explanations and steer the group in the right direction by intervening purposefully but sensitively. In short, provide scaffolding.

ICT and mathematical development

There is great scope for mathematical development in the Early Years context through utilising ICT. Numeracy skills can be fostered in a number of ways including:

- **the use of collaborative ICT-based activities to encourage mathematical language;**
- **the use of programmable robots and early Logo programs to explore position, direction, angles, shape and space;**
- **the development of data handling skills through the use of simple graphing programs.**

PROGRAMMABLE ROBOTS

The guidance actually makes specific reference to the use of these devices. One of the learning goals (in Knowledge and Understanding of the World) refers to children using 'programmable toys to support their learning'. These could be remote-controlled, radio-controlled models of some kind but usually refers to programmable robots such Pip or Pixie (both made by Swallow Systems) or, perhaps the most popular, Roamer (by Valiant Technology).

These floor robots (or turtles) were an innovation of the constructivist Seymour Papert who invented the Logo computer language and wrote one of the great educational computing books *Mindstorms*. Like Piaget he believed that children work through concrete experience to develop conceptual understanding. Thus, before children could be exposed to the *screen turtle* in Logo they had to use the *floor turtle* to prepare the way. So using a 3-D vehicle like the Roamer, and becoming confident with it, is excellent preparation for using a Logo program such as *RoamerWorld* (RM).

By its very nature, use of the Roamer can encourage the development of mathematical language in young children because it can address so many areas of mathematics. Instructional language is promoted because the Roamer must be given a sequence of instructions before it will move. Numeracy skills are fostered as a numerical input is required to specify how far you want the Roamer to travel or turn. Number recognition and the value of a given number will occur through the use of the Roamer. By experimenting, concepts such as direction, angle, shape and space, and the language associated with those concepts, are introduced to the young child. As with literacy, the value of talk in a numeracy setting should not be undervalued and should of course include the teacher/helper.

There are many good reasons for making use of a programmable robot such as the Roamer. Donahue (www.valiant-technology.com/) lists numerous pedagogical advantages and concludes by saying:

> In sum, the Roamer can serve as the basis of a powerful problem-solving curriculum that will help young children begin to develop the habit of creative, independent problem-solving while introducing them to the key technologies of the modern Information Age.

There are limitless innovative and creative ways that the teacher can use the Roamer. The BECTa website suggests using the Roamer in the context of a story. Many stories are suggested: *Rosie's Walk, Don't Forget the Bacon, The Shopping Basket, The Little Red Hen*. The children really enjoy dressing up the Roamer as a character from a story (removable covers for the Roamer can be purchased) and then programming it to travel around a specially created environment (perhaps a grid with painted on scenes from the story). When the Roamer appears as Postman Pat and has the challenge of delivering letters or as Santa Claus with the task of visiting all those chimneys, the learning taking place will be much more meaningful to the children.

Classroom story

Sally Smith (1997), an ICT co-ordinator at an infant and nursery school, shared her experiences of using the Roamer with young children. The school had two Roamers (christened Wilma and Rosie by the children!) Although the children were initially excited by the Roamers, interest began to wane and the possibilities were not being fully exploited. However, she 'experienced a turning point' when she got the class to decorate the Roamers as butterflies to link in with their work on The Hungry Caterpillar. By giving a 'butterfly' instructions it collected pollen from flowers. Sally and the children developed new games as their knowledge and confidence increased. The challenges they set became increasingly, well, challenging and now they look forward with great anticipation to their slot on the 'Roamer Rota'.

Floor turtles such as the Roamer are much more than toys for learning about going forward and backwards, left and right. They are open-ended, interactive devices that can promote learning in all sorts of areas not just mathematical development. Work on the computer using the screen turtle with older, more able, Foundation Stage children will go much more smoothly if they have covered the all-important ground work (if you'll pardon the pun) with a programmable robot.

DATA HANDLING IN THE FOUNDATION STAGE
Data handling activities are not beyond the capability of Early Years children and the software packages around make things quite easy for both teacher and pupils. Data handling skills should

be promoted from an early age by setting simple exercises such as counting the different coloured Smarties in a tube. Simple surveys can be introduced for instance 'Pupils' Pets', 'Favourite Colours' or 'How We Get To School'. These surveys, perhaps in the form of tally charts, can be taken across to the computer and, following teacher modelling, the data can be entered. The presence of an adult at this stage will be important and even more critical when it comes to generating a graph and discussing what it shows.

There are many straightforward graphing programs on the market today suitable for use in the Early Years. *PicturePoint* (Longman Logotron) introduces young children to data handling offering the facility to complete simple surveys and generate different graphs including the 'infant-friendly' pictograms. The graphs speak too, always a useful add-on for this age range. *RM Starting Graph* also offers simple surveys (tables) and the opportunity to produce pictograms (and other chart types) all at the click of a mouse (no need to use the keyboard in 'touch mode').

Suites of programs are now coming on to the market and one such, designed for the three to seven age group, is *Infant Video Toolbox* (2simple). The programs in this suite include *2count* (a simple data handling program to make pictograms), *2graph* (for producing block graphs, bar charts etc.) and *2question* (used to make simple branching databases). Working at a very straightforward level, a software kit like this can cater for all the practitioner's data handling needs and is easy for young children to master as there is no need for any great skill in reading.

ICT and other areas of learning

Although use of the computer is most obvious in the three areas of learning discussed above, there is plenty of scope for ICT in the three remaining areas of learning. In the 'Personal, social and emotional development' area the aim, amongst other things, is to develop a child's confidence through building positive relationships with peers and working well in various group situations, instil a positive disposition to learning and promote problem-solving skills. ICT can help in this process in a number of ways. It can:

- **promote a great deal of collaboration and discussion between children;**
- **be very motivating and lead to increased self-esteem;**
- **offer many opportunities to think about and solve problems.**

These benefits have already been made clear in this chapter. Teachers should be willing to look for links between stepping stones/Early Learning Goals and ICT. Under this area of learning, according to the guidance, practitioners will have the opportunity to encourage children to 'Have a strong exploratory impulse' (p32) which could be linked to 'Show an interest in ICT' (p92); to 'Seek out others to share experiences' (p36) could be linked to 'observe and talk about the use of ICT' (p93); and 'Show care and concern for others' (p38) could be linked to 'Show each other how to use ICT equipment' (p93).

These sorts of link can be found in the 'Physical development' area of learning. For example, if the children are to 'Respond to rhythm, music and story by means of gesture and movement' (p104) there will be an excellent opportunity to introduce the children to cassette or CD players and talking books. Using CD-ROMs and other computer software in the course of their meaningful play will develop hand-eye co-ordination through extensive use of the mouse. The mouse itself, of course, is an excellent example of a 'one-handed tool' (p114). Letting young children explore the computer, which should be as natural a part of the Early Years setting as it is in the home setting of many children, is often a good idea. They will enjoy pressing keys, and moving and clicking the mouse, and seeing the effects of their actions on-screen. As Smidt (1998) puts it, this is not 'messing about' but is essential physical exploration.

In the 'Creative development' area of learning ICT can help to enhance art and music activities in particular. They will enjoy any of the major painting packages available today. *KidPix Studio Deluxe* (Learning Company) is one of the most popular of this type of program. It has many simple, yet powerful, tools (complete with entertaining sound effects) that enable to children to be very creative and to develop their artistic skills. A colour printer is essential if the 'hard copy' is to be as impressive as the on-screen creation and self-esteem is to be increased. Even use of *Paint*, the basic package that comes with Microsoft Windows, is perfectly adequate for exploring shapes and colours, and for early 'mark making' where children might, for example, attempt to write their name with the brush tool.

A range of ICT equipment can be used to address stepping stones concerned with sound and music. Music cassettes and CDs for the youngest of children are ubiquitous today and will be used often in the Early Years setting. Tape recordings or video recordings of performances can be made and played back, much to the delight of the children. Programs such as *Beetles* (Brilliant) and *MusicMaker I* (Resource) introduce children to instrument sounds and many popular tunes, as well as giving them an opportunity to compose their own, with the usual engaging animations.

Using CD-ROMs in the Foundation Stage

The use of CD-ROMs is stressed a great deal in the guidance, particularly the Knowledge and Understanding of the World section of the document. CD-ROMs should not replace books of course (perish the thought!) but they do offer a whole new dimension to the process of learning and gathering information, to 'finding out'.

> Multimedia features such as sounds and video clips arouse intense interest, stimulating discussion. Spoken commentaries enable children to listen for information. Unlike a human speaker, the 'voice' may be paused, stopped or played repeatedly. (Smith, 1999:146).

There are numerous captivating titles around for use with young children on a variety of subjects and topics. Many address several areas of learning. Care needs to be taken when deciding on what will work for you. These packages offer opportunities for collaborative work and promote task-related talk. The quality of that talk will be improved with an adult present to provide essential scaffolding.

There has been an explosion in the availability, in recent years, of CD-ROMs for very young children. Many involve their favourite TV and book characters and the development of basic skills and are applicable across all six areas of learning. There are many that address the gaining of early literacy skills such as alphabet familiarity, letter recognition, letter shapes and sounds, phonics and spelling. Many more develop early numeracy skills of number recognition, counting and the exploration and creation of number patterns. Most are of the 'edutainment' variety, all singing, all dancing, multimedia extravaganzas! Motivation will rarely be a problem when using these content-specific, content-rich programs with their engaging animations and all-important sound prompts.

A leaf through any good educational software catalogue will reveal many more titles suitable for use in all the areas of learning. Titles involving *Noddy*, *Pingu*, *Spot* and *Winnie the Pooh* all offering a helping hand in the development of basic skills — what child could resist! However, teachers should not introduce any of these software packages without having first familiarised themselves with it. They should evaluate it and appraise its potential in helping children to achieve Early Learning Goals. The adoption of a 'try before you buy' policy is often a good idea. A browse through the Becta Educational Software Database (besd.ngfl.gov.uk) is also worthwhile.

The study by Collins et al (1997) found that teachers were generally 'cautiously enthusiastic' about this type of multimedia software and rightly so, we believe. However, practitioners should use them appropriately. Smidt (1998) asserts that many Early Years practitioners see the computer as 'an activity' when really they should be thinking 'How can it support learning?' Multimedia software can dazzle and delight children but teachers need to temper their own enthusiasm and examine the program, assess its value educationally and then, if they think it has potential, integrate it into the curriculum.

Not all theorists are convinced of the educational worth of 'flashy' multimedia CD-ROMs. Some maintain, for example Siraj-Blatchford (1998), that much of this software is of the old-fashioned 'drill and practice' variety based upon behaviourist learning theories that have been largely discounted these days. If the child gets the right answer they are rewarded with a sound effect and/or animation. If they get into difficulties, choices are lessened until the correct answer is found. He admits that this sort of 'arcade game' is popular, particularly amongst boys, but poses the question 'Are they educationally suitable?' The practitioner will have to decide for themselves. Certainly, in our opinion, the repetition and reinforcement such programs offer can be of great benefit to many young children.

There are many CD-ROM packages that we would like to recommend but space does not allow. However, if the reader would like to access this web address www.mmu.ac.uk/c-a/edu/primary/priweb/eycdrom.htm they will find numerous CD-ROMs, briefly reviewed, that cover all areas of learning.

Websites for use in the Foundation Stage

If there has been an explosion in the number of CD-ROMs available for the Early Years sector, then this has certainly been mirrored by websites on the Internet built with this age group in mind. Many of these websites offer the kind of multimedia experience you expect from CD-ROM-based software. Web technology is so advanced now that, as well as pictures and text, sites can provide sound effects, music, speech, animation and video. They are also akin to CD-ROMs in that they often have activities based around popular children's TV characters such as *Bob the Builder*, *Teletubbies*, *Tweenies*, *Postman Pat* and *Thomas the Tank Engine*. All of these attributes assist in grabbing the attention of the children, motivating them and increasing concentration spans.

There are websites suitable for use in all the areas of learning with young children. These will usually have a teachers' (or sometimes parents') section containing advice on using the site as well as printable materials and ideas for off-computer activities. The World Wide Web (WWW) is an ever-growing resource bank for teachers. The National Grid for Learning (NGfL) is now becoming the educational resource we always hoped it would. Early Years practitioners can get plenty of advice, ideas, lesson plans and worksheets from sites such as the Virtual Teacher Centre (www.vtc.ngfl.gov.uk/) and the British Educational Communications and Technology agency (www.becta.org.uk/). A useful collection of links for the Foundation Stage practitioner can be found at www.mmu.ac.uk/c-a/edu/primary/priweb/earlinks.htm. These will help in finding resources and researching topics.

The BECTa site is particularly good for ICT resources of all kinds. Information sheets (www.becta.org.uk/technology/infosheets/) are available on a number of topics of interest to the Early Years teacher including *Foundation Stage Education and ICT*. In the curriculum section of the site an extremely useful page can be found entitled 'Learning with ICT at the Foundation Stage'. A document mapping where ICT can support early learning goals in all six areas of learning can be downloaded.

Best of all, a lengthy list of lesson plans and associated resources are downloadable.

> These materials provide a framework to help nurseries plan for integrated use of ICT across all subjects of the curriculum and throughout the Foundation Stage. (BECTa/VTC)

All six areas of learning are covered by these resources but with an ICT focus. *Living Books* addresses literacy and gives guidance in using the talking story 'Just Grandma and Me'. *A Survey of Eye Colour* covers numeracy and knowledge and understanding of the world. *Creating A Maths Trail* would be excellent in providing a purposeful ICT-based activity both indoors and outdoors. *All About Me — My Body* aids physical development. *Colour Matching and Creating Flowers* promotes creative development. *Food, Glorious Food!* and *Our Place* address, amongst other things, personal and social education. They also demonstrate that ICT activities not only make use of computers and software but of other ICT devices such as digital cameras, video cameras, scanners, cassettes and CDs. It is important that young children realise that 'ICT' does not mean solely 'computer'. The computer is an everyday part of children's lives and should, therefore, always be available for role-play. *Class Café* and *School Office* are both examples of how ICT can be used in role-play to achieve teaching and learning objectives.

There are many websites that we would wish to recommend for use in the foundation stage as we think practitioners will be surprised at the quality of the material out there in cyberspace. Limitations of space prevent us from doing this here but links to excellent sites, with brief reviews, can be found at www.mmu.ac.uk/c-a/edu/primary/priweb/eyweb.htm.

ICT in the Foundation Stage:

a summary of key points

There is little doubt that ICT can be of great use in the foundation stage.

——— *It can motivate young children and enhance their learning experiences.*

——— *Though applicable to all six areas of learning it is particularly useful in developing literacy and numeracy skills and knowledge and understanding of the world.*

- *Practitioners would do well to utilise generic software packages such as word processors, data handling and graphics packages, as well as a range of CD-ROMs and websites especially designed with Early Years children in mind.*
- *Other ICT equipment, notably programmable robots, should also be introduced at this stage.*
- *The advantages of collaborative, co-operative learning should be exploited when using ICT, with the teacher or assistant intervening in a purposeful way to encourage meaningful talk and to provide scaffolding.*

Further reading

Sharp, J., Potter, J., Allen, J. and Leveless, A. (2002) *Primary ICT: Knowledge, Understanding and Practice* in the *Achieving QTS* series. Exeter. Learning Matters. Gives further information about planning ICT, and also assessing it, in the Early Years.

10 MONITORING, ASSESSMENT, RECORDING, REPORTING AND ACCOUNTABILITY: THE CHALLENGES FOR THE FOUNDATION STAGE TEACHER

Sue Egersdorff

Professional Standards for QTS

→ 3.2.1, 3.2.2, 3.2.3, 3.2.4, 3.2.6, 3.2.7

These Standards state that in order to gain QTS, teachers must be able to: use and devise a range of monitoring and assessment strategies to evaluate pupils' progress towards planned learning targets; give immediate and constructive feedback and use assessments to involve pupils in considering their own performance; accurately assess pupils' progress using the Stepping Stones and Early Learning Goals; use assessment to identify and support pupils who are falling behind and/or failing to achieve their potential in learning or who are experiencing behavioural, emotional and social difficulties; record pupils' progress and achievements systematically; and report on pupils' attainment and progress orally and in writing in a form accessible to parents, carers and other professionals.

You may also find it helpful to refer to the appropriate section of the Handbook that accompanies the Standards for the award of QTS, for further clarification and support.

By the end of the chapter you should:

- *understand the importance and value of assessment in the early years environment;*
- *know and be able to define the key terminology used in the assessment process;*
- *understand how planning and assessment work together to support teaching and learning;*
- *know what should be assessed and how purposeful records can be maintained;*
- *understand the benefits of quality assessment for children, teachers, parents and the whole school.*

Introduction

Monitoring of each child's progress throughout the Foundation Stage is essential to ensure that they are making progress and that particular difficulties in any of the areas of learning, whatever the cause, are identified and addressed.
(*Curriculum Guidance for the Foundation Stage*, DfEE/QCA, 2000)

The establishment of the Foundation Stage through the *Curriculum Guidance for the Foundation Stage* document is a significant development in Early Years education as it gives clear recognition to the critical importance of children's first experiences in nursery/Reception class. There is an emphasis on learning key skills, which will form a firm foundation for future learning and give all children the best possible start to their education. The document also provides guidance for the practitioner to support the planning and provision of teaching and learning opportunities of the highest quality, which involves ongoing assessment and review of practice. The aim of this chapter is to help you to recognise that assessment, recording and reporting are not burdensome, bureaucratic tasks but essential tools to ensure the diverse needs of all children are successfully met and your class area is a lively, vibrant learning environment.

Section 1: what is assessment and why is it important?

Assessment in the classroom

As Foundation Stage practitioners, we are all committed to positively engaging children in quality learning experiences. But how do we measure our success and how do we know if children are making progress?

Assessment is central to the learning process as it enables the teacher to:

- **focus on a child's strengths and weaknesses;**
- **analyse whether teaching programmes are successfully meeting a child's individual needs;**
- **ensure progress is being made and highlight children who may require additional support;**
- **consider how far the classroom organisation and management is supporting children and fostering independent learning.**

It also provides a process by which we can collect information and make judgements; informing, directing and improving our future planning and provision of learning opportunities to best meet the diverse needs of the children in our care.

Children develop at a rapid pace during their Early Years and this must be recognised when considering assessment practices. Assessment can take two basic forms: formative and summative.

FORMATIVE ASSESSMENT
This is an ongoing feature of everyday practice in the nursery/Reception class setting. It requires the teacher to use the following key skills:

- **observing;**
- **questioning;**
- **challenging;**
- **supporting;**
- **intervening;**
- **discussing.**

This form of assessment involves constant dialogue between teacher and child, through which the teacher can make decisions about how much the child understands and the direction of future learning. When such information is shared with the child it can be highly motivating, helping them to recognise their own potential and the part they must play in their own learning journey.

Not all such ongoing assessments will require to be recorded, as this would be far too burdensome and intrusive on teacher time. However, it is important to make a record of 'significant achievement' for a group of children or an individual child. This will be discussed in detail later in the chapter.

SUMMATIVE ASSESSMENT

This adds rigour to the assessment process and considers progress over time. It usually takes the form of a tracking system where significant information is recorded across the six areas of learning:

- **personal, social and emotional development;**
- **communication, language and literacy;**
- **mathematical development;**
- **knowledge and understanding of the world;**
- **physical development;**
- **creative development.**

This allows the teacher to give consideration to:

- **starting points – what the child already understands and can do;**
- **the transition between home and school;**
- **the experiences the child brings from the home setting;**
- **how parents support their child's learning;**
- **how the child learns best. For example, some children prefer to work outdoors and enjoy their own company, whilst others need to be in small groups with an adult close at hand for support and security;**
- **the progress or lack of progress made by the child over a period of time;**
- **the appropriate nature of the learning activities planned. For example, has the able child been suitably challenged? Is this reflected in the progress made?;**
- **children whose lack of progress may be causing concern and require further investigation. For example, co-ordination difficulties or speech and language problems.**

Schools and nurseries have been highly creative in designing tracking systems which meet their needs and work well in individual settings. Others have adopted published systems. Whatever system is used it must have the following key characteristics:

- **a focus on learning and teaching;**
- **include analysis of classroom observations to focus on what the child can do, knows and understands but most importantly the direction of future learning;**
- **be user friendly and not too time consuming to complete;**

- include comment from all those working with the child;
- involve parents, presenting information in a way that is meaningful for them;
- allow parents to contribute their views about their child's progress;
- enable evaluative judgements to be made of the child's progress and how well the child's needs are being met within the setting.

Statutory assessment requirements

Alongside the assessment procedures followed by individual settings are the Statutory Assessment Procedures which must be followed by all primary schools. These currently require schools to adopt a Qualifications and Curriculum Authority (QCA) accredited baseline assessment scheme to assess all new four to five year old pupils within seven weeks of starting primary school. This enables schools to assess children's progress over time against an entry baseline attainment judgement.

However, due to the introduction of the Foundation Stage the current baseline assessment arrangements are under review. It is proposed that statutory assessment should:

- be moved to the end of the Foundation Stage;
- be a single national scheme used by all to assess children's achievements in relation to the Early Learning Goals;
- include assessment of all six areas of learning included in the Foundation Stage Curriculum Guidance to ensure assessments cover the breadth of learning in which children have been engaged;
- be based on teachers' observations of children during everyday classroom activities;
- link appropriately with the range of other Foundation Stage provisions and assessments for children with special educational needs, acting as a trigger for further diagnosis where appropriate;
- be referred to as the 'Foundation Stage Profile';
- inform parents, with results reported to them before the end of the summer term;
- involve the collection and collation of national data to enable schools to compare their results with those of similar schools.

At the present time the QCA has commissioned an independent research company to undertake development work for the new assessment procedures. You can access more information from the DfES website at www.dfes.gov.uk.

The language of assessment

The following terms are frequently used when discussing assessment. It is important for you to be clear about the precise meaning of each term. The following definitions are intended to be a useful source of reference:

- *Monitoring* – a systematic checking process with a clear focus on:
  – teaching and learning;

- collecting and using evidence to improve practice and influence decisions;
- analysing the quality of provision and its impact in terms of educational outcomes.

- *Learning objective/ intention* – what the child *is expected* to know, understand or be able to do, having taken part in a planned activity.

- *Learning outcome* – what the child actually knows, understands or can do following a planned activity.

- *Pupil target* – a focused learning objective for an individual child based on a careful analysis of what the child can do and what constitutes the next steps in learning.

- *Teacher accountability* – the responsibility assumed by the teacher for the quality of provision within the setting.

- *Differentiation* – ensuring the needs of children are met by the careful matching of activity and teaching to the individual pupil.

- *Evaluation* – reflecting on teaching and learning outcomes by analysing, interpreting and making judgements which influence future actions and decision making.

- *Recording* – a systematic and agreed school procedure for the tracking and logging of individual progress over time.

- *Reporting* – closely linked to assessment and recording and the method by which information is passed to parents/teachers about a child's achievements and progress.

Section 2: what to assess

Establishing successful assessment practices across the Foundation Stage curriculum can seem a daunting task for even the most experienced practitioner. However, the more you are involved in observing young children and sharing your findings with colleagues, the easier it will become. It is important to take every opportunity to discuss and test your judgements against those made by others within the setting.

When deciding what needs to be assessed it is important to ask yourself the following questions.

- **Why do I need this information?**
- **What is my key focus for this assessment?**
- **How will I collect the information I need?**
- **What will I do with the information I collect?**
- **Has the assessment process made a positive difference to the quality of the teaching and learning process?**

The work of Pascal and Bertram (1996) is also helpful here. They have developed a framework to support observation, assessment and evaluation. It has three major areas of focus within the setting:

1. **The context** – looks specifically at features of the physical environment and how the classroom is arranged to support children's learning.

2. **The process** – gives consideration to what is happening within the setting. Findings are

Area of focus	Key questions
Context	• How is planning, assessment and recording managed to maximise learning opportunities for children? • Are all staff directly involved in the planning process? • How involved are parents in their child's learning? • Are the various learning styles of children catered for? • How does the setting 'feel'? Is the atmosphere consistently welcoming/calm/purposeful? • Are resources managed in a way that supports children's learning? • Are resources of good quality and in good condition? • Are there sufficient resources for the number of children in the setting? • Are children able to access the resources they need independently? • Do children understand and follow the basic routines of the setting? • Are all areas of the curriculum catered for? • Does the display work support and extend children's learning opportunities as well as celebrating achievement? • How well is the outdoor environment used to support all areas of the curriculum? • How well is time managed to maximise learning opportunity? • Is a policy of Equal Opportunities in place and evident in the day-to-day practice of the setting?
Process	**For the child (learning)** • What is the child's starting point? What knowledge, skills and understanding is the child already bringing to the learning experience? • Does the activity have a clear learning objective/intention? Is this appropriate and does it meet the needs of the child? • How involved is the child in an activity? Is there evidence of sustained concentration over a period of time? • How independent is the child in the activity? • Is the child able to talk about the activity? • Is the child aware of the expectations of the setting in terms of behaviour, noise levels and routines? • How well does the child interact with others in the setting – children and adults? • Does the child demonstrate initiative by selecting activities to become involved with rather than waiting for adult direction? • How curious is the child? • How is the child with special needs identified and integrated within the setting? • Is the child able to make a simple evaluation of his/her own progress or achievement? • Does the child demonstrate a dominant learning style? • Does the child know what to do to get help when needed? • Is the child happy, settled and secure in the setting? How do you know? • Is the child making progress in all areas of the curriculum – are there any gaps? **For the adult (teaching)** • Does the child understand my expectations? • Does the child understand my explanation of the activity? • Do I waste time because of poor organisation and management? • Do I differentiate the learning objectives and activities appropriately to accommodate all learners? • Do I use a variety of questioning skills? • Is the child stimulated by the work? Is concentration sustained? • Do I talk too much? Should I give the child more time to think, discuss and explain? • Am I aware of the noise level in the setting? Do I respond if it becomes too high? Is my response appropriate and successful? • Do I constantly make connections for children between new and prior learning? • Am I positive and encouraging at all times? • Do I use resources well to support learning and add depth to understanding? • Do I evaluate my work to assess whether learning objectives have been met/not met/partially met and what I need to develop with the child next? • Do I encourage the child to explain what he/she has learned? • Do I offer ongoing opportunities for the child to consolidate and reinforce prior learning? • Are children encouraged to investigate, take risks and solve problems? • Am I sensitive to the emotional needs of the child? Do I respond appropriately? • Am I aware of the importance of equal opportunities when I plan my work? • Do I have high expectations for children with identified Special Educational Needs within the setting? • How successful are my relationships with parents? How do I encourage them to become involved in the education of their child? • How do I involve the wider community? • What links have I developed with other similar Foundation Stage settings? • What do I do to develop positive relationships with my colleagues within the setting? Are adult relationships a strength of the setting or do they need further development? • Do I give enough consideration to my own further training needs? • Am I happy in my work? Do I sometimes let my mood affect the quality of my teaching and the relationships I have with children?
Outcome	• What steps do I take to ensure the quality of provision within the setting is consistently good? • Do I regularly seek the opinions of others about my performance and how it may be improved further? • Am I prepared to listen to and act upon feedback from others? • How regularly do I seek feedback from other stakeholders in the setting, for example, parents and the children? • Are the planning, assessment and recording procedures I use efficient and, above all, successful in supporting children's learning? • Are all children making progress? How do I know? • What am I doing about the children who are not making appropriate progress for whatever reason? • Do my lesson evaluations show any common themes? Is any action required as a result of my findings? • Do I use my lesson evaluations to inform my future planning? • Is my record keeping a useful tool when planning for individual children? If not, what needs to be improved?

Table 10.1 Assessing context, process and outcome (adapted from Pascal and Bertram, 1996)

recorded through two 'Observation Scales', one focusing on how involved the child is in the learning process and the other on the involvement of the adult and how the adult interacts with the child to support and extend learning.

3. **The outcome** – this reflects upon the 'end product' of the learning process from three distinct points of view:

    1. child;
    2. adult;
    3. setting.

Practical task

You may find Table 10.1 useful as a checklist of questions to ask yourself.

Consider the questions in relation to a setting you have experienced or a child you have worked with. What might your assessments have identified?

Practical task

Consider the following classroom stories. What might be the 'next steps' in teaching and learning for these situations and children? See if you agree with the ideas suggested.

Classroom stories

1. *Harry, age four, has just entered the Reception class. He has not attended any pre-school provision and is an only child. His mother is anxious about him starting school and this is very evident when she leaves him in the morning. He, in turn, is tearful every morning and clings to his mother.*

   When she has gone, he continues to need the constant support of an adult and refuses to choose any activity independently. His interactions with the other children are very limited but he will talk at great length to an adult he trusts.

2. *Mia, age three, has been in the nursery class for two terms. She is regularly found in the book area where she likes to pretend she is the teacher telling a story. She uses picture cues and memory to retell her favourite stories, and does so in great detail. She recognises much of the environmental print around the nursery and the letters in her own name.*

3. *Liam, age three, has just started nursery on a part-time basis. His mother is a teenage single parent. She wants the best for Liam but finds his constant demands very tiring and tends to let him have his own way. In nursery he finds it very difficult to share and can be aggressive with other children if he does not get what he wants straight away. However, he is curious and interested in*

everything around him. He particularly likes the attention of an interested adult and puts great effort into everything he does.

4. *Jamie, age four years (an August birthday), has joined your Reception class during the autumn term. His family have recently moved into the area. His previous school have forwarded records which suggest that staff found Jamie very difficult to manage as he refused to sit still, fidgeted and was unable to concentrate for any length of time. They suggest that Jamie made little progress and may have special educational needs.*

Important considerations

Classroom story I

- No pre-school experience.
- Never been separated from his mother.
- As an only child he has had limited interaction with other children.
- Lack of social skills.
- Over-anxious parent. Child worried by mother's responses and behaviour.
- Unsure of what school is all about in terms of what is expected of him.
- Highly dependent on mother for all aspects of his personal care.

Possible next steps

- Arrange a meeting with mother to discuss the issues and how her anxious behaviour is contributing to Harry's difficulties.
- Could someone else bring Harry for a while to avoid the separation upset?
- Perhaps mother could telephone at mid-day to ensure Harry is fine and alleviate her own worries.
- Suggest ways mother could support Harry by discussing school routines and expectations at home in a positive and exciting way. By appearing more confident herself she will lessen his concern.
- Arrange for yourself or another adult to be available to greet Harry every morning and explain what will be happening that day. Such a role could be developed so that Harry has a key worker in school who he views as his 'trusted adult'.
- Ensure Harry has someone to play with at play and lunchtimes. Some schools operate a 'buddy system', where older children are given the responsibility of caring for the more vulnerable younger ones.
- Provide opportunities for Harry to work in small groups with an adult, building his confidence and making friends at a pace he can cope with.
- Take every opportunity to encourage and praise Harry when he tries something new or completes a task by himself. Self-esteem is a key component of successful learning.

Classroom story 2

- Mia obviously enjoys books and recognises the power of the spoken and written word.
- She is aware that letters carry and communicate meaning.
- She notices and is stimulated by the environmental print displayed around the nursery.
- She is aware of reading strategies and how pictures often support the text.
- She has learned a lot about story telling from adults who have modelled the process for her.
- She understands how stories are structured and develop.

- Provide puppets and props for Mia to develop her story telling.
- Encourage her to make up stories for herself.
- Share stories, encouraging her to predict what might happen next, discuss her favourite characters, and explore and explain word meanings.
- Act as scribe to record her stories – model the writing process for her. Encourage her to edit the writing with you.
- Encourage Mia to use the writing area to record her stories for herself. Discuss the writing with her.
- Provide opportunities for Mia to tell her stories to others, using her props if she wants to.
- Work with Mia to make a book of her stories which she could illustrate and display in the book area.
- Provide a range of books for Mia to take home to share with her parents.
- Discuss with Mia's parents how they might support her rapidly developing literacy skills – for example, by joining the local library.
- Encourage Mia to use her skills across the curriculum. For example, making a label for her model, writing a recipe, writing a notice for the role-play area, making her own props and puppets.
- Play word games which encourage Mia to listen for and recognise sounds/letters.

Classroom story 3

- Liam's home situation has provided limited opportunity for him to experience positive interaction with other children.
- His mother has found it difficult to establish boundaries and behavioural expectations for Liam.
- His early experiences have provided little opportunity for him to develop a sense of his own identity and how his behaviours might affect others around him.
- Liam is not used to routine and finds it very difficult to understand the expectations of the nursery.
- His mother, although willing, needs guidance to support Liam's social and emotional development at home.

- Discuss the issues with Liam's mother. Work together to produce a structured programme of support to improve Liam's behaviour based on recognition and reward for positive behaviours.
- Suggest activities Liam and his mother could complete at home together which would focus Liam's attention in a positive way. For example, a trip to the park to feed the ducks or a model making session. In this way she will begin to enjoy his company more and respond to his demands more appropriately.
- Reinforce and model the positive behaviours expected in nursery at every opportunity.
- Catch Liam 'being good' and praise immediately.
- Allocate time for Liam to spend on a one to one basis with an adult every day. Encourage him to give feedback to the whole group about what they chose to do together and what happened.

Classroom story 4

- Jamie is a very young Reception aged boy. His immaturity may have been mistaken for poor behaviour.

- As a Reception aged boy he is unlikely to be able to sit still for long periods and may fidget because of a desire to be active.

- Movement is an important aspect of learning in the Early Years.

- Was the curriculum on offer to Jamie appropriate to his needs?

- Have his hearing and vision been checked recently?

- He needs to be given time to settle into his new surroundings before accurate assessments can be made about special needs.

- Discuss the previous school report and records with Jamie's parents. Have they experienced similar difficulties at home?

- When was his hearing and vision last tested? Encourage the parents to have them re-tested.

- What does Jamie like to play with at home? Does he appear to be a very active learner?

- Suggest calming activities which Jamie's parents could try at home.

- Make regular observations of Jamie within the class. Does he settle better to some activities than others? Are any significant patterns emerging in terms of his behaviour?

- Hold regular feedback sessions with all those involved? If concerns persist arrange for further support to help assess Jamie's specific needs.

- Encourage all adults to talk quietly and calmly to Jamie, modelling acceptable behaviours.

- Provide opportunities for Jamie to learn actively, which appears to be his preferred style. Do behavioural difficulties still persist?

- Develop his self-esteem and confidence by praising him whenever you can.

Section 3: involving others in the assessment process

The teaching assistant

Good Early Years practice has always recognised the crucial importance of appropriate adult/ child ratios within the nursery and Reception setting. Young children need adults around them to support, interact and extend their learning as well as making them feel safe, secure and settled within their new environment. The arrival of the Foundation Stage has helped to raise the profile of the Early Years within many Local Education Authorities and schools, and with this the need to ensure, and in many cases improve, staffing provision. As a student teacher and ultimately a teacher, you will find yourself working with support staff and it is important that you understand their role and what assistance you should expect from them with the assessment process.

The DfEE have produced a good practice guide, *Working with Teaching Assistants* (2000) which divides the work of the teaching assistant into four strands:

- **support for the pupil;**
- **support for the teacher;**
- **support for the curriculum;**
- **support for the school.**

These strands are intended to apply to teaching assistants working in any type of educational setting from nursery to secondary school. Table 10.2 is adapted from the DfEE guidance and is based on a survey carried out by the Centre for Educational Needs at the University of Manchester in 1999, which looked specifically at good practice in the management of teaching assistants in schools.

Effective practice	Form of support for children from the teaching assistant
Fostering the participation of pupils in the social and academic practices of the setting.	• Supervising and assisting small groups of children • Developing children's social and emotional skills • Implementing behaviour management policies • Spotting early signs of disruptive behaviour • Supporting the inclusion of all children • Keeping children interested and stimulated • Observing children's progress • Talking to parents
Seeking to enable children to become more independent learners.	• Showing interest • Assisting individuals with specific tasks and activities • Observing children's progress • Freeing the teacher to work with groups • Working in partnership with outside agencies • Modelling good practice and having high expectations of all children at all times • Assisting children with physical needs sensitively • Involving parents
Help to raise the standards of achievement of all children.	• Being involved at whole class level • Being directly involved in the planning and assessment process • Extending learning by making more ambitious and challenging activities possible • Providing feedback to teacher on observations made • Preparing materials and resources • Working with parents

Table 10.2 Working with teaching assistants

Outside agencies

We are currently at a very important pioneering stage in the development of Early Years services nationally. The *First Report on Early Years* from the Select Committee on Education and Employment (2001) referred to the success of integration initiatives such as the Sure Start and Early Excellence Programmes. These give consideration to the all-round care and education of the child, commonly known as 'educare' and are based on the rationale that care and education in the Early Years cannot be separated as one is directly affected by the other and vice versa. As a result they promote the joined-up working between education, health and social services.

As a Foundation Stage teacher you are likely to work closely with a range of professional colleagues, for example:

- **health visitor;**
- **school nurse and doctor;**
- **speech therapist;**
- **social worker;**
- **educational psychologist;**
- **clinical psychologist;**
- **learning support teacher;**
- **ESL teacher.**

Such relationships are of crucial importance as their success will have a direct impact on the progress, achievements and well-being of the children in your care. Refer to Chapter 3 for further detail and information.

Partnerships with parents

Many settings operate what they describe as an 'open door policy' for parents where they encourage ongoing dialogue and access to the setting and staff. Care is needed to ensure this is not a tokenistic gesture, as true partnership with parents requires constant effort, hard work and input from the setting. No matter how warm and welcoming you are, many parents still find it difficult to approach you with problems or queries. You will probably find that a small group of parents are very demanding of your time, while you barely converse with or see others.

It is important to remember that parents know their child best and have a wealth of information that will be of value to you to help your all-round understanding of the child. Refer to Chapter 2 for details of the many and varied roles that parents can be encouraged to play in the wider life of the school.

Practical task

Think about the useful information parents could provide about their child prior to entry to your setting. How and when would it be appropriate to collect this information? Note down your ideas and compare them with the sample parent questionnaire used by a nursery setting with parents at a pre-nursery taster session (see Figure 10.1).

Your child will soon be starting nursery with us. We would like this time to be special and memorable for them.

By completing the questions below you will help us to get to know your child and make sure they feel happy and settled from the start!

The sheet will also form part of your child's profile record.

Child's name... Date of birth ....

Parent's name...

Please complete Part 1 with your child.

PART 1: ALL ABOUT ME!

I am happy when...	
I really enjoy...	
My best friend is...	
My favourite time of day is...	
My favourite story is...	
My brothers and sisters are...	
I have pets...	
Other special things I want you to know about me...	

PART 2: PARENT SECTION

What name should we use for your child in nursery?	
What position are they within your family i.e. youngest, oldest?	
What does your child like to play with at home?	
Does your child enjoy playing alone or prefer company?	
Tell us about the stories your child enjoys.	
Has your child attended any other pre-school provision?	
Can your child go to the toilet without help?	
Is your child looking forward to attending nursery?	
Has your child any medical condition we should be aware of? ● Hearing/vision problems ● Attends speech therapy ● Asthma ● Food allergies	
What are your hopes for your child in nursery?	
Is there anything else you would like to tell us about your child?	

Sometimes there may be confidential information that you would rather not write down. Please feel free to make an appointment to see us. We are always happy to help. Thank you for taking time to complete the sheet. We look forward to welcoming you and your child to nursery.

Figure 10.1 Parent/child interview sheet

Practical task

Figure 10.2 shows a list of questions parents commonly ask. Before reporting back to them think about the information you may need and how your assessment procedures may support you.

- *My child does not want to come to nursery/Reception class. What should I do?*
- *All my child seems to do is play; when will he/she start proper work?*
- *My child says he/she has no one to play with. What's happening?*
- *Why do you let the children play outside? How do I know my child is safe?*
- *Why is my child bringing books home with no words?*
- *Other children seem to bring paintings and pieces of writing home from every session. Why doesn't my child?*
- *All my child wants to do at home is play on the computer and watch television. Is this normal, how can I encourage him/her to do other things?*

Figure 10.2 Common questions asked by parents

Parents as helpers in the classroom

There is no doubt that parents can be a tremendous source of help in the classroom and offers of assistance should be encouraged and valued. Every Early Years teacher welcomes an extra pair of hands. See Chapter 2 for details of how this can be successfully managed and support the provision of quality teaching and learning opportunities.

Parents may also be able to assist with the assessment process by giving you feedback about how particular activities were received by the children, what they felt was achieved and how individuals fared. However, it would not be appropriate to involve them in any more formal assessment or recording procedures.

Section 4: linking assessment and planning

Planning for specific curricular areas has been covered in earlier chapters. However, the importance of understanding how planning, recording and assessment work together to ensure quality teaching and learning opportunities cannot be overemphasised.

It is easiest to remember as a cycle incorporating the key features we have discussed earlier in the chapter (see Figure 10.3).

The close link between assessment and planning is highlighted in the *Curriculum Guidance for the Foundation Stage*:

> Assessment gives insights into children's interests, achievements and possible difficulties in their learning from which next steps in learning and teaching can be planned.

(DfEE/QCA, 2000:24)

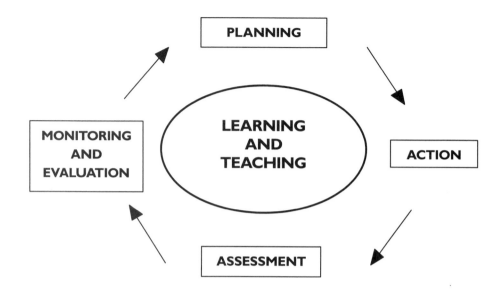

Figure 10.3 Linking assessment and planning

Practitioners need to share information gained from assessment to:

- inform their future planning;
- group children for particular activities and interests;
- ensure that the curriculum meets the needs of all children;
- promote continuity and progression.

Where practitioners are clear about what children know, the skills they have developed, the attitudes they have towards learning and the interests they have, they can plan how best to take the learning and teaching forward.
(DfEE/QCA, 2000:24)

Understanding 'significant information'

Much has recently been reported about teacher workload. Campbell (1993), working with a research team, looked at infant teachers and found that many assessment and recording activities were 'unduly complex, time consuming and often purposeless' (Campbell et al, 1993:88).

If you are to remain fresh, motivated and positive in the classroom it is important that the assessment, recording and reporting aspects of your work are:

- **valuable and valued as a tool for managing teaching and learning;**
- **useful and accessible to all stakeholders including the child;**

- time efficient and manageable;
- ongoing and focused.

Therefore, the information that you eventually record must be 'significant'.

The following points may help you to decide whether achievements are significant.

- **The child has demonstrated a skill for the first time.**
- **You feel the child has consolidated a concept after demonstrating proficiency on several occasions.**
- **The child has demonstrated clear understanding of a process, i.e. as a result of a problem-solving activity.**
- **The achievement may be significant for one particular child and should be defined for that child. For example, a child with speech and language difficulties may initiate a conversation with his peers for the first time.**
- **It involves talking with children about their achievements. Do they feel they are significant too?**
- **If it is truly a significant achievement, there will be implications for the planning of future teaching and learning opportunities for that child.**

Section 5: celebrating children's achievements

The *Curriculum Guidance for the Foundation Stage* recognises that in the Early Years children do not neatly compartmentalise aspects of their learning. For them, learning is connected, interrelated and centred around the 'here and now' of real life, practical experiences. In order to plan and meet individual needs effectively it is important to consider children's all-round progress in:

- intellectual development;
- physical development;
- social development;
- emotional development.

This means that record keeping will not be limited to academic progress alone but over time will build an accurate picture of the whole child. Through your assessment and recording processes you should have a clear idea of the level of knowledge, skills and understanding across the range of developmental areas.

Portfolios/records of achievement

In addition to teachers' records many Foundation Stage settings keep individual portfolios of work, sometimes called records of achievement, to demonstrate children's achievements across this broad range. These are ongoing records which are added to throughout the year. Care needs to be taken to ensure that they serve the purpose intended and do not become merely a collection of work produced by the child over a period of time. Criteria must be agreed within the setting for the selection of pieces, but may include:

- a significant achievement;
- a significant event, i.e. a trip, concert, birth of a sibling;
- evidence of personal qualities;
- evidence of preferred learning styles;
- evidence of particular interests and special aptitudes;
- favourite pieces selected by the child.

Such a portfolio, which celebrates progress and provides an ongoing record of what the child can do, needs to be shared. Bringing parents into the picture to view the portfolio is a powerful way to involve them in their child's learning from the earliest stages. All parents enjoy looking at work produced by their child and this provides a good starting point for discussion about progress, strengths, weaknesses and future targets.

Portfolios also encourage the child to take an interest and responsibility for self-assessment leading to the development of the key life-long learning skills of:

- ownership;
- organisation;
- decision making;
- personal choices;
- active v. passive learning;
- pride;
- communication;
- thinking skills;
- target setting.

What to include in a portfolio

Portfolios offer a creative way of recording progress and can contain a range of evidence including such things as:

Photographs	Responses to…	Drawings and paintings
Observation notes/ transcripts	Audio or video tapes	Investigations
Targets	Problem solving	Favourite books and book characters
Emergent writing	Friendships	Certificates or good news notes

By encouraging children to reflect on the learning process from the earliest stage of their education they begin to understand:

- **how they learn best;**
- **the processes and concepts involved;**
- **the strategies that help them;**
- **how others can support their learning;**
- **how to set targets and goals for themselves;**
- **self-motivation and a desire to succeed.**

Conclusion

Through the chapter I hope to have convinced you that monitoring, assessment, recording and reporting need not be dreaded, time consuming activities teachers put up with in return for the pleasure of working with young children.

In fact they are active components to successful, quality teaching and learning environments. Without constant evaluation and review how can we be sure we have planned future learning objectives which are appropriate to the needs of the children in our care and will move them on?

Recording and reporting also appear more manageable when we realise that others, namely parents, teaching assistants and the child, all have a valuable part to play in the process. It helps to view the package of monitoring, assessment, recording and reporting as a supportive tool-kit to assist you in fulfilling your core purpose of providing a learning environment in which young children can thrive academically, socially and emotionally.

> All children should be given the opportunity to experience the very best possible start to their education. We need to ensure that our children enter school having established solid foundations on which they can build. This will help to ensure that they continue to flourish throughout their school years and beyond.
> (Hodge, 2000)

Monitoring, assessment, recording, reporting and accountability:

a summary of key points

- *Be clear about the terminology of assessment.*
- *Have a clear focus for your assessments and understand why you are carrying out particular assessments.*
- *Remember the role of others in the assessment process, e.g. teaching assistants, parents.*
- *Ensure the outcomes of your assessments are reflected in your planning. Consider the impact of assessment on the quality of the teaching and learning opportunities you provide.*

——— *When recording assessment outcomes, keep it manageable and focused by remembering the importance of 'significant information'.*

——— *Recognise your achievements and those of your pupils by positively celebrating success and progress at all levels.*

Further reading

Wintle, M. and Harrison, M. (1999) *Co-ordinating Assessment Practice across the Primary School.* London. Falmer Press. Primarily for assessment co-ordinators but full of good practical ideas which keep children at the centre of the process.

Hutchin, V. (1999) *Right from the Start – Effective Planning and Assessment in the Early Years.* London. Hodder and Stoughton. Good practical advice on planning, assessment and record keeping, well illustrated with case studies.

Cleave, S. and Brown, S. (1992) *Early to School – Four Year Olds in Infant Classes.* London. Routledge. A useful book for Reception class teachers covering a whole range of topics, including a chapter on monitoring and recording progress.

Macintyre, C. (2001) *Enhancing Learning through Play.* London. David Fulton. Highlights the learning potential of play and helps the practitioner to understand and recognise the various stages of children's development.

By the end of this chapter you should:

- *understand what the idea of an effective teacher means in the Early Years context;*
- *see how effectiveness is a quality that is achieved through the Professional Standards for QTS;*
- *have an idea of ways of building your own style of effective teaching;*
- *be able to map out a personal plan by building a portfolio.*

Professional Standards

Achieving the new Professional Standards will make you an effective teacher. **All of the Standards contribute towards your effectiveness**. But your path of learning to this achievement will not be the same as your colleagues' or friends'. You will naturally be competent in some areas, while in others you will find the process more difficult. This is perfectly normal. The award of Qualified Teacher Status is not the end of the learning process – rather it is still the beginning. You will need support, mentoring, training, development, praise and time for reflection along the way.

The standards cover three main areas: **professional values and practice, knowledge and understanding**, and **teaching**. They detail a range of essential knowledge and expertise, laying particular emphasis on:

- subject knowledge;
- understanding of the high standards expected of pupils;
- the principles and practice of entitlement and inclusion for all pupils;
- planning and teaching with clear objectives and setting pupil targets;
- the core pedagogic skills of interactive teaching, differentiation and assessment for learning;
- principles and practice in the Foundation Stage;
- the National Strategies in Key Stages 1, 2 and 3;
- effective class organisation and behaviour management;
- support for pupils with special educational needs and those learning English as an additional language.

As previously, the new standards are accompanied by a Handbook of non-statutory guidance and exemplification. This is designed as a reference document setting out in greater detail the range of professional knowledge and skills relevant to each of the standards. You will find it useful to make reference to this in order to develop in the most effective way. So, in the twenty-first century the newly qualified teacher has more guidance and direction than ever before on the elements of good quality teaching. How to translate this into practical, sustained effectiveness is the question.

It is not the intention of this chapter to examine all the Standards in detail, for many Standards have been covered in previous chapters. I am more concerned with exploring the *idea* of effectiveness — a quality that is not only gained through achieving the standards but which is also enhanced by **the teaching and learning styles** of individual teachers. I am constantly fascinated by the way teachers teach. As a headteacher I never ceased to be impressed by the quality of the dedication, skill and commitment of busy teachers making a fantastic difference to the lives of the children they taught, by simply being effective. First, let's look at **teaching**.

Two of the significant Standards in this respect are:

1.1 in which teachers show that they have **high expectations** of the children they teach, respecting the diverse backgrounds and unique circumstances of every child and demonstrating a commitment to raising their achievement in every way;

2.1a in which teachers must demonstrate that they have 'a **secure knowledge** and understanding' both of the subjects they are required to teach and of the Foundation curriculum. This includes the aims, principles, six areas of learning and the early learning goals.

Without expert knowledge it is impossible to be effective. Now let's look at **learning:**

1.7 in which teachers must demonstrate their levels of motivation to achieve and to take responsibility, to demonstrate their ability to improve their own practice by self-evaluation, learning from others, from professional development, and from research. The degree to which you commit to achievement, self-improvement and professional development will directly affect your effectiveness as a teacher.

These Standards reflect a teaching style which is able to cater for every child, and which is effective in raising standards through having high expectations. The learning style is evident from the reflective nature of **1.7** enhanced by the *same commitment for improvement*. Note how **1.7** has strong similarities with the set of five competences that emerged from international research conducted by the Organisation for Economic Co-operation and Development (OECD):

- **knowledge of substantive curriculum areas and content;**
- **pedagogic skill, including the acquisition of and ability to use a repertoire of teaching strategies;**
- **reflection and the ability to be self-critical, the hallmark of teacher professionalism;**
- **empathy and the commitment to the acknowledgement of the dignity of others;**
- **managerial competence, as teachers assume a range of managerial responsibilities within and beyond the classroom.** (OECD, 1994)

Knowledge of teaching and learning

Implicit in these standards is **knowledge** and understanding: knowledge of the process of teaching, the subject base, the children and the learning process, as well as knowledge of self. As Smith (1994:109) declares, teachers need:

> knowledge and understanding of the teaching and learning processes, how to develop appropriate contexts, strategies and interactions which stimulate learning and development and subject-matter knowledge.

The word **knowledge** figures extensively in the Standards. Teachers must have knowledge of child development, knowledge of the Foundation curriculum and the National Curriculum for KS1, knowledge of appropriate teaching strategies and classroom management. The teaching of knowledge to children tends to be measurable. It is enabling children to acquire skills and inculcating desirable attitudes in them that makes defining effectiveness difficult. The theme of the knowledge base of effective teaching is argued expertly by many writers (Turner-Bisset, 2001).

This is undeniably the pursuit of excellence, which is twofold. Firstly the practice of the teacher becomes more expert and secondly the teacher, through the learning process, achieves personal and professional growth. The interface between learning and teaching becomes dynamic.

Defining effectiveness

The outstanding concept in this chapter is **effectiveness.** It is a popular term, much vaunted by researchers and writers in education. But it is interesting to realise that the majority of the research in recent years has been into *school* effectiveness rather than that of the teacher. Yet all teachers aspire to be effective in the classroom. It is what they aim for — it is what they expect and work hard to achieve. For consider the other side of the coin. What if teachers were not effective? What then? The picture emerges of children not making progress, not playing, working or interacting well, and perhaps not happy. Everyone would be well aware of what was going wrong. So are we equally aware of what is going right in the classrooms of young children?

Teachers of young children, as Edwards and Knight (1994) stress, have 'one of the most important and most difficult of educational jobs'. This job of teaching encompasses a set of skills, knowledge and understanding that is both wide and complex. The array of competencies, conditions, characteristics of good teaching, should I attempt to list them all, would be too lengthy for this chapter and, moreover, distinguished writers and researchers have already done so elsewhere (see Hay McBer, 2000).

Distinguished authors help when we strive to formulate definitions of effectiveness, for the word currently has high profile on the national agenda. LEAs as well as schools must demonstrate and be accountable for their effectiveness, and teachers must do so in the annual round of performance management. So what can help the new or inexperienced teacher define what it actually means?

MacGilchrist et al (1997:39) offer this definition:

> Effective teaching is comprised of a set of interrelated skills, knowledge and understanding in the mind of the teacher that interact with the skills, knowledge and understanding in the minds of pupils, to enable effective learning and high achievement to occur.

The **quality of the interaction** between teacher and child and the **emphasis on the learning** that takes place is what identifies the effective teacher.

Teachers are highly trained people but individual effectiveness is a quality that is sometimes difficult to define. Why? The reason is that effectiveness can only be judged to exist in actual teaching and learning situations and that these are as individual as human beings themselves.

> British school effectiveness research has increasingly been showing that the range of variation *within* schools dwarfs the range of variation between schools and that the influence of the teacher and of the learning level considerably exceeds that of the school'.
> (Muijs and Reynolds, 2001:ix)

Being an effective teacher

The art of being a teacher entails a myriad of exchanges with the child in a complex social setting in which the teacher seeks to motivate the children, organise activity, present information and stimuli, and provide security within which the child may learn. This is not a simple task! Consider this quotation from Turner-Bisset:

> Teaching is such a complex job that typically one is using a number of skills simultaneously, for example, choosing words carefully, listening to what children say, scanning the class to pre-empt order problems, and making mental notes for future action.
> (Turner-Bisset, 2001:160)

Certainly good teaching is 'a complex, highly skilled activity requiring judgments on how to act' (O'Hara, 2000:vii), or as Wragg puts it:

> Experienced teachers engage in hundreds of exchanges every single day of their career, thousands in a year, millions over a professional lifetime. Teaching consists of dozens of favoured strategies that become embedded in deep structures, for there is no time to re-think every single move in a busy classroom.
> (Wragg, 2001:vii)

What the new teacher needs to develop is the right choice of strategies within the boundaries of the Standards framework, which prove to be effective *for that teacher*, so that, above all, the children learn at an optimum pace, grow and develop confidently towards reaching their potential, achieving with pride the targets set before them.

Practical task

- *What 'favoured strategies' have you begun to form?*
- *On what basis are they your favourites?*
- *What links do they have with the Standards framework?*

Principles for Early Years education

In the document from DfEE/QCA entitled *Curriculum Guidance for the Foundation Stage* the following principles are set out and are 'evident in good and effective early years settings'. I have summarised them for you.

Principles for Early Years education

- *Effective education requires both a relevant curriculum and practitioners who understand and are able to implement the curriculum requirements.*
- *Effective education requires practitioners who understand that children develop rapidly during the Early Years – physically, intellectually, emotionally and socially.*
- *Practitioners should ensure that all children feel included.*
- *Early years experience should build on what children already know and can do.*
- *No child should be excluded or disadvantaged.*
- *Parents and practitioners should work together.*
- *To be effective, an Early Years curriculum should be carefully structured to include three strands: provision for children's different starting points, relevant and appropriate content, planned and purposeful activity.*
- *There should be opportunities for children to engage in activities planned by adults and also those that they plan or initiate themselves.*
- *Practitioners must be able to observe and respond appropriately to children.*
- *Well-planned, purposeful activity and appropriate intervention by practitioners will engage children in the learning process.*
- *For children to have rich and stimulating experiences, the learning environment should be well planned and well organised.*
- *Above all, effective learning and development for young children requires high-quality care and education by practitioners.*

With the principles above in mind, consider what elements of effectiveness are evident in the following story. Think about those three elements of *professional values and practice*, *knowledge and understanding* and *teaching*. What evidence can you spot of these elements? What styles of teaching are implicit in the information? What values and attitudes are being developed in the children and communicated to the parents? What are your impressions?

Classroom story

Mrs P, Reception class teacher, is welcoming the children into her classroom in the morning. The room is richly displayed, steeped in stimuli in the form of books, artefacts, labels and artwork. The children come in with whoever has brought them, and immediately go to the library book boxes to change the book that they have enjoyed or shared at home the previous evening. Parents and carers have the opportunity to share in the book choosing session.

Mrs P is chatting informally with parents, dealing with news and a few matters that need attention. Mrs R, the teaching assistant, is keeping a watchful eye on Chloe, who is feeling insecure, and invites her to look at the glass case where pupae are nearly ready to transform into butterflies. While distracted, Chloe's mum leaves, but the head teacher is outside the door, ready for a tearful mum with words of reassurance. More children gravitate towards the butterfly tank, as the excitement of an imminent event spreads.

Sanjit and Leanne ask if they can use the computer for a little while on the program about life cycles, which includes butterflies, and a lively conversation ensues, attracting eager onlookers. Meanwhile, the rest of the children settle down on the carpet, having parted from mums, dads and carers, ready to start the day. An argument breaks out in the group round the computer. Mrs P remains calm, and without raising her voice calls the children over, but two children linger. She starts a singing rhyme that they have been learning this week, and the music and rhythm bring the attention of the children together. Words related to the rhyme are on a board at the children's level, and art work related to the theme has been displayed the previous evening.

By the end of the rhyme there is an expectant hush. People look over at the lingerers who become aware of their lateness. Mrs P reminds them of the expectation that they shall do as they are asked first time. The children look crestfallen, but only for a little while as the now complete class take turns to discuss the long awaited emergence of the butterflies, prompted with sensitive and searching questions from their teacher.

This is a true story, repeated in infinite variations throughout the year. The atmosphere is one of calm, trust, security, respect, firm expectation, enjoyment, excitement and rest. This is the style of one highly effective Early Years teacher, whose children developed in both confidence and ability. The caring attitudes formed in this young class, this sense of purpose and quality, formed the foundation of the other classes as these children grew older.

Knowledge of the child

First and foremost the teacher must have effective **knowledge of the child**, for as Bruce (1997:v) emphasises,

> Unless we know and understand our children, unless we act effectively on what we know, we cannot help them very much.

The first eight years of life are fundamental to the child's development. The child comes to learn who they are, about those people upon whom they depend, and they become aware of their world. They begin to learn to absorb meaning, to participate, to create by exercising their fertile imaginations. They learn to co-operate, to share and they begin to work together. They learn to use their senses, their skills and their emotions. They learn through the physical activity of their bodies and through first-hand experience. They learn best when this rich diversity is shaped thoughtfully, carefully and sensitively by expert teachers and other adults, with the gift of knowing what interventions, explanations and directions will be effective at any particular moment. They learn best within a stimulating and challenging environment created by the teacher in such a way as to reflect the learning needs and interests of the children. They learn best when the high expectations of those around them are communicated in a positive, caring way, so that the child believes s/he *can* learn and revels in that knowledge.

Conditions such as these for learning have been depicted in a deliberately idealistic way in order to establish an easily identifiable goal in the mind of the developing teacher. Teachers should avoid the element of complacency, which stultifies development. Complacency at any stage of education is the enemy of effectiveness and high quality, and must be avoided.

Putting the ladder up against the right wall

Effectiveness means that the effort being made contributes to achieving the school's goal. It is the nature of goals that they are true to the values, aims and principles of the organisation, whether they originate from the outside, such as government legislation or community needs, or from within the school's particular philosophy. It means that the strategies employed in teaching bring about quality learning in the child. It also means knowing the extent to which this is happening, to which I shall return later. It means that when you feel you are making progress you must be sure that the ladder that you are climbing is up against the right wall.

The 'right wall' must be built upon what is right for the young child within the context of the philosophy and values of the school. The pre-conditions for Early Years education are well founded. The entitlement of the child to a broad and balanced Early Years curriculum in a safe and stimulating environment must be understood. Through much debate the curriculum has been through frequent revisions to achieve consistent quality for all. Agencies that have responsibility for the care and education of the young constantly strive to underline this very fact. Much attention has been given to the needs of children in several Acts of Parliament, e.g. The Children's Act (1989) and successive Education Acts from 1986 onwards, so that there is a well-defined framework of standards and expectations within which each teacher must work.

Learning styles

There is, moreover, no single way to teach because there is no single way to learn. As we know more and more about the way learners learn, the more we realise that one size cannot fit all. To understand the meaning of 'effective teacher' we have to understand what makes for effective learning, for both are inextricably linked.

The teacher must have knowledge of the different learning styles that children naturally display. There are many books on the subject, and one of the most accessible of these is by Shaw and

Hawes (1998) in which they summarise not only the various types of learning styles – visual, auditory, kinesthetic – but also multiple intelligences, brain mapping, and the way that teaching styles can be adapted to meet these factors. There can hardly be a more significant development in pedagogic theory than these ideas. Within the theory we come to understand why one child cannot sit still, why another is so predisposed to writing, why yet another learns better through using their hands. Teachers always knew the differences existed but new research, made possible by medical advances whereby the living brain can be examined in detail without damage, now provides us with answers.

Practical task

Watch how children use their eyes when they think. Eyes swivelled to the right indicates imagining, to the left signifies remembering.

Eyes up signifies an image, eyes level – a sound, eyes down means accessing feelings.

Being child-centred

When beginning to unravel the expectations of effectiveness the wise teacher starts with the child. We know that good teaching can only be judged by the extent and the quality of the learning that it brings about. The true curriculum, after all, is not always that which is planned, it is *what the child receives in actuality* and this is what Ofsted inspectors look for. MacGilchrist et al (1997:34) interviewed many youngsters in a number of schools about their views on their school experience. What they have to say about the child's viewpoint is, in my opinion, a useful starting point:

> Their answers to questions about how they learn are almost always the same
> whatever their age. They say they learn best with teachers who:
>
> - explain things well;
> - listen to them and are concerned about them as an individual;
> - show them how to get better;
> - keep control of the class;
> - have a sense of humour.

The simplicity of this is refreshing and I suggest that we never forget how much simpler the child's viewpoint is than ours and that, no matter how complex our intentions or professional knowledge, we must never lose sight of the child's expectations of what their education should involve. The younger the child, the more important this advice becomes.

It is interesting to compare the list above with the findings of the research by Hay McBer consultants, commissioned by the government to define teacher effectiveness (Hay McBer, 2000). As has been mentioned before, teacher effectiveness is linked to children's learning, or pupil progress, the extent to which effective teachers make a difference to their pupils, of whatever age or stage of development. They found three main factors within teachers' control that significantly affected the extent to which children progressed:

- **teaching skills;**
- **professional characteristics;**
- **classroom climate.**

Here we have distinct but interrelated areas upon which the developing teacher should reflect. It is the combination of these areas that 'provide valuable tools for a teacher to enhance the progress of their pupils'. What follows in the research report by Hay McBer is a detailed breakdown of these areas into micro-behaviours, characteristics of professional roles, and dimensions of classroom climate for our consideration. The report aims to simplify the complexity of the descriptors, to identify the most useful links that could be made between them and to produce a model of teacher effectiveness that could be used for professional development and career advancement at all stages of teaching. Its **dictionary of characteristics** encompasses a number of attributes grouped under headings:

- *Professionalism*: **challenge and support; confidence; creating trust; respect for others;**
- *Thinking*: **analytical thinking; conceptual thinking;**
- *Planning and setting expectations*: **drive for improvement; information seeking;**

[handwritten: Reflective Practice to read. E2]

...countable; managing pupils; passion for

...e; teamworking; understanding others.

...h teachers can enhance the difference that they make
...according to the report, for, as Croll and Hastings

...nakes a difference to the classroom experiences
...hrough these, to the outcomes of education.

[handwritten: Creative Chap 1 & 4]

...y meets the standards set but exceeds them in a style
...the child on his or her journey of learning and growth.

...ist et al (1997) for me captures the essence of the
...hese high expectations, this raising of self-esteem, the
...ished:

> The job of the school is: to motivate the learner; to encourage her or him to learn; to help the learner to understand how to learn; and to **believe it is possible** to do so.

'Know thyself' – teacher self-knowledge

But the effective Early Years teacher must match their knowledge of early childhood education and his or her knowledge of the child with **self-knowledge** as a professional – that ability to reflect and evaluate those characteristics and behaviours in order to refine them, improve them, so that they more critically match the learning needs of the children. Knowing when and how to intervene, knowing what to say, and in what tone of voice, can form a critical moment of learning for a child, a moment that can be truly captivating and rewarding for all. Take this description from Dunne and Wragg (1994:5), for example:

> When children learn something, there is often a magical quality about the excitement of discovery, the warmth of regard between teacher and taught or the novelty to the learner of what is taking place and the romanticism seems to be destroyed if teaching is seen as too deliberate, calculated, manipulated or over analysed.

The word 'magical' rarely if ever appears in official documentation to do with education, but every good Early Years teacher can identify with it readily. It is an important word referring to a moment of time, both exciting and significant, in the life of the child. The inspiration of such a moment is what drives many teachers to come to school every day, and the rewards of which far outweigh the usual positive factors in teaching. It earmarks the time when teachers really do feel that they have contributed to something significant, something worthy, proof that they have indeed made a difference.

> Good or bad lessons generate feelings: in good lessons those of euphoria, excitement, relief, satisfaction, hope; in bad lessons or those that do not 'go well', feelings of sadness, guilt, disappointment or even despair.
> (Turner-Bisset, 2001:109)

Teaching is hard work. Teaching very young children is demanding and challenging.

> Teaching as a job involves a huge investment of the self.
> (Turner-Bisset, 2001:109)

There really can be no effectiveness without the commitment of effort, and the sheer physical needs of young children demand that their teachers have plenty of energy!

The 'e' factors – what to bring to the classroom

The word *effort* brings me finally to some ideas for effectiveness that were first devised by Handy (1990:25). He suggested that motivation of employees depended upon the extent they were prepared to expend what he called **e-factors**, e.g. **energy, enthusiasm, excitement, effort, emotion.** I have found that this theory works exceedingly well in schools in terms of motivating all staff and children alike. There is nothing quite so infectious as enthusiasm. Learning is an exciting, emotional experience as well as an intellectual one. Teaching is hard work, it takes great commitment, energy and effort. It could be said that without the expenditure of such factors, the work done by any teacher could hardly be effective. Imagine a lesson taught in a lacklustre way, without enthusiasm, without excitement, unemotional, and with a tired countenance. Maybe we can remember being on the receiving end of such lessons ourselves encountering a dull teacher, but in the Early Years classroom? It is unthinkable in today's world where quality and accountability drive the education system inexorably towards improvement.

I suggest that the effective teacher already displays these e-factors and some more besides, such as: expertise, empathy, empowerment, enjoyment, encouragement, enquiry, ethos, evaluation, esteem, expectations and excellence. These words do appear in Hay McBer's report from time to time, but I feel that they are particularly important to the standards of effectiveness in the Early Years classroom.

Enthusiasm is infectious and generates positive attitudes in young children, who easily absorb its power. Enthusiasm drives out doubt and wavering, which is especially important in terms of adult assistants or helpers in the classroom. It can get people on board, carry them along and empower them through its motivating power:

> the more emotion attached to any experience the more memorable it becomes. Children learn most effectively (and remember more) when teaching engages their emotions.
> (Shaw and Hawes, 1998:15)

What we can learn about **emotional intelligence** (Goleman, 1996, 1998) will give the teacher a deeper understanding of the child especially in relation to the way the child handles anger and frustration.

Exciting lessons are the ones children most remember. The cutting edge that it gives to the learning outcomes is invaluable. In terms of the quality *impact and influence*, a teacher capable of creating exciting lessons is guaranteed to achieve both in full measure.

Practical task

Try asking Year 6 children what their earliest memories of starting school are, and note the type and characteristics of the events they remember. Also try asking your colleagues/fellow students.

Shaw and Hawes (1998:14) advise the teacher to connect into children's values:

> what will be exciting enough to compel attention, what will they consider interesting and important?

Most of us know when children display over-excitement, which can be a most unhelpful state for learning. So how can we be sure that the right level of excitement has been reached and that it can be safely controlled? Perhaps a better term for excitement would be **involvement** in terms of everyday activities. A useful guideline for assessing the children's levels of involvement has been devised by Laevers (1994) and these include *concentration, energy, creativity, facial expression and posture, persistence, precision, quick reactions, language, satisfaction.* Young children who are not only on task but displaying such levels of involvement could be said to be learning in that crucial proximal zone of development (Vygotsky) where learning is advanced.

Expertise

This encompasses the capacity for analytical and conceptual thinking. Knowledge of both the self as a teacher and of the children as learners is central to becoming an expert teacher. It means knowing one's subject area, knowing and understanding how the children learn, and it means knowing one's own strengths and weaknesses. Turner-Bisset's excellent book on expert teaching

(2001) gives a thorough discussion of the notion of the expert teacher. The teacher has to be thoroughly trained, informed and empowered in order to deliver the Early Years curriculum, and I would emphasise that this process is ongoing. Expertise makes us think especially of the craft of teaching, whereby the microbehaviours outlined in Hay McBer's *Teaching Skills* (Hay McBer, 2000) are refined and developed, such as the techniques for gaining order and quiet, the techniques for getting children to listen, stop and start. The techniques for establishing class routines, principles of fairness and respect.

Many of these techniques involve being able to **explain** concepts and activities to young children in a way that they can understand. Wragg (2001) expresses it well:

> The ability to explain clearly is a vital human talent, recognised and appreciated as such by children as young as two or three … At the beginning of a lesson, a teacher will often spend five or ten minutes setting up what may be an hour's, a day's, a week's or even a term's work, so time invested in establishing or improving the ability to explain is time well spent. Badly handled, this setting up phase may be followed by mayhem, as children, uncertain what they are supposed to do, or why they should do it, resort to asking one another, improvising or simply hoping the teacher will explain the task once more. Well conducted, however, a good explanation or introduction can motivate a class very effectively.
> Wragg (2001:1)

It is such a basic technique, explaining, and perhaps it is taken for granted. There is a great need for all teachers, not just those in Early Years classrooms, to reflect critically upon their techniques of exposition and explaining. Too many assumptions abound that the children 'must have understood'. Too many teachers just repeat themselves. Too few teachers take the time to find out how much of their explanations the child has understood. The waste of a child's time as s/he wanders aimlessly round the classroom looking for reassurance or clarification is one of the most damning indicators of an ineffective teacher.

Practical task

Tape record yourself working with children. Note the quality of your explanations. Watch for repetitions. If you find yourself repeating yourself, ask why? Was the repetition effective or did it just fill a gap? How did you deal with questions and interruptions?

Teach young children that they 'can do', give them confidence, autonomy and praise, make them responsible for simple tasks and trust them to perform them early on, with the expectation that they will meet the trust put in them.

I encourage the children in my class to believe in themselves as capable learners by:

- celebrating success;
- showing them that I value their work and achievements;
- taking every opportunity to acknowledge and identify progress;
- being very clear in my own mind that I believe in them as learners;

- raising self-esteem and encouraging self-evaluation;
- ensuring that each child knows the learning purpose of a lesson, and has a sense of how far it has been accomplished.

(Shaw and Hawes, 1998:18)

The expression of these principles in day-to-day teaching practice builds up the positive and caring ethos of the classroom. Though felt intrinsically, empowerment principles need to be expressed repeatedly for young children so that they come to expect and believe in them.

The teacher's enquiring mind

An effective teacher will ascertain as much information about the children in his or her class as possible. Social and family background, learning styles, friendship patterns, stages of development all contribute to the detailed profile which informs the teacher's planning, delivery and evaluation.

But in particular an effective teacher goes on learning, developing, refining their skills. The world is rapidly changing, and nothing more so than the explosion of information communication technology. One of the greatest threats to effectiveness these days is the admission that teachers are lacking in proficiency in this area, to the extent that children can be more proficient than their teachers, even in Reception classes!

The effective teacher continues to learn. S/he must continue to learn, or admit to complacency. Children are entitled to an education that evolves to meet their changing needs and this demands that, however tiring the job may be, continuing professional development is a necessity. This, moreover, demonstrates the skill of lifelong learning, providing a vital role model for the children, which animates them and keeps them young.

Evaluation

The developing teacher will find that evaluation is a process that can make or break the drive for high quality in effective teaching. It can break it if it is not conducted thoroughly, if it is not conducted regularly, if it is not conducted fairly and honestly. Teachers often bemoan the time taken for evaluation, yet without a system of evaluating, how can the outcomes of what has taken place in teaching and learning be other than a 'gut reaction'? I would refer readers to a research project named EEL – the *Effective Early Learning: An Action Plan for Change* (Pascal and Bertram, 1997). The authors argue that of all professional tools, evaluation is the most powerful when aiming to build quality Early Years provision:

> our experience has shown that to lay down precise, fixed, static definitions of quality is inappropriate. Rather, we have found that evaluation is more powerful, accurate and valid if it grows out of the shared and agreed perspective of those who are closest to the experiences being assessed.
> (Pascal and Bertram, 1997:7)

The authors conceptualise the process of evaluation within a framework answering the questions, *what, when, where, why* and *who?* I suggest that it is a useful device when faced with a bewildering task. It provides ten dimensions to which the teacher can relate, and these dimensions also provide useful headings for school improvement.

Classroom values and ethos

Effective teachers have classes of young children whose self-esteem is not dented by sarcasm or irritation. The ethos of the classroom heralds mutual respect, children feel trusted and feel that they will be heard when they want to voice their feelings. The teacher understands that the child wants to make sense of the world and is patient while this immensely valuable process emerges.

> Finding ways of teaching very young children that are going to result in positive
> feelings is one of the most important jobs we have as Early Years educators.
> (Ouvry, 2000:9)

Practical task

If you want to know what the ethos of a school is like, watch the beginnings and endings of the school day, and see how the children and their parents and carers act. Stop for a minute, the first time that you enter a school building and, using your senses, try to 'feel' what the school is like. Most people can detect a positive or negative feeling the minute they enter the main door.

In the classroom the ethos is clear from the visual clues as well as the way the children behave when they are working, or getting ready to go out to play. But one of the most telling ways is after the children have gone home. Stand in the classroom, very still and just soak up the atmosphere and look closely and critically at what meets your eyes. What does it say to you about the kind of class and the kind of teacher that works there? Is it saying what you want it to say?

Excellence

Children deserve the best that we as educators can offer. They deserve the highest quality, the best teachers, they need well-resourced and clearly organised classrooms. They deserve the best treatment, consideration and care. They need adults and teachers who are committed to them, who will 'go the extra mile' for them and who value the best in Early Years education. They need schools where the culture exalts the Early Years, where, if teachers are moved to teach there they do not refer to being 'moved down'. They need the highest quality of safety in their environment as well as stimulation through a sufficient variety of play materials. Young children need calmness and continuity. They need to feel that they know where they belong and that the school belongs to them. An early sense of pride in their own achievements teaches them what excellence really means and gives them an appetite for more. Consider this story, in which the teacher makes effective use of the **environment.**

Classroom story

Mrs T is taking her class on a regular trip to the local country park in order to do some experiential work on the seasons. Although it is early spring and still cold, the children are well prepared with stout outdoor wear and wellington boots.

Several mothers have offered to accompany the class and help to transport them the short distance to the park. The children are excited, naturally! But they are well versed in firm expectations for good behaviour, which is monitored carefully by the high number of adults. Mrs T talks to the children again, reminding them of all that they have done previously in the classroom on signs of spring, the shape of winter trees, blustery skies and the names of wildlife. Clutching bags for collecting fallen 'treasures' and a tiny sketchbook for a quick sketch, the children move off … each eager to be the first to spot a magpie, or a grey squirrel!

Back at school for dinner time, the children are breathless, excited and rosy cheeked. There is much stamping of feet and fussy removal of hats and coats. They call out to other children and the caretaker about where they have just been and what they have seen, but soon order prevails and they are mustered onto the carpet for some quiet but delighted reflection of their expedition.

In the afternoon Mrs T organises a variety of activities to suit the needs and abilities of her children – they use paint or pastel to create stunning impressions of dark trees, they write freely, they discuss, they find out more from books or the computer. Everyone seems more happily excitedly focused than is usual for a blowy, grey, March day …

Building your portfolio

Another requirement that is being increasingly demanded these days is the Personal Professional Portfolio. It is a requirement for newly qualified teachers to demonstrate the steps being taken to develop their career entry profiles. It is a requirement for teachers applying to go through the threshold. It is not beyond the bounds of possibility that soon the requirement will be right across the profession. The benefits of such a portfolio are in the reflection of achievements made by the teacher during her or his career.

Photographs, evidence of children's progress, details of courses taken and other professional development, the ways in which professional responsibilities have been undertaken, plus creative ideas all contribute to the ability of the teacher. It is an effective tool in itself. It sometimes amazes teachers when they compile all that they have achieved and of course it is invaluable to present such information at job/promotion interviews. Most of all it raises your self-esteem.

There is guidance available from the DfES about portfolio-building.

Be a reflective practitioner

The effective teacher will learn when her or his batteries are low. S/he understands the need for self-renewal and for balance in life, what Covey (1989) calls 'sharpening the saw'. In other words, if we want to cut a piece of wood, it is ineffective to do so with a blunt tool. So it is with the working life of teachers – without time for reflection, relaxation and self-renewal, the tool with which we seek to hone the cutting edge of effectiveness soon becomes dull and weak. Effective school leaders recognise this and strive to make some headway to provide thinking and reflection time for their teachers against the tide of the constant urgent agenda for decision-making and reform.

Writing down your own thoughts is recommended by several writers (e.g. Bolton, 2001). Much as teachers are constantly thinking and planning, very little time is usually afforded for reflection. Teachers are very tired at the end of the day and staff meetings now have full agendas of information sharing and policy reform stretching away through the school year. Lunchtimes are frenetic and the modern teacher often hardly has time to draw breath. All the more reason, then, to strive to create some 'time out'. It cannot be overstressed that the act of writing is a cathartic, problem-solving tool much overlooked in today's busy world. However, the onset of e-learning and e-conferencing does provide another way. There is a growing number of online discussion groups in which teachers can share good practice and gain mutual support. The high tech nature of this will appeal to the young graduate who is no doubt proficient with e-mail and chat rooms. Although no replacement for the personal journal, it does provide a fertile ground for teacher development, reflection and learning.

Conclusion

Effectiveness in teaching is sometimes considered as a gift, but more often than not it is the result of systematic improvement, evaluation and reflection. Effectiveness is usually measured by the progress in learning made by the children in terms of targets met in the Early Years curriculum. But I suggest that this is not the whole picture. Effectiveness as far as young children are concerned, must include evidence of some of the other factors discussed in this chapter, such as esteem, excitement, excellence, and enjoyment. For high self-esteem is not easily measured in young children, yet its presence accelerates learning. Children learn particularly well when they are happy, when their needs are met and when purposeful activity offers them a challenge. Effective teaching provides evidence of all of these.

The effective practitioner is a developing professional who avoids complacency and seeks to improve her or his practice in the light of effective self-evaluation, whereby the unique collection of learning needs and potential of the children in the class is at the forefront of planning, delivery and review. It requires both skill and commitment, but also a drop of magic encased in a good sense of humour.

Moreover, effectiveness is readily identified by others. Where it occurs, it needs to be identified and praised, and then good practice should be shared in a sensitive way amongst other practitioners. This is best achieved in a school that could be deemed to be a **learning organisation**, in which *all* practitioners, including the head teacher, can be seen to embrace the lifelong learning ethic. The learning school adopts the principles expounded here, and seeks as a whole organisation to grow in its achievement of quality and effectiveness. To be in such a school affords the highest opportunities for learning as a teacher, because learning is seen as an end in itself. But that is another chapter.

What makes an effective Foundation Stage teacher?:
a summary of key points

- *Effectiveness is doing the right things, making the right choices, decisions in the knowledge that we are going in the desired direction which is right for the child, right for the school and which conforms to the thrust of legislation.*

- *Concentrate on achieving the Standards in order to achieve effectiveness.*

- *Know the children – know all that you can about them, their family background, their learning potential, their achievements, interests and emotional character.*

- *Deepen your knowledge of teaching by making reference to recent research, by personal reflection and by learning from the craft of other practitioners.*

- *Develop your own style as there is no single way to teach, remembering always that the true curriculum is that which the child receives. Understanding of the way children learn and the evaluation of the learning that they demonstrate is vital. It is the quality of the interaction between teacher and the young child with the emphasis on learning that is vital.*

- *Continue to learn as all schools are learning organisations.*

- *Create a personal Professional Development Portfolio -- it will enable you to reflect upon your own performance and growth as well as providing evidence of your success!*

Anning, A. and Edwards, A. (1999) *Promoting Children's Learning from Birth to Five*. Buckingham. Open University Press.

Association of Educational Psychologists (2001) *The Role and Functions of Educational Psychologists – an AEP response*. Durham

Aubrey, C. (1997) Children's early learning of number in school and out, in Thompson, I. (ed) *Teaching and Learning Early Number*. Buckingham. Open University Press.

Barnes, P. (ed.) (1997) *Personal, Social and Emotional Development of Children*. Buckingham. Open University Press.

Barriere, I., David, T., Gouch, K., Jago, M., Raban, B., Ure, C. (2000) *Making Sense of Literacy*. Stoke on Trent. Trentham Books.

BECTa/VTC Learning with ICT at the Foundation Stage. Available at www.curriculum.becta. org.uk/docserver.php?docid=2666

Bennet, N., Wood, E. and Rogers, S. (1997) *Teaching Through Play: Teachers' Thinking and Classroom Practice*. Buckingham. Open University Press.

Bielby, N. (1994) *Making Sense of Reading: The New Phonics and its Practical Implications*. Leamington Spa. Scholastic Publications Ltd.

Bilton, H. (1998) *Outdoor Play in the Early Years*. London. David Fulton.

Blenkin, G. M. and Kelly, A. V. (eds) (1996) *Early Childhood Education*. London. Paul Chapman.

Bolton, G. (2001) *Reflective Practice*. London. Paul Chapman Publishing.

Brown, M. in Wetton, P. (1997) op cit.

Browne, A. (1979) *Developing Language and Literacy, 3–8*. London. Paul Chapman.

Bruce, T. (1997) *Early Childhood Education*. 2nd edn. London. Hodder and Stoughton Education.

Bruce, T. and Meggitt, C. (1999) *Child Care and Education*. London. Hodder and Stoughton.

Bruner, J. (1980) *Under Five in Britain. The Oxford Pre-School Research Project*. Oxford. Grant McIntyre (Blackwell).

Bruner, J. (1981) What is representation?, in Roberts, M. and Taburrini, J. (eds) *Child Development 0–5*. Edinburgh. Holmes McDougall.

Bruner, J. S. (1983) *Childs's Talk: Learning to Use Language*. Oxford. Oxford University Press.

Bryant, P. E. and Bradley, L. (1985) *Children's Reading Problems*. Oxford. Basil Blackwell.

Cambourne, B. (1988) *Story – Natural Learning and the Acquisition of Literacy in the Classroom*. Sydney. Ashton Scholastic.

Cameron, C., Moss, P. and Owen, C. (1999) *Men in the Nursery: Gender and Caring Work*. London. Paul Chapman Publishing.

Campbell, J., Evans, L., Neill, S. and Packwood, A. (1993) The National Curriculum and the management of infant teachers' time, in Preedy, M. (ed) *Managing the Effective School*, London: Paul Chapman Publishing.

Caudrey, A. (1985) Volunteer army steps into the firing line. *TES*. 12 April: 8

Central Advisory Council for Education (1967) *Children and their Primary Schools*. (Plowden Report) London. HMSO.

Clark, M. in Tizard, B. (1974) *Pre-school Education in Great Britain: Research Review*. London. SSRC.

Clay, M. M. (1979) *The Early Detection of Reading Difficulties: A Diagnostic Survey*. Auckland. Heinemann Educational Books.

Collins, J., Hammond, M. and Wellington, J. (1997) *Teaching and Learning with Multimedia.* London. Routledge.

Cook, D. and Finlayson, H. (1999) *Interactive Children, Communicative Teaching.* Buckingham. Open University Press.

Covey, S. (1989) *The Seven Habits of Highly Effective People.* London. Simon and Schuster.

Croll, P. and Hastings, N. (1996) *Primary Teaching: Research-based Classroom Strategies.* London. David Fulton.

De Boo, M. (2000) *Science 3-6: Laying the Foundations in the Early Years.* Hatfield. ASE.

Department for Education and Science (1990) *Starting with Quality: A report of the committee of enquiry into the quality of educational experiences offered to 3–4 year olds.* (The Rumbold Report) London. HMSO.

Department of Education and Science (1986) *The Education Act.* London. HMSO.

Department of Education and Science (1988) *The Education Reform Act.* London. HMSO.

Department of Education and Science (1991) *The Parent's Charter. You and Your Child's Education.* London. HMSO.

Department of Health (1989) *The Children Act 1989. A New Framework for the Care and Upbringing of Children.* London. HMSO.

Department of Health (1991) *An Introduction to the Children Act.* London. HMSO.

DfE (1994) *Code of Practice on the Identification and Assessment of Special Educational Needs.* London. HMSO.

DfEE (1999) *All Our Futures: Creativity, Culture and Education.* Sudbury. National Advisory Committee on Creative and Cultural Education.

DfEE (2000) *Working with Teaching Assistants.* London. DfEE Publications.

DfEE (2000) *Draft Code and Guidance.* London. DfEE Publications.

DfEE/QCA (2000) *Curriculum Guidance for the Foundation Stage.* London. Qualifications and Curriculum Authority.

DfES (2002) *Useful Lessons Plans and Resources.* Available from: http://www.teachernet.gov.uk

Donahue, T. *Pedagogical Advantages of the Roamer.* (www.valiant-technology.com/)

Duffy, B. (1998) *Supporting Creativity and Imagination in the Early Years.* Buckingham. Open University Press.

Dunne, R. and Wragg, E. C. (1994) *Effective Teaching.* London. Routledge

Edwards, A. and Knight, P. (1994) *Effective Early Years Education: Teaching Young Children.* Buckingham. Open University Press.

Finch, J, (1984) *Education as Social Policy.* London. Longman.

Fisher, E. in Scrimshaw, P. (ed) (1993) *Language, Classrooms and Computers.* London. Routledge.

Gelman, R. and Gallistel, C. R. (1978) *The Child's Understanding of Number.* Cambridge, MA. Harvard University Press.

Goleman, D. (1996) *Emotional Intelligence: Why It Can Matter More than IQ.* London. Bloomsbury.

Goleman, D. (1998) *Working with Emotional Intelligence.* London. Bantam.

Goswami, U. (1993) Orthographic analogies and reading development. *The Psychologist.* July.

Goswami, U. and Bryant, P. (1992) *Rhyme Analogy and Children's Reading*, in Gough, P. B. et al (eds) *Reading Acquisition.* London. Lawrence Erlbaum Associates.

Griffiths, A. and Hamilton, D. (1984) *Parent, Teacher, Child: Working Together in Children's Learning.* London. Methuen.

Gulbenkian Report (1982) *The Arts in Schools: Principles, Practices and Provision*. London. Calouste Gulbenkian Foundation.

Hall, N. and Robinson, A. (1995) *Exploring Writing and Play in the Early Years*. London. David Fulton.

Handy, C. (1985) *Understanding Organisations*. London. Paul Chapman Publishing.

Handy, C. (1990) *Inside Organisations*. London. BBC.

Hardy, C. (2000) *Information and Communication Technology for All*. London. David Fulton.

Harlen, W. (2000) *The Teaching of Science in Primary Schools*. 3rd edn. London. David Fulton.

Hay McBer (2000) *Report into Teacher Effectiveness*, Report No 216 (www.dfee.gov.uk).

Hodge, M. (2000) in *Curriculum Guidance for the Foundation Stage*. London. Qualifications and Curriculum Authority.

Hohmann, M. and Weikart, D. P. (1995) *Educating Young Children*. Ypsolanti, MI. High/Scope Press.

Houghton, D. M. and McColgan, M. C. (1995) *Working with Children*. London. Collins Educational.

Hughes, M. (1986) *Children and Number*. Oxford. Blackwell.

Hughes. M. and Westgate, D. (1997) Teachers and other adults as talk partners in nursery and reception classes. *Education 3–13*. March.

Jacques, K. and Hyland, R. (eds) (2000) *Achieving QTS. Professional Studies: Primary Phase*. Exeter. Learning Matters.

Joy, A. M. (1994) *An Evaluation of Talking Pendown*. Unpublished MSc thesis, University of Southampton.

Laevers, F. (1994) *Defining and Assessing Quality in Early Childhood Education*. Leuven. Leuven Univeristy Press.

MacGilchrist, B., Myers, K. and Reed, J. (1997) *The Intelligent School*. London. Paul Chapman Publishing.

Maxted, P. (1999) *Understanding Barriers to Learning: A Guide to Research & Current Thinking*. London. Campaign For Learning.

Mayall, B. and Storey, P. (1998) A school health service for children. *Children and Society*. 12: 86–97.

Medwell, J. (1996) Talking books and reading. *Reading*. April:41–6.

Mercer, N. (1995) *The Guided Construction of Knowledge – Talk amongst Teachers and Learners*. Clevedon. Multilingual Matters Ltd.

Moyles, J. (ed) (1994). *The Excellence of Play*. Buckingham. Open University Press.

Muijs, D. and Reynolds, D. (2001) *Effective Teaching: Evidence and Practice*. London. Paul Chapman Publishing.

Munn, P (1997) Children's beliefs about counting, in Thompson, I. (ed) *Teaching And Learning Early Number*. Buckingham. Open University Press.

Munro, B. and Smith, I. (2000) *Making the Mouse Roar: Teaching for Effective Learning Using ICT*. (www.svtc.org.uk/mouse/)

Muter, V., Snowling, M. and Taylor, S. (1994) Orthographic and phonological awareness: their role and significance in early reading development. *Journal of Child Psychology and Psychiatry*, 35, 293–310.

Neaum, S. and Tallack, J. (1997) *Good Practice in Implementing the Pre-school Curriculum*. London. Stanley Thomas Ltd.

OECD (Centre for Educational Research and Innovation) (1994) *Making Education Count: Developing and Using International Indicators*. London. Organisation for Economic Co-operation and Development.

O'Hara, M. (2000) *Teaching 3–8: Meeting the Standards for Initial Teacher Training and Induction*. London. Continuum.

Ouvry, M. (2000) *Exercising Muscles and Minds : Outdoor Play and the Early Years Curriculum*. London. National Early Years Network.

Pascal, C. and Bertram, T. (1997) *Effective Early Learning: Case Studies in Improvement*. London. Paul Chapman Publishing.

Pascal, C. and Bertram, A. (1996) *Effective Early Learning Research Project*. Worcester. Amber Publishing Company.

Pugh, G. (ed) (1996) *Contemporary Issues in the Early Years: working collaboratively for children*. 2nd edn. London. National Children's Bureau.

Pugh, G. and De'Ath, E. (1989) *Working Towards Partnership in the Early Years*. London. National Children's Bureau.

Pugh, G., Aplin, G., De'Ath, E. and Moxon, M. (1987) *Partnership in Action: Working with Parents in Preschool Centres*, Volumes 1 and 2. London. National Children's Bureau.

Reay, D. (1998) *Class Work: Mothers' Involvement in their Children's Primary Schools*. London. UCL Press.

Rodger, R. (1999) *Planning an Appropriate Curriculum for the Under Fives*. London. David Fulton.

Roffey, S., O'Reirdon, T. (1998) *Infant Classroom Behaviour. Needs, Perspectives and Strategies*. London. David Fulton Publishers.

Rogers, C. R. (1983) *The Freedom to Learn in the 80's*. Columbus, OH. Merrill.

Schaffer, H. R. (1996). *Social Development*. Oxford. Blackwell.

Scrimshaw, P. (ed) (1993) *Language, Classrooms & Computers*. London. Routledge.

Select Committee on Education and Employment (2001) *First Report on Early Years*. London. Parliamentary Publications.

Sharp, J., Potter, J., Allen, J. and Loveless, A. (2000) *Primary ICT: Knowledge, Understanding and Practice*. Exeter. Learning Matters.

Shaw, S. and Hawes, T. (1998) *Effective Teaching and Learning in the Classroom*. Optimal Learning

Siraj-Blatchford, I. (ed) (1998) *A Curriculum Development Handbook for Early Childhood Educators*. Stoke on Trent. Trentham Books.

Smidt, S. (1998) *A Guide to Early Years Practice*. London. Routledge.

Smith, E. A. (1994) *Educating the Under-Fives*. London. Cassell.

Smith, H. (1999) *Opportunities for Information and Communication Technology in the Primary School*. Stoke-on-Trent. Trentham Books.

Smith, S. (1997) *Getting the Roamers out of the Cupboard*. MicroScope 50.

Snowling, M. J., Hulme, C., Smith, A. and Thomas, J. (1994) The effects of phonemic similarity and list length on children's sound categorisation performance. *Journal of Experimental Child Psychology*. 58:160-80.

Stacey, M. (1991) *Parents and Teachers Together: Partnership in Primary and Nursery Education*. Milton Keynes. Open University Press.

Starkey, P. (1987) *Early Arithmetic Competencies*. Paper presented at the biennial meeting of the Society for Research in Child Development. Baltimore, MD, April.

Stringer, J. (2001) We haven't got a computer. *Primary Maths and Science Magazine*. January:35–36.

Tizard, B. and Hughes, M. (1984) *Young Children Learning: Talking and Thinking at Home and at School*. London. Fontana.

Tizard, J., Schofield, W. N. and Hewison, J. (1982) Collaboration between teachers and parents in assisting children's reading. *British Journal of Educational Psychology*, 52:1–15.

Trevarthan, C. (1995) The child's need to learn a culture. *Children in Society*. 9(1).

TTA (2000) *Using Information and Communications Technology to Meet Teaching Objectives in English*. London. TTA Publications.

Turner-Bisset, R. (2001) *Expert Teaching*. London. David Fulton.

Vincent, C. (2000) *Including Parents? Education, Citizenship and Parental Agency*. Buckingham. Open University Press.

Wegerif, R. and Scrimshaw, P. (eds) (1997) *Computers and Talk in the Primary Classroom*. Clevedon. Multilingual Matters Ltd.

Wetton, P. (1997) *Physical Education in the Early Years*. London. Routledge.

Whitehead, M. (1996) *The Development of Language and Literacy*. London. Hodder and Stoughton.

Whitehead, M. R. (1990) *Language and Literacy in the Early Years*. London. Paul Chapman Publishing.

Williamson, P. A. and Silvern, S. B. (1988) Thematic fantasy play and story comprehension, in Christie, J. F. (ed) (1991) *Play and Early Literacy Development*. Albany. State University of New York Press.

Wolfendale, S. and Bastiani, J. (eds) (2000) *The Contribution of Parents to School Effectiveness*. London. David Fulton.

Wragg, E. C. (2001) *Explaining in the Primary School*. London. RoutledgeFalmer.

Yopp, H. K. (1988) The validity and reliability of phonemic awareness tests. *Reading Research Quarterly*. 23:159–177.

Achieving QTS

Our *Achieving QTS* series now includes nearly 20 titles, encompassing *Audit and Test*, *Knowledge and Understanding*, *Teaching Theory and Practice*, and *Skills Tests* titles. As well as covering the core primary subject areas, the series addresses issues of teaching and learning across both primary and secondary phases. The Teacher Training Agency has identified books in this series as high quality resources for trainee teachers. You can find general information on each of these ranges on our website: www.learningmatters.co.uk

Primary English
Audit and Test (second edition)
Doreen Challen
£8.00   64 pages   ISBN: 1 903300 86 X

Primary Mathematics
Audit and Test (second edition)
Claire Mooney and Mike Fletcher
£8.00   52 pages   ISBN: 1 903300 87 8

Primary Science
Audit and Test (second edition)
John Sharp and Jenny Byrne
£8.00   80 pages   ISBN: 1 903300 88 6

Primary English
Knowledge and Understanding (second edition)
Jane Medwell, George Moore, David Wray, Vivienne Griffiths
£15   224 pages   ISBN: 1 903300 53 3

Primary English
Teaching Theory and Practice (second edition)
Jane Medwell, David Wray, Hilary Minns, Vivienne Griffiths, Elizabeth Coates
£15   192 pages   ISBN: 1 903300 54 1

Primary Mathematics
Knowledge and Understanding (second edition)
Claire Mooney, Lindsey Ferrie, Sue Fox, Alice Hansen, Reg Wrathmell
£15   176 pages   ISBN: 1 903300 55 X

Primary Mathematics
Teaching Theory and Practice (second edition)
Claire Mooney, Mary Briggs, Mike Fletcher, Judith McCullouch
£15   192 pages   ISBN: 1 903300 56 8

Primary Science
Knowledge and Understanding (second edition)
Rob Johnsey, Graham Peacock, John Sharp, Debbie Wright
£15   224 pages   ISBN: 1 903300 57 6

Primary Science
Teaching Theory and Practice (second edition)
John Sharp, Graham Peacock, Rob Johnsey, Shirley Simon, Robin Smith
£15   144 pages   ISBN: 1 903300 58 4

Primary ICT
Knowledge, Understanding and Practice (second edition)
Jane Sharp, John Potter, Jonathan Allen, Avril Loveless
£15   256 pages   ISBN: 1 903300 59 2

Professional Studies
Primary Phase (second edition)
Edited by Kate Jacques and Rob Hyland
£15   224 pages   ISBN: 1 903300 60 6

Teaching Foundation Stage
Edited by Iris Keating
£15   192 pages   ISBN: 1 903300 33 9

Teaching Humanities in Primary Schools
Pat Hoodless, Sue Bermingham, Elaine McReery, Paul Bowen
£15   192 pages   ISBN: 1 903300 36 3

Teaching Arts in Primary Schools
Stephanie Penny, Raywen Ford, Lawry Price, Susan Young
£15   192 pages   ISBN: 1 903300 35 5

Learning and Teaching in Secondary Schools
Edited by Viv Ellis
£15   192 pages   ISBN: 1 903300 38 X

Passing the Numeracy Skills Test (third edition)
Mark Patmore
£8   64 pages   ISBN: 1 903300 94 0

Passing the Literacy Skills Test
Jim Johnson
£6.99   80 pages   ISBN: 1 903300 12 6

Passing the ICT Skills Test
Clive Ferrigan
£6.99   80 pages   ISBN: 1 903300 13 4

Succeeding in the Induction Year (second edition)
Neil Simco
£13   144 pages   ISBN: 1 903300 93 2

To order, please contact our distributors:

BEBC Distribution,
Albion Close
Parkstone
Poole
BH12 3LL

Tel: 0845 230 9000
Email: learningmatters@bebc.co.uk